Managing
Artificial Intelligence
and
Expert Systems

Selected titles from the YOURDN PRESS COMPUTING SERIES
Ed Yourdon, *Advisor*

BAUDIN   Manufacturing Systems Analysis with Application to Production Scheduling
BELLIN AND SUCHMAN   Structured Systems Development Manual
BLOCK   The Politics of Projects
BODDIE   Crunch Mode: Building Effective Systems on a Tight Schedule
BOULDIN   Agents of Change: Managing the Introduction of Automated Tools
BRILL   Building Controls into Structured Systems
BRILL   Techniques of EDP Project Management: A Book of Readings
CHANG   Principles of Visual Programming Systems
COAD AND YOURDON   Object-Oriented Requirement Analysis
CONNELL AND SHAFER   Structured Rapid Prototyping: An Evolutionary Approach to Software Development
CONSTANTINE AND YOURDON   Structured Design: Fundamentals of a Discipline of Computer Program and
      Systems Design
DeMARCO   Concise Notes of Software Engineering
DeMARCO   Controlling Software Projects: Management, Measurement, and Estimates
DeMARCO   Structured Analysis and System Specification
DeSALVO AND LIEBOWITZ   Managing Artificial Intelligence and Expert Systems
DICKINSON   Developing Structured Systems: A Methodology Using Structured Techniques
FLAVIN   Fundamental Concepts in Information Modeling
FOLLMAN   Business Applications with Microcomputers: A Guidebook for Building Your Own System
FRANTZEN AND McEVOY   A Game Plan for Systems Development: Strategy and Steps for Designing Your Own
      System
INMON   Information Engineering for the Practitioner: Putting Theory into Practice
KELLER   Expert Systems Technology: Development and Application
KELLER   The Practice of Structured Analysis: Exploding Myths
KING   Creating Effective Software: Computer Program Design Using the Jackson Method
KING   Current Practices in Software Development: A Guide to Successful Systems
LIEBOWITZ AND DeSALVO   Structuring Expert Systems: Domain, Design, and Development
MARTIN   Transaction Processing Facility: A Guide for Application Programmers
McMENAMIN AND PALMER   Essential System Analysis
ORR   Structured Systems Development
PAGE-JONES   Practical Guide to Structured Systems Design, 2/E
PETERS   Software Design: Methods and Techniques
RIPPS   An Implementation Guide to Real-Time Programming
RODGERS   UNIX Database Management Systems
RUHL   The Programmer's Survival Guide: Career Strategies for Computer Professionals
SCHMITT   The OS/2 Programming Environment
SCHLAER AND MELLOR   Object-Oriented Systems Analysis: Modeling the World in Data
THOMSETT   People and Project Management
TOIGO   Disaster Recovery Planning: Managing Risk and Catastrophe in Information Systems
VESELY   Strategic Data Management: The Key to Corporate Competitiveness
WARD   Systems Development Without Pain: A User's Guide to Modeling Organizational Patterns
WARD AND MELLOR   Structured Development for Real-Time Systems, Volumes I, II, and III
WEAVER   Using the Structured Techniques: A Case Study
WEINBERG   Structured Analysis
YOURDON   Classics in Software Engineering
YOURDON   Managing the Structured Techniques, 4/E
YOURDON   Managing the System Life Cycle, 2/E
YOURDON   Modern Structured Analysis
YOURDON   Structured Walkthroughs, 4/E
YOURDON   Techniques of Program Structure and Design
YOURDON   Writing of the Revolution: Selected Readings on Software Engineering

Managing Artificial Intelligence and Expert Systems

EDITORS

Daniel A. De Salvo
MCI Telecommunications Corporation

Jay Liebowitz
George Washington University

YOURDON PRESS
Prentice Hall Building
Englewood Cliffs, New Jersey 07632

Library of Congress Cataloging-in-Publication Data

```
Managing artificial intelligence and expert systems / edited by Daniel
  A. De Salvo [and] Jay Liebowitz.
      p.  cm. -- (Yourdon Press computing series)
    Bibliography: p.
    Includes index.
    ISBN 0-13-551789-3
    1. Artificial intelligence. 2. Expert systems (Computer science)
  I. De Salvo, Daniel. II. Liebowitz, Jay. III. Series.
  Q335.M36  1990
  006.3--dc20                                       89-8556
                                                       CIP
```

Editorial/production supervision
  and interior design: Karen Bernhaut
Cover Design: Karen Stephens
Manufacturing buyer: Mary Ann Gloriande

© 1990 by Prentice-Hall, Inc.
A division of Simon & Schuster
Englewood Cliffs, New Jersey 07632

The publisher offers discounts on this book when ordered
in bulk quantities. For more information, write:

> Special Sales/College Marketing
> Prentice-Hall, Inc.
> College Technical and Reference Division
> Englewood Cliffs, NJ 07632

ISBN 0-13-551789-3

Prentice-Hall International (UK) Limited, *London*
Prentice-Hall of Australia Pty. Limited, *Sydney*
Prentice-Hall Canada Inc., *Toronto*
Prentice-Hall Hispanoamericana, S.A., *Mexico*
Prentice-Hall of India Private Limited, *New Delhi*
Prentice-Hall of Japan, Inc., *Tokyo*
Simon & Schuster Asia Pte. Ltd, *Singapore*
Editora Prentice-Hall do Brasil, Ltda., *Rio de Janeiro*

To our families

Elaine, Dominick, and Robert De Salvo

and

Janet and Jason Liebowitz

Contents

PREFACE   ix

Part 1 Teamwork   1

    CHAPTER 1 STAFFING YOUR NEW AI GROUPS   1

        Daryl J. Furno, Halbrecht Associates, Inc.

    **CHAPTER 2 APPRENTICESHIPS AND TECHNOLOGY
                  TRANSFER**   21

        Jeff C. Tanner, Intellicorp

    **CHAPTER 3 YOU TOO CAN BECOME A KNOWLEDGE
                  ENGINEER IF...**   38

        Jay Liebowitz, George Washington University

CHAPTER 4 **THE ARCHIVIST'S ASSISTANT: FROM THE EXPERT'S PERSPECTIVE** **53**

Renee M. Jaussaud, Archival Consultant

Part 2 **Strategies** **80**

CHAPTER 5 **EVOLUTION OF THE KNOWLEDGE SYSTEMS MARKETPLACE: THE INTELLICORP EXPERIENCE** **80**

David J. Mishelevich, Intellicorp

CHAPTER 6 **COST JUSTIFYING EXPERT SYSTEMS** **93**

Donna M. Thompson, ICF/Phase Linear Systems and Jerald L. Feinstein, ICF/Phase Linear Systems

CHAPTER 7 **A CRITICAL REVIEW OF LEGAL ISSUES IN ARTIFICIAL INTELLIGENCE** **122**

Janet S. Zeide, Attorney at Law and Jay Liebowitz, George Washington University

Part 3 **Tactics** **138**

CHAPTER 8 **AI CORP ENTERS THE MARKET** **138**

Larry R. Harris, AI Corp

CHAPTER 9 **MANAGING THE DEVELOPMENT OF GENERIC EXPERT SYSTEM PRODUCTS** **146**

Walter Reitman, Rensselaer Polytechnic Institute

CHAPTER 10 **DEVELOPMENT OF NATURAL LANGUAGE PROCESSING SYSTEMS FROM A MANAGER'S PERSPECTIVE** **170**

Antonio Zamora, IBM Corporation and Elena M. Zamora, IBM Corporation

CHAPTER 11 **STRATEGIES FOR MANAGERS TO REDUCE EMPLOYEE FEAR WHEN INTRODUCING A NEW TECHNOLOGY** **189**

Deborah A. Glazer, Independent Consultant in Social and Organizational Behavior

INDEX **207**

Preface

The authors who share their ideas and experiences in this book are eminent practicing professionals in the field of artificial intelligence and expert systems. Their combined expertise extends from the research laboratory to the most hardened bottom-line–oriented business group.

The contributors present their unique perspectives on a new industry as it is taking shape. The research community's efforts to study and create computer intelligence has produced a wealth of new knowledge about the practice of computing: new algorithms, data structures, and hardware configurations. In the last few years, we have seen the emergence of AI from the laboratory into the mainstream of data processing, helped along by a new class of technical entrepreneurs who recognized the power of these new tools and packaged them for commercial use. Their products are being readily accepted into even the most conservative data processing organizations.

A mathematician will happily explain that a system can be either complete or consistent, but not both. This scientific oddity translates into a source of useful tension in the world of management. On the one hand, we struggle to impose clear and ordered policies. On the other, we regularly disrupt policies to gain the advantages of a new tool or technique.

The contributing authors' experiences and expertise in managing these conflicting priorities are reflected in their chapters. Each contributor has been deeply involved in the introduction and acceptance of this new technology; each has been the person responsible within their organization.

Consequently, their writings provide first-hand accounts of successful professionals who have broken ground in an emergent industry. We believe that these unadulterated viewpoints are valuable to anyone interested in how a new technology moves from the laboratory to the shop, and in particular to the reader trying to make sense out of the AI industry at a time when it has not yet—thankfully—spawned any grand theories of management.

Daniel A. De Salvo
Jay Liebowitz

PART ONE: TEAMWORK

1

Staffing Your New AI Groups

DARYL J. FURNO, Halbrecht Associates, Inc.

To get a better grasp of how to staff an artificial intelligence (AI) group, we must reflect on how it was done in the past. Examples will be presented of the successful—and unsuccessful—ways in which organizations have recruited AI professionals. The types of managers and professionals needed will be detailed. In addition, recruiting and interviewing techniques characteristic of the field will be reviewed.

The subject of staffing new AI groups is tied to the rise to prominence of AI technology from university research laboratories, which began around 1980. This rise to prominence was stimulated by the emergence of manufacturers of hardware dedicated to Lisp, one of the first AI computer languages. The first visions of AI technology with a commercial payoff arose with this hardware.

Originally, the major efforts in AI were located in a few widely spread universities and nearby research labs, the most prominent of which were the Massachusetts Institute of Technology (MIT) in Cambridge, Carnegie-Mellon University (CMU) in Pittsburgh, and Stanford University in Palo Alto, California. The adjacent private research labs were the Xerox Palo Alto Research Center (PARC), nearby SRI International, and a robotics laboratory at CMU.

With internal funding and some government grants, these initial groups were almost always staffed by professors and their students, mostly Ph.D. candidates. Many of the brightest students were plucked right out of the classroom and offered good salaries and leading-edge projects, which they accepted at the expense of continued formal education.

The tendency to acquire the best talent among computer science students accelerated with the formation of the dedicated AI hardware companies and continued later with the start-ups in expert systems and natural language software. One of the early proponents of AI technology, Marvin Minsky of MIT's AI lab, frequently spoke out in 1982 and 1983 against this drain of students from university research labs. Minsky was one of the few professors of his caliber who did not get involved with some of the early start-ups. However, several years later, he helped form an AI company in which he then participated.

The nature of those working in the universities and quasi-university research labs is pertinent. They were predominantly Ph.D.s dedicated to their own projects. These often were a continuation of earlier thesis work. If they found positions as assistant or associate professors, they tended to stay with the university, teach, and pursue their research. Otherwise, they usually went to the research labs set up in conjunction with the universities that were funded by industry or government.

Examples of the most prominent labs were the Information Science Institute (ISI) in Marine del Rey, which is associated with the University of Southern California, and SRI International in Menlo Park, California. If masters-level students were hired, they were primarily assigned to programming, the most tedious part of projects directed by those with doctoral degrees. The first work in these labs was done on conventional computers. The hardware was usually DEC 10s from Digital Equipment Corp. (DEC) of Maynard, Massachusetts. At that time, there was a need for hardware that was more responsive to the kind of languages these researchers were working in. In the United States, the language was predominantly Lisp.

As university and quasi-university research groups began to develop their own hardware, they realized that there was a market for it. This led to the creation of new computer makers such as Lisp Machine, Inc. (LMI) and Symbolics, both of Cambridge, Massachusetts. In addition, xerox created some of these new machines. LMI and Symbolics were founded by a score of scientists from MIT's AI lab. These scientists tended to be Ph.D. students, their professors, or young, brilliant computer hackers.

As knowledge of these new companies and their products crept into the marketplace, other companies began stepping up their AI efforts. The early AI research labs, such as that of Schlumberger-Doll (Ridgefield, Conn.) and GTE Labs (Waltham, Mass.), bought Xerox machines initially because they were the first available. Later, other labs were able to buy machines from LMI and Symbolics.

Most of these early labs running Xerox hardware were staffed by Ph.D.s from the three major universities devoted to AI (MIT, Stanford, and Carnegie-Mellon). These scientists found comfortable places to continue their research in environments very similar to the ones they had left. They anticipated that eventually less-expensive delivery vehicles would implement practical applications of their work. The main technology to be commercialized or likely to be was the expert system. A model in an early medical system, called MYCIN, was developed at Stanford University.

One of the first start-ups in Palo Alto was Teknowledge, formed mostly by Stanford professors and their students. They used MYCIN as a model to develop expert systems for customers. They hoped that these prototypes would be developed into larger systems. At the same time, they wanted to develop a shell (a computer-aided design tool for expert systems).

As Teknowledge began to build its dedicated software tools, other groups soon realized that this was the way to go. One of these groups was Inference Corp. (Los Angeles, Calif.), with a founder from the University of Southern California. Another was Intellicorp, founded by former Xerox researchers and others from the Palo Alto area. At the same time, DEC, which had a very strong connection with CMU and its robotics lab, was looking closely at AI, but not for the same reason Xerox sponsored AI work at PARC, which was to augment its product line and provide future leading-edge products.

DEC, on the other hand, chose to use the technology to improve its operations. It did so by means of an expert system called R1, used by the marketing group. R1 is a good example of successful technology transfer. It was created by a team of managers from DEC and top scientists from CMU's robotics lab. The more difficult parts of the expert system were worked out at CMU, but professionals with only masters or bachelor's degrees at DEC did a good part of the knowledge engineering, selected the rules, and carried them through to delivery of the system. Of course, this was under the continual guidance of the group at CMU.

THE BEGINNING OF THE GREAT SHORTAGE

The question can now be asked, When did the shortage of AI professionals first begin? It appears that it was somewhere around 1983 and was based on the activity stimulated by the new hardware companies. In MIT circles, it was no secret that a push toward a new technology was emerging. Some of the consultants from the Cambridge-based Index Group (now called Index Systems), were quick to see the potential commercial possibilities of this new technology. With advice from several MIT professors, who eventually became members of their board of directors, Index Group started a new company called Applied Expert Systems, now known as Apex. Most of the administrative staff and original planners of Apex were former Index employees and principals. They were the first company to try to develop off-the-shelf applications and then sell them to interested American corporations. Because Index originally specialized in the financial-services industry, Apex also aimed its initial applications at that industry. Under great secrecy, they brought in some industrial partners with particular application needs. A major one was selected for the first product. Meanwhile, several prototypes being considered for the liaisons were not with Wall Street, as was first assumed, but with insurance carriers. At first, Apex was served technically by its original university advisers. Early on, it was able to hire the manager of the development group from a nearby research lab. But soon, just as the pressures of product development came into play, hiring qualified staff became more difficult, because more groups were attempting to get into this new technology. To find Lisp-proficient computer scientists willing to move to a commercial software company, Apex had to seek outside help. In this case, Apex officers followed the example of their previous employer and hired an outside executive search firm. Although at this time no outside firm had the in-house AI technical expertise to assess candidates technically, they were able to employ conventional search methodology for this project. That paid off. Apex was able to attract a young, bright, associate professor who helped to get the project out the door. Apex also attracted one of the few gurus in the field. Because Apex could not have attracted this person without the help of a third party, it is interesting to see the process that was involved in the successful search.

To better understand AI technology, the firm sent representatives to various AI seminars. This was in the early 1980s, so the firm had few representatives to send. Apex also approached a large number of professionals in the field. In all of these places, they left either a verbal or a written description of the opportunity at Apex. As information about this opportunity spread, several AI professionals inquired into these positions. Among them was a senior scientist who, by coincidence, was working at the company from which Apex's hiring manager had originally come. When the name of the hiring company was revealed to the senior scientist, he did not lose interest, although he was quite surprised that there was such a senior-level position open at Apex.

In turn, the hiring manager was amazed that someone who was a former close associate of his, whom he believed was aware of his mission at Apex, would surface as a candidate through a search firm. The senior scientist had been attracted by the generic description of the career opportunity. When the name of the hiring company was revealed, he felt more comfortable with the initial inquiry coming through a third party, because his past relationship with the hiring manager would not become invalid. In this case, the hiring manager welcomed the candidate. They subsequently worked successfully as a team to create the company's first few products.

GROWING COMPETITION FOR PROFESSIONALS

Meanwhile, the other newly formed software companies were finding the personnel marketplace very limited and becoming more so. At this time, the best place to find AI computer scientists was around Stanford. Besides the university itself, there were qualified professionals doing innovative work at research labs such as SRI International, Hewlett Packard Company, and Xerox PARC. This facilitated the easy staffing of the AI start-ups in that area, especially those spun off by professionals from the abovementioned institutions. The northern California software companies were able to bring in the technical talent they needed by means of their network of friends and the qualified professionals in the area. Word also got out to universities throughout the country active hiring was going on in this area. Soon the most qualified Ph.D. students began to apply.

Inference Corporation, located in Los Angeles, had a slightly different problem. One of the two founders of Infererence, Alex Jacobson, was a visionary entrepreneur from the business world who previously had been involved with software development. Early on, he saw the possibility of offering an AI-dedicated tool.

Jacobson teamed up with a very strong technical student working on a Ph.D. thesis leading in the same direction. Unlike its competitors in northern California, this team did not have a national reputation in AI; they were virtually unknown. When it came time to staff their company, they could network into the local universities and the scientists at ISI. However, they discovered that there were not enough qualified professionals available locally.

Inference did not have the kind of reputation that would attract qualified young professionals. Inference solved this problem by forming a technical advisory board made up of the most famous AI researchers. This was not difficult, because its initial product, ART, was very sound. When the product concept was demonstrated, the AI visionaries were impressed with its potential. As soon as Inference unveiled its technical advisory board, the job of attracting Lisp professionals became much easier. Applicants who wanted to know about Inference's plans, its vision, and the long-term potential of its products could contact one of these gurus and ask these questions during the hiring process. This technique proved invaluable during the hiring process. These gurus also served as technical advisors for the company during the first project. Another contribution they made was to give technical credibility to the company in the eyes of venture capital investors.

Inference had another hiring problem. Although many qualified people from other parts of the country were interested in working in AI, they were reluctant to relocate in the Los Angeles area. Living costs were very high. Of greater significance, most AI professionals in California were in the northern part of the state. Inference had to convince applicants from other states that it was blessed with a concentration of AI people and excellent weather. The company was able to attract several excellent people from CMU. This success was partly because of the quality of the company, but also because the weather in Los Angeles was superior to that in Pittsburgh.

One lesson to be learned from this experience and from that of the other companies in the early days of AI is that once a company got one or two leading AI computer scientists on board, it was easier to hire others. Brilliant young professionals who may not have had a reputation would come to work on a team with someone they respected.

THE PROFESSIONALS' WISH LIST

About this time, some invaluable information was developed that was to be of help in recruiting. A group of AI scientists from the Gould Corporation (Amherst, N.H.) ran a workshop on AI. At the workshop, they revealed the results of an informal survey of AI professionals assessing what was important to them in a work situation and what they would look for in a new job. Their priorities, not in any particular order, were

1. a parking spot near the entrance to the workplace and a key to the building;
2. the chance to work in one's lab any time of the day or night, and proper heat and air conditioning;
3. an unlimited supply of free coffee;

4. an informal atmosphere and no unnecessary meetings;
5. more computer memory and better tools;
6. availability of some discretionary funds, especially for hiring;
7. substantial reward for any significant contributions.

The significance of the wish list is that these professionals were not concerned about salaries matching what they considered their worth, but they did want to make sure that when they achieved their objectives, they would be financially rewarded. Based on these revelations, start-up corporations were motivated to give the first cadre of scientists and administrative people a piece of the action in the form of stock. In some instances, vesting in stock options was very quick, sometimes immediate. These perks helped attract staff.

In the early days, salary escalation was inevitable because of the great demand for talent. Hiring corporations that were not located near the major universities specializing in AI found that they could barely compete when offering only the same salaries. If they needed to hire someone, they had to pay a premium. In some cases, they would provide the little extra in the form of stock options or other perks.

A very high salary scale for both experienced and fledgling AI professionals was established in the early 1980s. Since then, AI salaries have stayed at about the same level, mainly because many more qualified people are available, and many more universities are offering graduate studies in AI. In addition, qualified people, especially in expert systems development, have been able to gain needed experience within research labs and in industry. This means that the early salary structure set the salary structure that exists today.

Although salaries for AI specialists have not escalated much from the mid- to late-1980's, they are nevertheless considered very high, especially as compared with those of other computer scientists and analysts. Even today, salaries for AI specialists are higher than those for other professionals with as much education and experience.

In 1983–1984, with the AI start-ups actively recruiting, the established research labs were affected for the first time. With AI catching on, the military and other government agencies began to look into this appealing new technology. Funding from these agencies was growing very rapidly at this time. This was an incentive for the traditional research groups to start AI groups and share in the bonanza. Companies that had the facilities to promote AI research, such as Mitre (Bedford, Mass.), Lockheed (Burbank, Calif.), Boeing (Seattle, Wash.), ITT (Shelton, Conn.), and GTE Labs, were now able to establish small, active AI groups or expand their work in AI. This expansion put a lot of pressure on the supply of available Ph.D. and research scientists in the universities. The universities were losing professionals not only to start-ups but also to these new opportunities in the commercial research labs. In addition, professors with AI expertise either started businesses themselves or were working as consultants. The marketplace for professionals in the established research laboratories became very competitive. Companies committed to AI began to find it more difficult to attract qualified people. At the same time, some of their own employees, such as those who left Xerox PARC to head up several start-ups in the Palo Alto area began to recruit staff from their former employers. This further inflated salary scales for research professionals.

INTERVIEWING TECHNIQUES

The model for interviewing AI candidates came from the early research labs. In general, recent Ph.D. graduates would be invited to come for a day and meet the expert who headed the group for which they were being considered. Perhaps other professionals who specialized in their field would also be brought into the process. Part of the day would always include a presentation, in which candidates would present a synopsis of their Ph.D. thesis. This was similar to the way they defended their dissertations. This procedure revealed the level of their research and their depth of knowledge of the topic, as well as their ability to organize and communicate their ideas. After the presentation, company experts would ask detailed questions about the research and get a chance to do a fairly rigorous technical evaluation of the candidate. The candidates would then sometimes meet with peers. If they were being considered for project management or for other management positions, they might even meet with those who would be on their team and whom they would supervise.

When entrepreneurs left the universities to establish software development companies, they followed the same procedure. They would ask candidates to do a technical presentation as a basis for judgment of their technical depth. The entrepreneurs would do this in addition to (and sometimes instead of) reviewing examples of their work or asking them questions in a personal interview or reading their theses. This evaluation method not only persists, but in many AI groups is applied to applicants for marketing and other nontechnical positions. A candidate for a marketing position could talk about the marketplace for AI. An applicant for a management position might talk about staffing an AI group, the method of developing a team, and the kinds of technologies the group could develop.

FUNDING SHAPES STAFFING

The source of funding for AI research and development has helped to configure the kinds of groups and the staffing of the groups. The Defense Advanced Research Project Agency (DARPA) and other government agencies have always been interested in leading-edge research of value to U.S. defense.

These agencies were some of the earliest funders of the projects at MIT, CMU, and Stanford. They also were very active in supporting early projects at SRI and at Bolt, Beranek & Newman, Inc., in Cambridge, Massachusetts. Those advanced computer-science projects overlapped all through the 1970s and early 1980s and eventually coalesced into what is now called AI. As more and more interest in AI developed, there was in turn more funding from the government. This encouraged the companies long serving the government to realize that they would better establish their own AI facilities. Companies like TRW (Cleveland, Ohio), FMC Corp. (Chicago), Lockheed (Burbank, Calif.), Boeing, and Mitre all began to back some AI effort in their research labs. The staffing of these labs was, in a way, more difficult for them. They did not have stock to offer, and they could not ignore their established salary scales to hire qualified AI experts, much less the top people they really needed. They had to look to other solutions to staff their labs. Other economic constraints helped them in this effort indirectly. For example, the cost of the new dedicated hardware was very expensive, close to prohibitive. In some of the early work at these labs, there was no need to hire professionals well trained and experienced in Lisp, because no Lisp hardware was available. Thus, they frequently attempted to staff their early efforts with some very bright computer science students working in traditional computer languages.

Some companies, such as Amoco (Tulsa, Okla.) and Lockheed, were able to use professionals already on staff and working in familiar computer languages and techniques. They attempted to build shells that would get them started in AI. The shell developed by Amoco in coordinating with IBM became one of IBM's early non-Lisp expert system shells. Researchers at Lockheed developed a product called LES (Lockheed Expert Systems), which also was a product of its best talent working in a traditional language.

THE BOEING MODEL

Another way these companies were able to staff their labs was by following the Boeing model. The aerospace giant had excellent internal education and training facilities, as did many other large corporations at that time.

While companies like Aetna Life & Casualty (Hartford, Conn.) and General Electric (Bridgeport, Conn.) continued to offer traditional training and executive management courses, Boeing introduced a one-year AI graduate program. Boeing permitted its own employees—managers as well as young programmers—to take time off work to participate in the innovative program. Thus, Boeing trained much of its own staff to lead its AI efforts. At this time, these AI labs were also hiring Ph.D.s out of the universities. They acted as master teachers under which these newly trained people could apprentice.

THE CONSULTANT ALTERNATIVE

Another way these groups were able to afford to bring in good people was not to put them on staff. They were hired instead as consultants. It has always been ironic that American businesses may find it impossible to hire staff professionals at salaries that fall inside the company's existing salary scale, but they are able to pay the same professionals far more as consultants.

One of the early staffing innovations was at Lockheed, which borrowed AI scientists from Inference Corporation and assigned them to work directly on projects as if they were Lockheed employees. This tactic enabled Lockheed to use professionals who were paid substantially more than they would ever be paid on a yearly salary basis. These highly paid consultants worked side by side with Lockheed's people and trained them.

Lockheed also became a major investor in Inference, which gave them favorable access to consulting. This investment also gave Lockheed access to Inference's products and proprietary tools. This strategy helped Lockheed meet its contractual obligations with the National Aeronautics and Space Administration and other governmental agencies.

Lockheed's method of bringing in top talent through consulting assignments and also supporting the source of the talent was soon copied by Framatone in Paris and Detroit-based General Motors Corporation, both of which became major investors in Teknowledge. In the same vein, Ford Motor Company (Detroit) invested in both Inference and Carnegie Group (Pittsburgh).

These liaisons between the software development companies with consulting groups and the giants of industry allowed the latter to bring in top-quality staff. In turn, these arrangements helped the software houses support and maintain their high salary scales. Thus, industrial research groups were perpetuating the high salaries of AI professionals at the same time that these high salaries prevented the labs from hiring the same AI professionals directly. There was one compensating advantage, however: When a research group hired consultants, it did not have to worry about what to do with those highly paid AI professionals if the project had to be aborted.

Not all industrial research labs could afford the luxury of having their parent corporation invest in an AI start-up or consulting group. Nor were they able to afford to hire outside consultants to augment their own AI work. These labs had to either hire young students right out of school at rates within their salary structures and hope that they would become AI superstars, or else they had to attempt to attract more experienced professionals for reasons other than money.

One of the major "other" reasons then, as now, is location. As previously mentioned, if an AI lab was located in a prime territory, such as around Palo Alto, then that lab had an extra means of attracting professionals. Palo Alto is a prime location, not only because of the attractive ambiance and weather, but also because of the heavy concentration of AI professionals and many prestigious companies active in AI.

A close contender to Palo Alto is the Boston area, which also has most of the same attractions plus proximity to sailing and skiing. Pittsburgh, on the other hand, is generally not rated as exciting as Boston, although it has much the same weather and also a major AI-oriented university in CMU.

The more geographic attractions a locality offers, the larger the number of professionals that should be drawn to it. When Martin Marietta Corporation started a large research effort in Denver in early 1980, it hoped to attract professionals through its desirable environment, by providing support, and interesting work in many projects. However, Martin Marietta was limited by the salaries it could offer. It touted Denver as an attraction. Perhaps some candidates who skied and liked the West and its mountains would be interested in the potential in AI.

Could AI affect the bottom line or even become a competitive weapon for these industrial giants? One of the first industries not funded by government to look at AI was the oil industry. One pioneer was Schlumberger-Doll, which was supporting research to help it service the oil industry. In turn, oil companies, such as Standard Oil of Ohio (Cleveland), Exxon (Florham Park, N.J.) and Amoco (Tulsa, Okla.) became interested in this technology and added small AI groups to their research efforts. These oil giants encountered much the same staffing problems as the large defense-related companies. They, too, were burdened by established salary structures that could not accommodate higher priced AI talent.

AI'S APPEAL TO FINANCIAL SERVICES

The financial services industry also began to look at AI for much the same reasons as had other industries. For the former, the bottom line is paramount, closely matched by the need to gain competitive advantage. However, financial services were accustomed to rewarding employees who could affect the business. One hiring obstacle for the financial services was their lack of research facilities. When they needed new technology, they usually bought it off the shelf or in a state almost ready to use. For these companies, an AI research group was out of the question. The notion of selecting a project and then spending six months to two years or more waiting for results was not their way. They might hire one or two professionals to study a technology of interest, and then hire one or two pros to create some protoypes or small systems. Some financial services also dabbled with consultants. In fact, the banking industry supported a very elaborate AI project at Arthur D. Little, Inc. (ADL), (Cambridge, Mass.). In all cases, the AI efforts on behalf of the financial services proceeded haltingly. They did not take off in 1984 and 1985 when larger companies with research labs and the ability to sponsor some long-term projects were really sinking their teeth into AI.

OTHER CONSULTING SERVICES

From the very beginning, Teknowledge and the other AI start-ups (including Inference) who were building tools were also offering consulting services. Sometimes their intent was to sell their tools, but it was also just to show potential customers the value of the technology. These AI companies offering consulting, for whatever reason, soon found this part of their business very lucrative. As a result, the established consultancies, such as ADL and subsequently the "Big Eight" accounting and consulting firms, began to view this new technology as an area of expertise they should be offering to their clients.

Initially at ADL, the head of the AI practice would go out to potential clients and sell the assignment by building a small prototype or at least by outlining a rough design for an expert system. The intent would be to use the staff the partner had in the group, some of whom were not trained AI people or who were fairly new to the technology. When the assignment was sold, ADL would in turn supplement the group with experienced professionals or at least Lisp programmers from nearby universities on a part-time basis, possibly professors or graduate students. Hiring this high-quality part-time help was certainly very efficient for ADL but not inexpensive. One of the early Big Eight accounting firms that established an AI effort was Arthur Andersen in Chicago. Traditionally, Arthur Andersen hires the majority of staff right out of college, trains them in its methodology, and then promotes the most qualified until they achieve partnership. Andersen decided to use the same approach and build an AI group from scratch, despite the fact that there were not many qualified AI graduates in the Chicago area.

After they were given some standard Arthur Andersen in-house training, the trainees were then sent to be trained by the software tool companies in the use of tools. Thus, Andersen slowly started to build an AI capability to serve clients. Some proprietary tools were also developed that could be used with present clients and to acquire new ones.

This approach to building an AI capability and consulting practice was very slow. However, Arthur Andersen started doing this very early and therefore was able to build a well-integrated and very successful group before its rivals. Andersen's approach became the model for the other Big Eight firms. But first, the other firms had to hire experienced AI professionals to match Arthur Andersen's capability. Later, when the other consultancies decided to staff up for AI, they couldn't wait to train their own people from scratch; they tended to hire experienced expert systems developers called knowledge engineers. One of the reasons they could do this successfully is that they were staffing an AI group two or more years after Arthur Andersen's initial efforts. In the intervening years, a large pool of experienced knowledge engineers had evolved.

SUMMARY OF HIRING PRACTICES

The start-up AI groups in the defense industry did not merely hire Ph.D.s. They also hired students with master's degrees and anyone who could be trained, had experience as a knowledge engineer, or was able to quickly pick up new computer languages. The level of the person hired depended on the budget of the particular project or on the extent of the research grant from DARPA or one of the other branches of the military.

The main ways of finding qualified people for the defense research labs industry were generally through conventional channels. These were companies with established personnel departments that are accustomed to hiring technical people. These departments have long-established procedures for recruiting right out of universities or by networking throughout the industry. They knew enough to advertise in the technical journals and magazines read by the candidates they wanted to attract. Thus, they were able to solicit a fairly good flow of qualified candidates. Contingency recruiting agencies would also read these ads and call the personnel department or hiring manager to get more detailed descriptions and would in turn begin to supply other qualified candidates.

Financial institutions, on the other hand, had no traditional research model. Therefore, hiring was more difficult for them. Their personnel departments did not have the ability to network or recruit technical people. Because Wall Street had been interested in expert systems for some time, it did hire some very well-known and talented AI professionals who were willing to work for the high-paying financial services. These AI experts applied the technology in exciting ways to investment banking, financial planning, and trading.

In most cases, these Wall Street firms chose to bring in people who were very mathematical and had strong AI experience. The notion of training people from scratch had no appeal to them. Their hiring was mostly done through agencies and some word of mouth because they did not have the same hiring capability as the industrial research labs.

Other organizations, such as those in manufacturing and process control and who were not defense oriented, often had research labs. These research labs tended to hire mostly Ph.D.s or some very bright students with master's degrees who had at least worked in the technologies of interest.

Up to this point, we have been mostly discussing companies that found AI attractive. They hoped the technology would enhance their business or their products. Higher level management decided that this technology should be explored further. Such executives were of three types: the one in charge of the research lab; the one responsible for tracking future technologies or planning; and, occasionally, the one in what used to be called operations research. Through this leadership, the AI groups would be established with the backing of higher level company executives. Then the personal computer changed the situation. More and more AI tools became available, not just for the large dedicated hardware, but also for personal computers. As a result, a whole new motivation evolved toward establishing AI groups. The early efforts were hampered because the tools and the hardware they ran on were very expensive. No matter where the push for AI came from, it had to be approved eventually by top management because of the heavy funding and expensive staffing.

THE EXPANSION OF THE EXPERT SYSTEM MOVEMENT

One company where an expanded expert system movement began to burgeon was DEC. DEC was one of the first companies to build a large and now-famous expert system, R1, since renamed XCON. Since XCON, DEC has built several other, related systems for its marketing group. The success of these systems was known to all of DEC's employees. DEC's top management was very positive about AI. Almost any employee in any division of DEC could get a green light from his or her manager to go ahead with an expert systems project. A grass-roots movement sprang up to develop expert systems across the board within DEC.

Reinforcement from top management was easy because it hoped for the same satisfactory results it was reaping from XCON. Recently, DEC reported that some sixty expert systems were being built by different business units or divisions using their own personnel. Of course, this is easier to do in a company in which most of the employees are trained in computers and are computer scientists or professionals with a computer science background.

Another company that was able to successfully employ expert systems to support the core business with similar ease was Texas Instruments, Inc. (Richardson, Tex.) Originally, TI applied AI to its product line. Many employees were building not only AI-dedicated hardware, but also their own proprietary tools to run on this hardware. TI also signed contractual agreements with Intellicorp (Mt. View, Calif.), Inference, and Carnegie Group to port their AI tools to TI hardware. To sell its hardware, TI supported its customers very cleverly. In many instances, TI assigned its own knowledge engineers, some of whom had worked on the development of the tools or at least were very versatile in the use of the tools, to work with customers and get them started in building expert systems.

These knowledge engineers helped build sophisticated prototypes or carried the customer through to a finished system by taking either a management role or perhaps building almost the whole system themselves. At the same time, TI emulated DEC and applied AI to internal operations. Naturally, these divisions and business units used TI's own products to build these expert systems. These internal systems have not been publicized as widely as the ones TI built for customers. However, those internal systems have been said to have paid off. As for DEC, it was easier at TI for this kind of grass-roots movement of building expert systems internally to spring up throughout the company because the professionals who work at TI happen to be predominantly computer scientists or computer-trained people.

The mid-1980s saw the emergence of AI tools that run on the personal computer (PC) and are much easier to use. This stimulated a grass-roots movement: Individuals without AI training started to experiment with expert systems and apply them without top management awareness because substantial funding was unnecessary. In some cases, top management was aware and even condoned and encouraged it, especially if they had no intention of buying expensive tools or hardware. Many staffers were encouraged to build expert systems, as long as they did it on their own time and within their own budgets.

At the DuPont Company, in Wilmington, Delaware, top management also found AI attractive but was inhibited initially by the expense of dedicated hardware and sophisticated AI professionals. The PC approach was more appealing. DuPont did work initially with the University of Maryland on some small projects, but in general it put its own managers in charge of this effort. Many of its engineers and scientists already had access to PCs. DuPont provided them with PC-based expert system tools to build expert systems throughout the company. To this day, DuPont may have the largest number of small expert systems—numbering in the hundreds—successfully built or on the drawing board. It appears that this flood will continue. The grass-roots approach has been so successful that many other corporations are emulating it. Meanwhile, DuPont is looking into more sophisticated tools and is beginning to build some larger and more complicated systems.

Because of the way DuPont went about building its AI capability, it did little or no hiring of AI professionals. DuPont tended to use shells, train its own people, or hire young professionals who desired the training. What DuPont did that made a difference was to select people with knowledge, called the experts, and give them the training to create their own expert systems. DuPont selected its most knowledgeable people, and it was those people who recorded their own expertise. This cut down on the number of people needed to build the system and also raised the quality of the rules that are an essential part of any expert system. DuPont has been a good model for how small expert systems should be built.

THE EXPERT SYSTEM TEAM

To build an expert system, you need an expert whose expertise is to be replicated. This expert would work closely with a technical person—a knowledge engineer who either knows how to use the tool or can build a tool. A knowledge engineer would configure the expertise in a way that would be usable in either the tool or a custom computer shell system developed by a computer scientist. Three individuals comprise the team: the expert, the knowledge engineer, and the technical computer person building the tool or using his or her knowledge to get the most from the tool. In some situations, the computer person and the knowledge engineer are the same person. Sitting down with an expert, he or she quickly builds the knowledge structure that is needed to get the information into a form that fits into the tool they are using. As projects get more and more complicated, it is advisable to depend more on a team with the people who are better at working with the experts becoming the knowledge engineers and extracting the knowledge. They can then turn the information over to the computer scientist, who inputs it properly.

The original vision of AI expert Edward Feigenbaum of Stanford University marked the knowledge engineer as the most valuable person in this trio. The knowledge engineer would work with the expert and would then download the knowledge into a convenient computer shell. Feigenbaum's vision has come true to a large extent. Combined with the grass-roots movement, this vision has greatly affected the staffing of AI groups. This, in turn, has made the role of the manager much more important. The manager who directs all of these grass-roots movements is also the person who is making sure that divisional people who are generating these systems are getting the support they need on time and within budget.

There is still a place for a very technical computer person, especially during delivery. At this time, when the expert system has moved successfully through the prototype stage and has been completely developed, problems can arise. Some real problems at this stage are getting the system to run in real time, to tie into existing databases, or simply to interface properly with existing hardware. This creates a need for a very good technical systems, architectural person who understands hardware and software very well. Often, companies did not view this as a separate position, because the very talented computer scientists who were building the tools were also working with the experts and acting as knowledge engineers one day and tool builders the next. When it became time to deliver these products, they were the ones who solved the porting and connection problems. Today, it is understood within these groups that when large systems or several systems are being built, a team member must be available to work solely on the problems of connecting it and getting it to deliver smoothly.

The need for excellent documentation people is growing. It is more and more important, not only for the shell products being built, but also for applications, that the documentation and user interface get attention at the beginning. As a result, positions are now being created for professionals with interfacing and documentation skills. They will be hired as part of the AI team.

THE SPREAD OF AI INTO MANAGEMENT INFORMATION SYSTEMS

AI is spreading beyond the Fortune 500 companies to medium-size and small companies. Expert systems, in particular, is a technology that is proliferating beyond the research lab or those technically trained in grass-roots movements. It is beginning to affect corporate management information systems (MIS). Chief information officers (CIOs), whatever their titles, are beginning to recognize that these new expert systems are not like the operational and administrative support systems that MIS traditionally developed, but are more like the traditional decision support systems. What were the more advanced systems of the late 1970s and early 1980s have now begun to contain some AI. If smart, the head of this group is a manager who is presently working to establish the leadership for the company's AI group. The desire to hire knowledge engineers suggests a maturing of the technology. In general, the early expert system technology that spun off YCIN at Stanford has become fairly sophisticated, deliverable, and usable by many. Therefore, layers of technical people are not as necessary when one gets to this stage, especially when the AI group is an applications group within MIS.

THE PC EXPERT SYSTEM SHELL COMPANIES

AI-expert systems technology has progressed to the point where it can enter the mainstream of MIS because of the second generation of software start-ups. After the original hardware companies and major software shell builders came a plethora of small companies. They are attempting to build useful shells that will run on PCs. This allows expert systems to be developed and delivered at a reasonable cost. One of the earliest of these was M.1, a shell that Teknowledge developed. It runs on PCs and was designed to permit users to build fairly sophisticated prototypes to prove the viability of the system. Customers were to use M.1 and then advance to Teknowledge's more powerful shell, called S.1. One surprise, however, was the customers who wanted to go to larger shells did not necessarily choose S.1. Instead, they frequently chose ART (a product of Inference), KEE (a product of Intellicorp), or one of the other shells. What was even more surprising was that many who used M.1 to successfully build small prototype expert systems decided that they liked those systems. Although the systems solved only small problems, they were put to use. This development quickly opened the door for the other start-up companies that were attempting to build PC shells. An example is Nexpert, one early, affordable PC shell. It helped stimulate the previously mentioned grass-roots movement in expert systems development.

One other very successful computer shell that ran on a PC was TI's Personal Consultant. It was conceived essentially as a shell that would demonstrate the power of expert systems. In a sense, it was a throw-away developed to raise interest in expert systems and also sell TI's new AI hardware, which supported more sophisticated AI tools. Again, this product was a pleasant surprise, because it was bought for itself. Quite a few successful expert systems have been built using Personal Consultant.

From a staffing point of view, the kinds of professionals who were employed in these second-generation start-ups were similar to those in the earlier, tool-building groups. They were mostly AI-trained Ph.D.s or else brilliant hackers who could use Lisp or Prolog to develop tools.

THE MAINFRAME EXPERT SYSTEM SHELL COMPANIES

One movement in the industry has been the attempt to build expert systems shells and products that allow the user to develop and deliver expert systems on mainframe computers, especially IBMs. This is the strategy of a company in northern California called Aion (Palo Alto, Calif.), originally staffed predominantly by former employees of IBM, and Artificial Intelligence Corp. (AIC) (Waltham, Mass.). Both Aion and AIC have introduced mainframe expert system shell products. Although they run on traditional hardware, they have been created by a combination of AI Ph.D.s and hackers plus experts in traditional computer languages and architectures.

AI APPLICATIONS COMPANIES

Another kind of company that has existed from the very beginning is the dedicated AI product company. Its products are decision support systems or expert system applications that have been targeted toward a particular domain or application within an industry or even a sector of an industry. The earliest of these companies was Applied Expert Systems (Apex). The staffing profile of Apex was discussed earlier. Other companies that operated from the very beginning on the premise of building sophisticated expert systems dedicated to a particular application were Palladian (Cambridge, Mass.) and Syntelligence (Palo Alto, Calif.). Many of the early contributors to the success of the products of Apex and Syntelligence have left those companies. Those companies are now at the stage of selling their existing products or attempting to perfect and sell them. Meanwhile, there has been a second-tier of start-ups trying to develop and sell applied products. These newer companies tend not to emphasize the expert systems part of their products. Expert systems are embedded in what appear to be traditional products. They appear more user friendly and useful to those who buy them. Examples of these kinds of products are found in the new wave of AI start-ups, such as Bachman Systems (Cambridge, Mass.), but they also are beginning to be seen in some of the products being developed in more established companies, such as Lotus and Apple.

What are the staffing configurations of these companies building dedicated products? Again, they are composed of the same variety of professionals: well-trained Ph.D.s working side by side with those trained in the computer sciences. Because these are dedicated expert systems based on true-life situations, knowledge engineers played a major development role under the direction of excellent technical managers.

STAFFING ADDITIONS TO THE AI GROUP

It took a lot more people besides the technical AI people discussed so far to staff all the different types of AI groups. From the very beginning, there has been a large number of marketers. Some marketed research and development to government agencies while investigating the market for all of the product companies. These marketers became very knowledgeable about AI. They did "yeoman" work in presenting the AI story to the marketplace. Another professional useful to the AI movement was the product development manager. As the vendors of both hardware and software began to develop products, they often found that they needed more than project managers.

Because there was a need to manage the product from conception to delivery, AI houses began to promote the most talented managers or to seek beyond in-house software expertise and bring in software product development managers not familiar with AI.

There also was a tremendous need for professionals skilled in training and customer support. These specialists were needed not just by the software vendors to support customers, but also in the large research labs where there was a big effort to train technical staff in AI languages and tools.

Later on, AI groups began to designate human resource professionals. These people frequently began as researchers but ended up supporting most of the hiring. Or they were hired specifically to handle all recruiting. Some were originally internal people who handled this responsibility as part of another job. In the earlier start-ups, some of the personnel people came from the computer science development ranks and took on personnel work because they understood the company's technical needs. But sometimes they were administrators or even secretaries who took on the added responsibility of helping with the staffing of the company.

As the industry became more mature, AI companies began to hire human resource professionals. They came from other software companies or even other technical industries. This has brought more knowledge and experience to the human resource function.

As AI has developed, the role of the technical leader has become increasingly important. The title of chief technical officer is beginning to appear not only in the start-ups, but also in the AI research labs. Sometimes, the chief technical officer is called the chief scientist or the senior scientist, depending on the extent to which the person is involved in management.

For the first time, there are several chief financial officers (CFOs) in the AI industry. They came mostly from other software companies. However, some started as controllers and worked their way up to CFO.

The role of chief executive officer (CEO) or chief operating officer (COO) has become increasingly important. In the start-ups, the CEOs and COOS were the early founders. As their operations matured, these people grew in their ability to take the company to its next milestone, or else they stepped aside (or were pushed aside) and replaced by executives with track records in growing technical companies.

WHERE AI PROFESSIONALS CAN BE LOCATED

We have reviewed all the staff roles needed in the AI movement thus far in its history. We will discuss the problem of locating qualified professionals. Obviously, a key criterion is the kind of company one is trying to staff. Let us begin with the highly technical positions requiring Ph.D.s. Today, they are found in a wide variety of places; in the early 1980s, qualified Ph.D.s were found only in universities or in highly AI-oriented research labs, private or government. Now qualified Ph.D.s are found in many start-ups, a larger number of university research labs, many more universities than at first, and certainly government labs. They are also found in all of the companies that are servicing the government, including those clustered around Washington, D.C. They can also be found in Fortune 500 companies.

Good computer science hackers with few credentials can be found anywhere. In general, the best of them can be found near university centers happily doing the creative work that they are so good at. They are less likely to be found within traditional MIS groups in industry.

Qualified knowledge engineers, on the other hand, are a product of a wide variety of university master's programs or possibly of the in-house training programs in larger companies or research labs. Sometimes, they were sent to the shell companies for training. The AI consulting groups in software companies, the Big Eight and industry is where they are presently located.

Technical managers come from two backgrounds. Most come from an AI background, where they have taken on progressively more responsibility. The other source are managers who have been working in more traditional computer companies or engineering or one of the other sciences, perhaps even business. Once given a leadership role in an AI research group or an AI start-up, they have established track records that qualify them to be AI technical managers.

Marketing and salespeople almost always come from the ranks of people trained in other software and hardware disciplines. A few bright people with master's degrees and even some AI-oriented PH.D.s have chosen to switch to the sales and marketing side because they are very business oriented. There were some very bright young people at Inference, Intellicorp, and Teknowledge who have developed into excellent marketers. Most AI marketing and salespeople have remained in the AI industry. However, some of them have already moved back to companies selling more traditional hardware and software. Some have even returned to other industries where they were previously employed.

The people involved in early development were often given the opportunity to move from an AI technical position into management and product development. Frequently, when they conceived and worked on a product, then went on to take it to delivery. Thus, they become quite skilled at product development. There are also MBAs and those with computer science degrees with experience in product development who joined the AI community.

When they succeeded, they became experienced product developers. Today, they are spread among the existing AI product development groups, although some have returned to traditional software houses. It is a little easier for a manager to move in and out of AI development groups than it is for the developer to do so. Developers who have worked with sophisticated AI languages such as Lisp or Prolog tend not to return to the traditional languages. There is a movement of the sales and marketing, product development, and technical managers in AI to move to other industries. This makes it more difficult to locate them. In contrast, the traditional AI types who build systems (the Ph.D.s and hackers) tend to remain in the Lisp-based operations they prefer.

The people involved in early training and customer support usually were hired from similar positions in other software houses. Of course, there were technical development AI people who found that they preferred the training and customer support side of the business. This does not necessarily mean they were not good at what they did before: They were simply choosing to narrow their interests a little. In general, many of the good trainers and customer support people were the same people who, when in the university, were very devoted teachers. They found training as rewarding as developing systems and products.

Documentation specialists have diverse backgrounds mainly because many of these people work free-lance. Documentation is full-time work at a large vendor like DEC. In such situations, the documentation specialist gets involved during the early phases of software design.

On the other hand, many smaller companies and start-ups do not build enough products to need a documentation specialist on staff; at least, they don't believe they need one. Small companies often hire documentation people on a free-lance basis. If a small vendor needs to create documentation, it should consider free-lancers and consultants.

Chief technical officers, CFOs, COOs, and CEOs were usually original founders, or at the least one of the first persons to be hired. As the company or the research division grew, they were able to increase their knowledge of the position and grow with it to take on the official titles of chief technical officer, CEO, and so on. These people are easy to target because of the level of their positions. In addition, their successes and failures have been well documented. Some of these AI-experienced chief technical officers, CFOs, and CEOs did come from traditional hardware/software companies and were hired particularly to bring in outside expertise. If one was looking to hire someone for these reasons from outside the AI industry, one would have to look very carefully and attempt to bring in someone who would feel comfortable in promoting and managing AI technology.

In general, the natural language groups follow much the same pattern as other groups in AI. But other aspects of AI have grown quite substantially in this decade. Certainly, the growing emphasis on user interface and human factors has been influenced by AI. Work in vision and optical-character recognition plus the auditory and speech input-output work have been notable. These advances have come from start-up companies such as Kurzweil Applied Intelligence, Inc. (Cambridge, Mass.), and some of the large research labs.

The current interesting technologies are parallel processing, connectionism, and neural networks. Here we see the same progress in these technologies characteristic of expert systems. A combination of work is going on in the research labs, in start-ups, and in the dedicated product development areas. The same types of people are found working in all of these companies. The accent originally was on the technical people; then the emphasis slowly shifted to the marketing people and the traditional administrative and chief executive officer types of positions.

HIRING AI PROFESSIONALS

How does one go about hiring people for AI groups? Is it just a matter of advertising? Targeting the appropriate candidates and letting them know about the job sounds like a simple process. Actually, advertising is one of the most difficult aspects of hiring. A common misconception of those in hiring positions is that advertisements automatically produce qualified candidates. What is less obvious to many personnel people is that some applicants know little or nothing about the hiring establishment, including its structure, goals, and aspirations. Some companies don't sell themselves as enthusiastically as they should. They are too shy, feeling that talking about the company will be regarded as bragging. This is one reason why hiring managers often rely on the personnel staff, or the personnel staff itself relies on professional recruiters to bring the company's message to qualified candidates. In fact, professional recruiters are particularly good at recognizing difficult-to-find AI professionals and can also be helpful in conveying the message of the client and detailing its advantages and disadvantages. They contribute strongly to the total hiring process of AI staff because of the kind of professional support they bring to that process.

Once qualified candidates have been found and convinced that they should come in for an interview, it is important that the interview be conducted in an organized and sensitive manner. In a good interview, the candidate's abilities and technical strengths are assessed, and the candidate is given all the information he or she needs about the available position and the company as a whole. Once this has been done successfully, and client and candidate appear to be interested in each other, an attractive compensation package must be put together.

Obviously, competitive compensation must be offered. Expect to pay at least 10 to 15 percent more than a candidate's previous salary to get the person to move to your company. An alternative is to pay the same salary as an established group but hire professionals with less experience. Agreeing on compensation is a sensitive part of the hiring process.

Then there are the problems and traumas of relocation. This tends to be an ever-present factor unless local people are the only candidates. After a compensation package has been agreed on, the candidate must also agree on the job description and the goals of the job. If these items are negotiated successfully and the candidate decides to accept the position, the company is responsible for orienting the new person properly to the job. Each employee must understand the corporate culture and be given an opportunity to grow within the corporation.

Staffing an AI group is a responsibility that goes beyond hiring talented people to carry out organizational goals. It is a company's responsibility to bring in the best people to accomplish the operation's goals, people whom the corporation will support with both proper working environment and the encouragement to achieve success.

2

Apprenticeships
and Technology Transfer

JEFF C. TANNER, IntelliCorp

INTRODUCTION

The availability of object oriented software development tools such as IntelliCorp's Knowledge Engineering Environment™ (KEE®) has created the need for mechanisms to reduce ramp-up time to use such tools for purchasers' applications. To meet these needs, IntelliCorp has provided two mechanisms: (1) training courses which are important to present a basic syntactical walk through of a tool and how it can be applied to generic applications, and (2) apprenticeships which are an effective vehicle for clients to receive a technology transfer, which is directly applicable to their problem, from an experienced Knowledge Systems Engineer (KSE).

WHAT IS TECHNOLOGY TRANSFER?

When one buys consulting, the consultants will (1) build a turnkey system whereby the client is involved only in providing specifications and test data, and (2) work alongside the client like an experienced "buddy" who leads and tutors throughout system development. The latter is technology transfer in the context of learning as a by-product of doing something useful.

PROVIDING TECHNOLOGY TRANSFER THROUGH
APPRENTICESHIPS

An apprenticeship at IntelliCorp is a twenty-day plus session staffed by the Applications and Research Division whereby a KSE provides technology transfer of knowledge system design and implementation to a client. Unlike consulting, in which the consultant is asked to perform one specific task without technology transfer, an apprenticeship is the opportunity for developing KSEs to participate in all the steps necessary to construct a demonstrable knowledge system prototype. Unlike training, in which trainers introduce the tools for developing knowledge systems, experienced KSEs show how to effectively use the tools for domain-specific applications.

After building knowledge systems for more than four years, completing eighteen such apprenticeships and a half-dozen major consulting contracts, the author can reasonably present the experience of knowledge systems engineering. The following discussions are a distillation of some of the author's experiences.

The profile of services that a KSE can provide in an apprenticeship is as unique as each client. A client may want to construct a knowledge system using one of the following three approaches:

1. *Following a well established AI methodology such as model-based reasoning.* A KSE will assist the client by elaborating on actions performed during such functions as modeling the knowledge system, Lisp programming, and tool utilization. This technology transfer is developmental. The majority of IntelliCorp's apprenticeships are of this type.

2. *Following a recently documented AI methodology such as qualitative reasoning.* A KSE and the client must develop a firm understanding of the logical foundations of AI to interpret and apply this methodology. This technology transfer is applied theoretically. Few clients are academically prepared to understand the results of such services provided by a KSE. The client must understand the risks of attempting to apply any recently discovered methodology. Such risks are:

   a. Most recent methodologies have been applied only to small domains, and they may not be applicable to large domains.
   b. Limitations in the new methodology that may not be apparent or known before will be discovered.

The majority of the apprenticeship time is used in evaluating the methodology, not in actual knowledge system development and contruction.

3. *The client is looking for a "buddy."* A client may already have an extensive background in knowledge system construction, but could use an experienced person to review and comment on the approach taken in developing the knowledge system. Such requests come from client KSEs who are working by themselves and could use a sounding board for a few weeks. Or the client is in need of experience in building a certain part of the system; it could be in data access, interface, or delivery. In such apprenticeships, the client and the KSE will be building different parts of the knowledge system concurrently. Daily, the KSE should explain enhancements of his/her part of the system and review the client's part. Such apprenticeships are quite exhilarating because of the high caliber of the participants involved.

BUILDING A KNOWLEDGE SYSTEM BY CONTRACT CONSULTING

In contract consulting, a client asks a KSE to build a knowledge system, and the client is not interested in technology transfer, or such transfer is not the major component. In such a case, the KSE is responsible for developing well-documented code so that the client or another KSE may be able to debug or enhance the knowledge system in the future. The KSE should be responsible in delivering a report indicating theoretical background, operational instructions, and system structure.

This service is most productive in developing client-specific code, but it is least effective in providing technology transfer to the client. Even with the best documentation, few clients would perform their own enhancements to a knowledge system built by a KSE. The client is dependent upon the KSE to provide future servicing and updating. This is potentially not as cost effective to either the client or the KSE's company. If the responsible KSE should not be available for future work, the client has ultimate responsibility for maintaining its software.

So, if the intent of the client is to acquire technology transfer, then the author strongly recommends that the client close the contract with an apprenticeship when the KSE is ready to deliver the knowledge system. In such an apprenticeship, the system developer KSE will explain in detail the internal structure of the system and assist the attending participants in adding modification and enhancements.

ARRANGING AND SCHEDULING AN APPRENTICESHIP

Apprenticeships are best held outside the client's site for the following reasons:

1. Ready availability of other resources as the need arises. When apprenticeships are held at IntelliCorp's headquarters, these resources can be other KSEs with experience pertinent to the client's application, additional systems. product engineers, and managers.

2. A minimum of interruptions to the client who has become relatively inaccessible by needs at the home office.

Most apprenticeships for clients of IntelliCorp are held at the IntelliCorp site. Even when an apprenticeship is not held at IntelliCorp's headquarters, it can still be held outside the client's site. For example, a Scottish customer chose as the location a hotel-castle in the Scottish Highlands and arranged for scrumptious five-course luncheons to be prepared daily by the hotel's gourmet chef at a very reasonable cost.

HOMEWORK BEFORE AN APPRENTICESHIP

All too frequently has the excitement about a computer technology come before establishing a need for it. It is like the enthusiastic purchaser of a potato slicer forcing the instrument to open bottles before the purchaser discovers the best use for a potato slicer.

Before starting a major consulting or apprenticeship with a client, the client should prepare a detailed technical design and feasibility review to be informally presented to the assigned KSE to the apprenticeship. Such preliminary reviews begin a successful relationship with clients. The client should cover the following knowledge system preconstruction issues during the feasibility review. However, most importantly, the client should state specific expectations of the knowledge system upon completion.

Knowledge System Preconstruction Issues

Present a model of the selected domain.

Determine if a production system is expected or if the work is being done to explore the technology.

Present the expected benefits of building a knowledge system focusing on this domain.

Explore the reason artificial intelligence (AI) was selected over conventional software approaches.

Identify how domain experts will be made available for consultation during system building.

Determine the necessary level of abstraction.

Decide what knowledge needs to be directly accessible (be in the knowledge system) or indirectly accessible (be in a data base).

Show that test data are available for comparing results.

Ascertain what is being sought in the proposed Knowledge System: knowledge accessibility, increased problem-solving speed, a domain tutor, or some other feature.

Identify the expected end-users of this knowledge system.

Resolve what platform this system will eventually be distributed upon.

Decide upon expected frequency of querying the knowledge system as well as the expected response time.

Present a rough schedule from initiation of system development to when the system is to be on-line in production.

Determine the half-life of the domain knowledge; i.e., when this knowledge will become obsolete.

Have a clear idea of how upper management views this project.

Understanding of a domain is essential for both the client and the KSE. If knowledge of a domain is weak, then the KSE will not have much to go on to define any structure. It is recommended that this preliminary review be held at the client's site as a preapprenticeship consultation so that the KSE can have full visual and other pertinent familiarity with all the components and actions that are a part of the domain. It can be a great visual breakthrough to see better how the pieces of the domain fit together as the expert points out the components and processes.

The main purpose of this initial review is to determine and realistically manage expectations; these are crucial to project success and vital for client-KSE relations.

PARTICIPANTS IN AN APPRENTICESHIP

In any apprenticeship, there usually will be a group of participants given active responsibilities. In some instances, only a single individual may be involved. Those who are not active participants will hinder the technology transfer process for others. A KSE can work most effectively with a maximum of three people per apprenticeship. One should be an expert and the other two should be developing to be KSEs. There should be no more than two people to a computer terminal. If the domain is large and complex, more advisory KSEs will need to be involved. Some of the participant's functions can be overlapped to keep groups small; for example, the interface designer and the end-user expert could form one team.

The group of participants a client should send to an apprenticeship are

1. Two participants who have an interest in KSEs. These participants should know the knowledge system tool, its underlying programming language, how to develop programs in the development environment, and be familiar with the expected delivery environment(s). If these participants do not meet the requirements above, then they need to take the necessary steps to learn these skills prior to the apprenticeship. or technology transfer will be remedial.

   a. One participant will construct the core knowledge representation of the domain.
   b. The other participant will be concerned with user and environmental interface issues, such as whether or not the knowledge system needs to acquire data from an external source (data base or modem).

Another advantage of having two developing KSEs is that it is good to have a "buddy system" when developing knowledge systems. The initial conceptualization during system modeling can be mind boggling; thus, the buddy system reduces individual stress and allows for sharing of ideas with somebody who also understands knowledge systems engineering. It also leads to better coding practices; if a KSE knows that the work will be reviewed and possibly modified by another KSE, then the code will be less esoteric, well commented, modular, and lucid.

2. Participants (or a participant) with the domain expertise needed for the success of building a knowledge system.

   a. Participants should have an in-depth current involvement in the domain under scrutiny to assist the core programmer.
   b. Participants should also possess an intuitive feel for expected end-users and the goals of the target system to assist the interface programmer.

In some cases, the expertise may have to be provided by more than one person. The domain expertise may be provided during only a portion of the apprenticeship time. In other cases, one of the client's KSEs may also be a domain expert.

When working in complex domains, it is advisable to bring into an apprenticeship a junior domain expert: somebody who has been recently trained and has been working in the domain for a maximum of two or three years. A junior expert will provide two qualities to the apprenticeship: empathy and assistance in the KSE's struggle to grasp the domain's fundamentals. He or she can also serve as a translator between the KSE and the expert. Junior experts can usually spend more time on the apprenticeship because they are much less costly than experts. The most significant benefit clients receive in bringing junior experts into apprenticeships is close association with both the expert and the KSE.

WHAT MAKES A GOOD KNOWLEDGE SYSTEMS ENGINEER?

The KSE must have the ability to grasp the essence of a client's domain knowledge and problem, to present a clear vision of the apprenticeship's direction, to communicate enthusiasm, and to gain confidence as an apprenticeship leader almost immediately. At IntelliCorp, an apprenticeship is typically twenty days. So, IntelliCorp's KSEs must demonstrate all of the above abilities within a few days in order to make the client feel confident and leave with a demonstrable prototype at the end of the apprenticeship.

To instill this confidence and vision into the apprenticeship, the KSE should have a strong background in the logical foundations of artificial intelligence (a master's degree in AI or cognitive science, or a minor in one of these fields with a strong computer science background). This person should also be a very good listener, an inquisitive sleuth, a near-neurotic stickler for knowledge consistency, a strong programmer with an exemplary and lucid style, an experienced project leader, an expert in one field or a semi-expert in a few fields, and, on rare occasions, a group psychologist and referee. Also, without exception, the KSE must have constructed and delivered several knowledge systems before attempting an apprenticeship.

The following may be evangelical, but the author finds the title of Knowledge Engineer quite silly because it implies too much hocus-pocus. The author does not design knowledge, he designs systems which manipulate knowledge. Hence the title Knowledge Systems Engineer seems more appropriate.

CONFINING A DOMAIN

How does one determine the necessary level of abstraction from a domain for a knowledge system?

A domain is like an onion with many layers of knowledge, with each layer more fundamental than the last in its knowledge. A KSE is an onion peeler, studying the domain layer by layer with the assistance of the domain experts, and then confining the knowledge system to resolve problems within a limited set of layers.

Let us take the domain of a electrical plant where the client wishes to build a knowledge system for its maintenance. The first layer is the basic plant operations that expert operators would know. Experts at this layer could supply rules that guide the KSE in making judgements. Typically, the rules involve "if-then" scenarios. It may be the case that these experts do not understand why they do what they do. If this is important in constructing the knowledge system, then the knowledge system requires more fundamental reasoning, which would be in the next underlying layers of the domain onion. Usually only a small subset of experts can explain the relationship of the deeper layers of knowledge to the higher layers. The deeper the need to understand this relationship, the harder it is to model the knowledge system and to find an expert who can articulate it. Therefore, the KSE must use discretion as to how deep the reasoning of the knowledge system must be.

Simply, given a set of observations, the KSE must determine how many layers of domain knowledge a well-modeled knowledge system will require to reach the same conclusion as the domain expert it was designed to mimic. Or put another way, what layers does the client wish to encapsulate into a knowledge system? Focus on the layers which the intended end-users wish reasoning assistance. Define the design constraints of a knowledge system by defining the wedge cut from the domain onion. Have the top layer of this wedge be the intended viewpoint of the end-user and go down only as many layers as necessary to provide reasoning and explanations that are understandable and useful to end-users.

SELECTING EXPERTS

The domain expert is the key participant for the success of a knowledge system project. The ease of building the system is proportional to the strength of the knowledge model gained from an expert. Ideally, do not attempt to build a knowledge system if a client does not have access to a good domain expert—an expert who is knowledgeable across all layers of the domain's defined constraints (or get the participation of more than one expert) and who can express this expertise with lucidity.

Sometimes a KSE will face a situation in which the client wishes to bring a semi-expert into an apprenticeship. This person may be chosen because of availability (e.g., retired) or expendability (e.g., member of a recently terminated project). These domain experts may tend to be weak, obsolete, or limited in the proposed domain. Suggest that the client avoid selecting these domain experts who are not currently active. Currently nonactive domain experts are fine for assisting in the initial modeling of a knowledge system and for providing generally agreed-upon knowledge of the domain. However, currently active domain experts must be made available to establish legitimacy and confidence in the accuracy in the knowledge system, to verify a current need for the proposed knowledge system, and to provide current test data.

There are experts who have mastered, possibly over several decades, an obscure specialty, and in the eyes of a client, this expertise is very valuable—too valuable to risk losing. In effect, clients desire to clone the expert's knowledge at any cost. Yet, a client's management is typically too reluctant to release its experts for any significant amount of time. It is necessary for the client to use a domain expert with discretion to appease management.

It is not necessary to pull domain experts away from their standard activities for long periods of time. An expert is vital in the first stage of knowledge system development to ensure a proper foundation for the knowledge model. This should take a couple of weeks of the expert's time initially (not necessarily in one chunk of time). After that, the expert can often be made available by phone or fax. When a model is established, the expert should be available to critique, provide tests with a logical explanation for expected results.

HANDLING AN EXPERT

Experts can sometimes be difficult people with whom to deal. The KSE must gain an expert's respect at all costs. The easiest way to do this is to listen attentively at all times. The KSE should try to avoid repeating questions, especially questions basic to a domain. One way to avoid repetition is to tape the conversation with the expert and have it transcibed. The KSE must pick up the common-sense fundamentals of a domain quickly and unquestioningly.

Being a good listener does not mean having the ability to recall every statement a domain expert utters. To listen is to simultaneously piece together a puzzle and detect inconsistent facts as the expert presents them. A good listener is initially unbiased and receptive. Gradually, the KSE should be able to effectively probe with relevant questions, and appropriately and nonjudgmentally challenge the expert about the domain with sincere interest and enthusiasm. *To listen is to understand.*

Again, an expert wants to feel important. An expert is divulging the precious secrets of his or her private realm, and he or she wants to be appreciated for sharing this accumulated knowledge. Promote the idea of a personal legacy of the expert by naming the system after the expert, such as the "Kelly Dam Maintenance Project."[1] The expert thus becomes fully (or even emotionally) involved with the success of the project because of personal identification and ownership. The KSE should discuss with the client's management providing special recognition to the assigned domain expert. This is because the assigned expert is a major contributor to the success of the project; without this expertise, the knowledge system project would not have been possible. This will reduce significantly an expert's fear of divulging his or her specialty.

Experts can find the interrogations troubling. Sometimes they will wonder if the KSEs understand what they are saying. Experts will be frustrated by the lack of communication because, most likely, KSEs will be inexperienced in the domain under study. Everything about the domain may be new to a KSE: the vocabulary, the components, and the processes. All of this has to be crudely understood prior to building a model of the domain reasoning. This is where a client's junior expert can be very helpful.

Experts tend to be tactiturn, and may wish not reveal enough about the domain. Though seemingly willing, an expert will listen to questions and reply simply yes or no. Explanations, when given, may tend to be uninformatively brief. Experts may believe they are being cooperative with the KSEs, but they may act unconsciously reluctant to part with their own expertise.

They best way to open up an expert is to go out socially. Dine and interact with the expert about topics other than the domain under study. Allow the expert to be relaxed and comfortable with the KSE as a sociable and intelligent person, not as an interrogator.

At times while interviewing an expert, the KSE may find that the domain knowledge is inadequate, incomplete, or inconsistent, and the expert is stymied as to how to resolve the situation. Such situations can be quite embarrassing to an expert. Tact and courtesy are of utmost importance in keeping an expert at ease. The expert should feel that he or she is a valuable resource contributing to the success of this project. Ask the expert to whom he or she would look for advice when all personal resources have been exhausted. Then have the client arrange meetings with this new expert immediately.

An expert's time is usually precious and limited, so the KSE and the other participants must spend time judiciously with the expert. Present the expert with the recommended basic knowledge representation model that will be implemented in the knowledge system and improve it until it meets the approval of the expert. Don't bog the expert down with programming details as to how the knowledge system will be built; basically, keep the expert informed about only the rudimentary details of the system and focus on building the best model of the domain. Keeping the experts uninformed about the programming environment and language constraints allows the experts to present an unhampered view of their domain. Otherwise, they will feel compelled to present a view which will work within these constraints. Making the domain view fit within the system environment's constraints is an issue for the KSEs and not the experts.

---

[1] Wall Street Journal, August 12, 1988, page 1, column 1.

ASSESSING THE COMPLEXITY OF KNOWLEDGE SYSTEM

A knowledge system is made up of five parts: structure, reasoning, data access, interface, and delivery. For each part to be delivered in the demonstrable prototype, allow ten days to discuss and construct it in an apprenticeship. An apprenticeship typically covers in twenty days only two parts in depth and others only partially.

If the client wants a demonstrable prototype, the KSE must allow the interface part to be covered in depth, allowing only one other part to be covered with reasonable completeness. This second is usually a choice between structure or reasoning. The choice is easily made by assessing the complexity of these parts. Structural complexity is the detail level of abstraction (class, member, attribute, facet) of the components and data that the system needs to handle. Reasoning complexity includes the depth and breadth of the reasoning and the methodology chosen. In other words, is the component abstraction high but reasoning simple or is the abstraction low but reasoning complex?

Typically an apprenticeship deals with singularly complex systems, allowing the first ten days to focus on the singular part that is of highest complexity and anxiety, and the second ten days to focus on interface, data access, and delivery issues. If the domain is highly complex in both parts, then a presentable prototype is not feasible in the twenty days of apprenticeship, and an additional ten days would be required.

COACHING MANAGEMENT

An important rule in apprenticeships is that managers should not be present in the development sessions. Managers tend to get so nervous observing the occasional negative details of any system development. For example, in one apprenticeship when a bug in the system code was discovered, the attending manager held his breath until the bug was fixed, and it was fixed quite promptly to avoid seeing the manager turning an unpleasant shade of blue. The point is tension eventually rubs everybody, especially when working in close quarters for an extended period.

Managers have very vital roles outside apprenticeships. They should be acquiring resources (experts, data, machines, etc.), reviewing apprenticeship contracts, and discussing apprenticeship problems with the attending KSE's management.

CASE STUDIES OF APPRENTICESHIPS

In this section are presented case studies of knowledge systems engineering assisting in piecing together the knowledge that is to be assembled into a cohesive reasoning package called a knowledge system. All case studies are of actual apprenticeships, and all use the same knowledge system building tool: KEE®. These apprenticeship case studies will focus primarily upon group dynamics, interactions with experts, domain abstraction, knowledge acquisition, and leadership by the KSE; technical detail of domains and knowledge systems will be presented only to gain a better understanding of the focus issues.

1.   Case Focus: Well Prepared Participants

Knowledge System: Power plant diagnostic system

Domain: Nuclear power plant control station

End-User: Station operators

Description: Provides operator assistance during malfunctions for at least two hours until an operations expert can arrive on the scene.

This client, whose company was still in its early start-up stage, brought in its entire staff of four members, to build an application for nuclear-power-station diagnosis. This was a "perfect" apprenticeship because each participant was very experienced in the expected task in building the knowledge system. The duty of the KSE was simple: to come up with a model of the domain, build additional programming tools which would assist the client programmers, and question the experts. One domain expert in this apprenticeship was a university professor in AI. When the gathering of expertise was on hold, he also participated in programming the code. The client had come well prepared, having cataloged the knowledge and explored reasoning alternatives. In this apprenticeship, technology transfer was focused on domain modeling and how to reason over uncertainty.

2.   Case Focus: Undertaking a new AI Methodology

Knowledge System: Propellent process expert

Domain: Propellent production facilities

End-User: Senior operators, junior and senior chemical engineers

Description: If a production operator notices that a certain monitored value of a batch of propellent has moved outside established constraints (such as excessive temperature delta), then the system operator requests what would reverse this undesirable trend.

The domain included a huge vat, which was attached to a mixer, containing a stable batch of an organic substance. The temperature of the batch is maintained by a water-cooling jacket surrounding the vat. During the production, different reagents are added to the batch to complete the chemical makeup of a propellent. So, a basic overview of the propellent production is that reagents were added to the batch while it was mixed and the temperature was maintained to produce a vat of propellent after one week. During this week, the production is broken up into a dozen phases. Each phase has a different set of processes (mixing, reagent adding, etc.) and limits on externally measurable variables (temperature, mixer power, viscosity, etc.). At the start of production, a batch is worth about $2000, but at the end of a week, processed material is worth approximately $250,000, based upon labor, facility, and reagent costs. If, during any production phase, the batch is processed outside any of the established limits for the appropriate length of time, then the batch must be thrown out. Thus, there is an unrecoverable loss of a quarter of a million dollars.

Recoveries were handled by senior operators referring to a well-used manuscript that provided a different set of solutions to similar sets of problems that may occur for each phase of the production. What the client initially wanted was a system in which a senior operator could enter in its erroneous variables of a production phase and the system would bring up recovery measures verbatim to the established documentation. Such a system has little value, and no knowledge is gained. In effect, it would eventually either constrain availability of knowledge, or the system would not be used at all because the operators would return to using the printed document.

However, the document had its limitations; it could not recover new, undocumented problems. In such cases, a senior chemical production engineer was brought in to perform the recovery. The steps for recovery recommended by this expert were similar to other recovery operations. What was not being learned by any of the operators or junior chemical engineers was the rationale for choosing the steps towards recovery of a batch.

After interviewing the domain expert for five days, it became evident that the expert took all the processes that could control the production of a batch and simplified them to a naive physics viewpoint. During this apprenticeship, the model used for representing the domain expert methodology was qualitative processes (QP).

Take, for example, a pot full of water on a heating element as a stage for explaining QP. At any stage, there are various variables that can be accessible (measurable), inaccessible (calculable), or controllable (by a switch or knob). An accessible variable is temperature, which can be measured using a thermometer; an inaccessible variable is heat transfer between the element and the pot; and the controllable variable is the knob that controls the heating intensity of the element. If the heating element is turned on by a controlling variable (the knob), then the pot will get hot by the process of heat transfer. As the pot is increasing in temperature, then the water in the pot will get hot by the same process. Eventually, the water will change to a gaseous state by a different process called boiling, which will occur only if the accessible variable exceeds a certain value.

Such an approach (i.e., QP) for doing knowledge system modeling is not recommended for the novice knowledge system development group. However, because the client's developing knowledge systems programmer had high-caliber Lisp programming skills and basic AI knowledge, the KSE felt comfortable that a complex system could be maintainable without the KSE's assistance. So, the apprenticeship set its course to take a qualitative approach to this project. For the first week, because it was difficult to come up with a structure for the domain model based upon QP, the interaction with the expert took place in the morning, and the KSE presented him each afternoon with a differently highlighted tour map of San Francisco to keep him entertained in the afternoons.

What transpired in the end was a knowledge system with a process toolbox that could be used by chemical-production engineers to see how the characteristics of the propellent batch could be altered if subjected to a different arrangement of processes. Even the domain expert could use it as a proof-of-concept system to check a production process configuration based upon his own qualitative viewpoint of processes.

System development took fourteen person-weeks, which included the eight person-weeks for the apprenticeship. Three different QP approaches were studied and tried by Colin Campbell (Evens and Sutherland), a superb programmer, and author with supportive assistance by QP notables a Johan de Kleer, Ken Forbus, and Conrad Bock (IntelliCorp).

3. Case Focus: Managing Disagreements

Knowledge System: Network configuration system

Domain: Telecommunications

End-User: Network operators

Description: If a communication link goes down, the first objective is to maintain customer satisfaction by rerouting calls through operating links as quickly as possible; the second objective is to establish the cause of failure; and the third is to initiate repair.

Apprenticeships can be a pressure cooker experience. Put multiple experts who have never worked together into a small room with a dapper KSE, the author, for a month, and without question, some stress and aggravation for all participants is bound to be a byproduct from knowledge acquisition.

The KSE is likely to be a gullible, unbiased participant as long as the knowledge gathered is logically consistent. If it is not consistent or a disagreement between experts ensues, the KSE acts as an impartial judge allowing the apprenticeship participants to act as lawyers presenting cases with supportive evidence for their heuristics over a domain.

When disagreements between experts get too heated, the domain is put aside and there is a switch to manipulations and emotions to sway the development of the knowledge system. The initial thought of a KSE is to have readily available a gun with N-1 bullets, and leave it in the room with the N disagreeable experts, so as to only have to deal with one disagreeable expert. Alternatively, it is best that the KSE should be willing to jump into the cross fire and act as an arbitrator showing the inconsistencies in the arguments.

Most of the time, disagreements are a positive sign of special-case situations. A similar situation in the domain has been observed by different experts, each of which viewed it differently because of his or her personal experience and study. The job of the KSE is to diffuse the heat, and allow each expert to state his or her case. What usually comes out of such special-case discussions is an expansion of the knowledge system with very specialized expertise to be included with the general expertise. This is great. However, if the special-case discussion comes to no avail within a short allotment of time (two hours maximum), then allow for the continuation in areas of the domain that is in more agreement, and return to the disputed matter later.

This apprenticeship had five experts in constant attendance for a month. All heated disagreements led to positive developments in the knowledge system and frequent application of aspirin by the author.

4.   Case Focus: A Demonstrable Prototype

Knowledge System: Probe-design assistant

Domain: Temperature probes for engine testing.

End-User: Test engineers

Description: An engineer wants to install a temperature probe that must measure at a set temperature range within a certain degree of accuracy for use in a special environment and confinement.

Some apprenticeships are an opportunity for participants to build a knowledge system that will prove feasibility of its utility to their domain. The participants in this apprenticeship requested that the feasibility prototype must sell upper management to assure future knowledge system development work to their department. In other words, their department was on probation until they could prove their worth to their company.

If such is the case, a majority of development time should be spent on interface that can be presented to management as a demonstration. The system's presentation during a project's design review should be limited to ten to fifteen minutes; anything longer creates inattentiveness among management and shows unnecessary detailing by the presenters. The system's utility should be apparent and intuitive to the viewing management. Build an interface that is primarily visual as opposed to textual; textual information slows down a presentation to allow viewers time to read. Too much textual information could be disastrous if text has to be read at a distance by management crowding around a computer terminal.

It is recommended when building a knowledge system that communicates through a highly visual presentation to include an artist or graphic designer to assist in reducing the technical separation between technology and the novice users.

5. Case Focus: Away with the Nonactive Participants!

Knowledge System: Remote repair advisor

Domain: Transmitter substations

End-User: Local service representatives

Description: A local service representative wants to connect into a centralized knowledge system to determine the current procedure for diagnosing and repairing a fault in a transmitter substation. The knowledge system would maintain a record of reported transmitter failures, and repair practices could be immediately updated by the central office whose representatives have to call to initiate the repair program.

There is only so much knowledge system design information that can be transferred in an apprenticeship. Therefore, the amount of information effectively used can be inversely proportional to the number of client participants. If there are participants who are not actively involved, this will be a detriment to others who are building the knowledge system. These nonactive participants should not be sent at all. Even if they know they will be active in the process after the apprenticeship, the currently active participants should arrange to transfer the acquired knowledge to them later.

With unnecessary and unskilled participants, the KSE is compelled to make them necessary and skilled. This is a detriment to the others who are necessary or skilled. Proper establishment of need for all participants and the appropriate preparation of those who do participate is mandatory.

6. Case Focus: Very Very Disagreeable Experts

Knowledge System: Factory scheduler

Domain: Manufacturing plant

End-User: Production managers and schedulers

Description: Never agreed upon.

This apprenticeship was quite a trying experience. In terms of the professional milieu, there were too many experts (five) with conflicting views of their domain. There was no part of the domain that the experts would not dispute over.

The KSE eventually sent the experts home after three days because of frustration in not coming up with a unifying domain model on which all experts could agree. It was noted at times that the cause of lack of agreement was animosity between the experts; for the sake of face, they would not agree with each other. The KSE soon became an arbitrator rather than a facilitator. The KSE requested that the apprenticeship should reconvene when the team of experts had done the following:

1. acquired knowledge system programmers or delegate that function within the experts (with those selected getting the appropriate training);
2. arrive at a group-endorsed model of the domain;
3. provide a set of test data from each expert;
4. delegate one expert to be present at the apprenticeship for the initial construction of the knowledge system.

7. Case Focus: Luxury of Very Accessible Experts

Knowledge System: Remote diagnosis and service scheduler

Domain: Office machines

End-User: Local service managers

Description: Nightly, a knowledge system would automatically connect to a remote office equipment, e.g. photocopier, via a modem and run through a maintenance check. The knowledge system would have access to the equipment's maintenance record and locally available service representatives via a data base.

The expert queried was a senior field service representative. He provided consistently 85 percent of the domain's putative knowledge. When either the KSE had found reasoning inconsistencies or the expert was stymied, the expert would query his contacts by phone for their more specialized expertise.

The expert was present throughout the apprenticeship. This was quite a luxury and not usually necessary; a junior expert would have been almost as sufficient. As inconsistencies were found, having him immediately available markedly expedited knowledge system development.

The KSE kept the expert active by entering nitty-gritty details into the system, refining and enhancing the domain model, and testing finished system components. Infrequently, when the expert had nothing to do, the author would call a local tennis instructor to pick the expert up to improve his backhand. After a couple of hours, he would be ready for another "match" of queries.

CONCLUSION

We have been told that the clients get further in six weeks through the apprenticeship program then they would in six months to a year on their own. The apprenticeship is a powerful start to building a knowledge system. Appropriate problem selection, careful selection of the participants, appropriate preparation by the participants, and good will are important ingredients. Of course, there must be management of expectations as well. This goes for the participants, their colleagues, and client management. As is evident in the case studies, *communication is proportional to success*.

The apprenticeship is an important vehicle for the client team to learn by doing. Such technology transfer has been and continues to be an important component of the Applications and Research Division and IntelliCorp's offerings overall.

3

You Too Can Become
a Knowledge Engineer If...

JAY LIEBOWITZ, George Washington University

It is extremely important for any manager to have a competent team to develop an expert system. The job is not unlike that of the president of the United States, who enhances his knowledge by surrounding himself by a competent, knowledgeable team of advisers. For an expert systems development project, the knowledge engineer—whether at senior or junior level—plays an influential role in the success of an expert system's development and implementation. The knowledge engineer is responsible for acquiring the knowledge from the domain expert and also is instrumental in the problem selection, knowledge acquisition, knowledge representation, knowledge encoding, and knowledge testing and evaluation phases of the expert system's development process.

This chapter discusses key attributes that a good knowledge engineer should possess. It will first discuss some steps and guidelines for successfully initiating and managing an expert systems project. Then, the individuals who make up the knowledge engineering team, particularly the knowledge engineer, will be explained. Last, various case studies looking at the role of the knowledge engineer will be discussed.

GUIDELINES FOR MANAGING AN EXPERT SYSTEM PROJECT

Most expert systems development follows the rapid prototyping approach. The approach is to "build a little, then test a little" until the knowledge is refined to meet the acceptance standards determined by the users. The focus is initially on a demonstration of feasibility, and then the domain knowledge is expanded in the expert system to meet user acceptable performance standards and utility. Freiling and co-workers (1985) state six steps to building an expert system prototype:

Knowledge Definition Phase	*Project Document*
1. Familiarization	Paper knowledge base
2. Organizing knowledge	Knowledge acquisition grammar
3. Representing knowledge	Internal knowledge base formats

Prototype Implementation Phase	*Project Document*
4. Acquiring knowledge	Knowledge base
5. Inference strategy design	Inference engine
6. Interface design	Interface

Weisman (1987) also describes a six-step approach to expert system prototyping:

1. Interviews
2. Initial implementation
3. Case analysis
4. Knowledge refinement
5. User sign-off
6. Documentation

An important aspect of expert systems building and acceptance is to work on problems that the experts actually want solved. Also, the expert systems should be constructed in such a way that they do not have a negative impact on the standard field computing environment (Smith, 1984). By using an incremental building process, as through rapid prototyping, the problem could be scoped gradually and user and management could be convinced of the expert system's validity.

There are several barriers to commercializing expert systems and having management use this technology. Kaplan (1984) cites some of these obstacles:

- Abstract quality of artificial intelligence—Many people do not understand artificial intelligence technology and either think it is ludicrous or might overstate its potential;
- Unrealistic expectations about the actual capabilities of the technology and the length of its gestation period;
- Slow growth of the technical prerequisites and development of expertise;
- Imagination and creativity required to identify artificial intelligence (AI) opportunities.

Several steps could be followed to sell AI to overcome some of these barriers. McCullough (1987) discusses six such steps:

1. Build a foundation of awareness.
    a. Speak in the jargon of the person to whom you are talking.
    b. Strive to communicate, not to impress.
    c. Don't waste time.
    d. Don't force a response or ask for closure.
2. Understand how your strategy for introducing AI fits in with the corporate strategy; that is, what does your boss' boss think?
3. Explain how AI can meet your boss' needs.
4. Focus your response on an important, doable project.
5. Continue to spread the gospel of AI.
6. Move the technology toward profit-and-loss impact.

An important part of the process is to determine how AI expert systems can be used to help the firm to provide better products and services. AI technology might be used to (Harmon, 1987):

- improve conventional mainframe applications;
- improve or develop midsize micro or workstation applications;
- support users who want to purchase or develop small- to medium-sized applications;
- implement major new strategic applications that will transform the way a company does business.

After deciding how AI expert systems technology might help the company in determining to start an expert systems project, some guidelines for successfully initiating and managing an expert systems project from its inception to its completion should be followed. Badiru (1988) presents some useful guidelines:

1. Definition of problem area
    a. Define problem domain using keywords that signify the importance of the problem to the overall organization.

   b. Locate domain experts willing to contribute expertise to the knowledge base.
   c. Prepare and announce the development plan.

2. **Personnel**
   a. The project group and the respective tasks should be announced.
   b. A qualified project manager should be appointed.
   c. A solid line of command should be established and enforced.

3. **Project initiation**
   a. Arrange organizational meeting.
   b. Discuss general approach to the problem.
   c. Prepare specific development plan.
   d. Arrange for the installation of needed hardware and tools.

4. **System prototype**
   a. Develop a prototype system.
   b. Test an initial implementation.
   c. Learn more about problem area from test results.

5. **Full system development**
   a. Expand the prototype knowledge base.
   b. Evaluate the user interface structure.
   c. Incorporate user training facilities and documentation.

6. **System verification**
   a. Get experts and potential users involved.
   b. Ensure that the system performs as designed.
   c. Debug the system as needed.

7. **System validation**
   a. Ensure that the system yields expected outputs.
   b. Validation may be performed by
      (1) evaluating performance level (e.g., percentage of success in a certain number of trials);
      (2) measuring the level of deviation from expected outputs;
      (3) measuring the effectiveness of the system output in solving the problem under consideration.

8. **System integration**
   a. Implement the full system as planned.
   b. Ensure that the system can coexist with systems already in operation.
   c. Arrange for technology transfer to other projects.

9. **System maintenance**
   a. Arrange for continuing maintenance of the system.
   b. Update knowledge base as new pieces of information become available.
   c. Retain responsibility for system performance, or delegate to well-trained and authorized personnel.

10. Documentation
   a. Prepare full documentation of system.
   b. Prepare user's guide.
   c. Appoint a user consultant.

By following this framework, the success of an expert system project should be increased. However, an important element of this process is picking the right team. The next section examines the team members of an expert system project, especially the knowledge engineer.

EXPERT SYSTEM PROJECT TEAM MEMBERS

A typical team to develop an expert system consists of a manager, a senior knowledge engineer, a junior knowledge engineer, a programmer, and a domain expert. The team will comprise a variety of skills, including domain expertise, knowledge engineering, expert system tool design, and programming support. The team requires at least one member to interact with the domain expert(s) and encode domain knowledge. The team also requires someone with a detailed understanding of the design and implementation of expert systems—someone who can construct the underlying framework in which to encode domain knowledge (Smith, 1984).

A typical AI group will have an eight-rung ladder, beginning with the Lisp programmer to the system programmer to the knowledge engineer to the senior engineer to the technical staff to the project manager to the individual contributor to the manager (Kay, 1987). The AI programmer is a person knowledgeable in symbolic and conventional programming who also has the technical ability to integrate the expert system into pre-existing systems. The system programmer is not only proficient in programming, but also is able to perform some of the design functions of the expert system. A junior knowledge engineer is someone with one to four years of experience in developing expert systems from the problem selection stage to the knowledge testing and evaluation stage. The knowledge engineer may never write programs in the work environment; however, he or she will need to possess a great deal of interpersonal communications experience and some mathematical or other modeling knowledge (Kay, 1987). A typical senior knowledge engineer has five years of experience or more in expert systems development and is specifically adept at acquiring knowledge from the expert. He or she can draw out information, as well as explore and understand the expert. The technical staff member might possess a certain area of expertise, such as knowledge representation or uncertainty methods, and may be called on to give advice on that aspect of the expert systems development. The project manager oversees the development process of the expert system, specifically from the viewpoint of meeting budgets, milestones, and deliverables. An individual contributor to the project might be an outside consultant called in to lend guidance or expertise to the project. The manager oversees the project manager and is interested in seeing that the expert system is delivered on time, within cost, and to the user's satisfaction. The manager is also interested in furthering the project in the long term.

A question often asked is, Do you need AI people to do expert system applications? Winston (1987) offers this advice:

> There is a widespread myth that only AI experts, trained practically from the cradle, can build expert systems. This is wrong. Often the best exploiters of AI technology are people who are not expert in AI but who need AI technology to solve a problem of importance to their work and hence to their careers, for these are the people with the most intense motivation. Also, the basic principles of AI can be learned much faster than domain expertise in most cases. A person with some programming experience and skill with computers can do useful AI work in a year, and occasionally less. To become good at anything for which experience counts can take many years....While implementers need not have extensive backgrounds in AI, their leaders should, for those leaders are ultimately responsible for pruning projects that are too hard to do from the possible-projects list.

Winston (1987) continues by saying that the best people for tackling AI problems are those who cope well with things that lack precise definition. The skill of understanding confused, ill-defined situations is an important trait in solving AI problems.

The key player of the expert systems team is the knowledge engineer. The next section describes the important attributes that a good knowledge engineer possesses.

KNOWLEDGE ENGINEER CHARACTERISTICS

The knowledge engineer (KE) is the key member of the expert systems development team. The KE has the central role of scoping the problem, acquiring the knowledge from the expert, determining the inferencing strategy and knowledge representation scheme, selecting an appropriate method for handling uncertainty, designing the user-machine interface, and performing knowledge encoding, testing, and evaluation. The key attribute that a KE must possess is interpersonal communications skills. According to Kay (1987): "...we need someone (i.e., the KE) who can draw out information, as well as explore and understand the expert; your conventional Fortran programmer wants to know what the syntax is and where the register numbers are." Most good knowledge engineers are inquisitive and are very good interviewers.

A good KE should possess several characteristics. These include the following (Hart, 1986; Faden, 1986; Taylor, 1985):

- The KE has to be able to pick out what is of value quickly and understand the emphasis in the words the expert uses;
- The KE needs to be able to spot when the expert is being ambiguous, and to do that he or she needs not only a good knowledge of English (or the relevant natural language) but a precise understanding of the language;
- A KE needs to ensure that the expert feels he or she is benefiting rather than being threatened;
- The KE should have good analytical skills needed to structure the mass of information that has been collected;

- The KE must be able to pick up, hold, and manipulate the information; he or she must be able to start to build the attribute hierarchy (tree) immediately, but be open-minded enough to restructure it later if it begins not to fit;
- The KE must have a wide knowledge of the tools that could be used (i.e., expert system shells) for helping in expert systems development;
- The KE must have the ability to listen well;
- The KE needs not only analytical skills but also the flexibility to be able to conceptualize using the particular reasoning style of the expert;
- The KE needs to understand what can be achieved with current technology;
- The KE must possess the ability to prompt and explore in a nonintrusive way;
- The KE must analyze the strategies and concepts involved, understand the social setting of how and with whom the expert works, understand the business setting, and integrate, if needed, the expert system into existing data processing and information systems;
- The KE must possess the skills required to grasp quickly how new information can be included in the system within a short period of time;
- The KE must have the social skills needed for projects that typically take a longer time and involve a closer contact with the client than conventional systems;
- The KE must possess intelligence, tact and diplomacy, empathy and patience, persistence, logicality, versatility and inventiveness, self-confidence, domain knowledge, and programming knowledge;
- The KE should have a broad understanding of the issues, principles, and tools of AI technology and their current and potential application in the domain environment;
- The KE should have familiarity with the syntax and application of several AI tools and languages;
- The KE should understand the behavioral and organizational issues and skills related to introducing technological change successfully.

It takes many years to perfect these knowledge engineering skills. Novice knowledge engineers typically make the following mistakes (Wielinga and Breuker, 1986):

- inadequate recording—Often, the novice knowledge engineer neglects to record on tape the utterances or actions of the expert;
- inadequate transcription;
- inadequate planning;
- wrong technique;
- too much involvement;
- putting the expert into tutor mode—The expert recites the textbook knowledge rather than verbalizing his or her genuine expertise.

Another question often asked is, Can a systems analyst become a knowledge engineer? The answer is a conditional *yes,* contingent upon the systems analyst's being able to learn many or all of the skills of a knowledge engineer previously described. Hart (1986) believes that a system analyst's main function is analogous to that of a knowledge engineer. A systems analyst helps a user design computer systems that carry out specific procedures; a knowledge engineer helps design systems that incorporate knowledge from an expert. However, some people, such as Winston (1987), feel that systems analysts sometimes find AI too much to bear because they are accustomed to an orderly process of precise specification, followed by precise implementation. One skill the systems analyst must unequivocally possess to become a knowledge engineer is good interpersonal communication skills. The ability to elicit information from an expert and get along well with people are important characteristics of a knowledge engineer.

Now that guidelines for managing an expert systems project and the key expert systems personnel have been described, we can look at some case studies involving the knowledge engineer.

Case Study 1:   *The Novice Knowledge Engineer*

After one or two university courses on expert systems development, Jay, the knowledge engineer, set out to develop his first expert system prototype. After carefully selecting the problem domain and appropriate task within the domain, he decided that an expert system prototype was needed to determine software functional requirements for command management activities for NASA-supported satellites. Software must be developed to generate and send commands to satellites to take pictures of the earth, send scientific data, or perform some other function. Before the software can be developed, the functional, performance, and operational requirements first need to be determined. Because few experts have the necessary knowledge and experience to develop these requirements in the command management area, an expert system approach was used to capture this experiential learning. The expert system prototype would generate up to three levels of software functional requirements for a satellite's command management system (CMS).

This true case study briefly describes some of the obstacles the novice knowledge engineer encountered. Even with these initial barriers, however, the expert system prototype proved to be accurate, easy to use, and well-liked among its users. It was a success, but some important knowledge engineering lessons were learned along the way.

There were several bottlenecks during the initial development of the expert system prototype. The first major problem in the knowledge engineering process concerned a commitment from the expert. The novice knowledge engineer made a fundamental error—not seeking the support and commitment from the expert's boss. After about a month into the knowledge acquisition process, the expert said that he could no longer work on the project. The expert was a contractor for the government, and his boss felt that the expert system project was taking up the expert's valuable time, which they needed for "funded" projects. As a result, the expert could not spend the time on developing the expert system, even though he sincerely wanted to participate. The situation was remedied by being able to seek the commitment from an expert on the government's side. Two important lessons learned were (1) always get the commitment and support from both the expert and the expert's boss, and (2) make sure there is a backup expert; at least one other expert will be needed, anyway, for testing purposes.

The second major obstacle for the novice KE was being very familiar with the problem domain. Fortunately, the KE had about two years of experience in the NASA environment and therefore knew most of the acronyms, terminology, and concepts applicable for the task used for expert system prototyping. There were, however, some acronyms and terms that were specific to the command management area, and the KE had to read other manuals to understand this area more thoroughly. The novice KE knew that he was not as familiar with the terminology as he should have been when first interviewing the expert. An important rule of thumb is that the KE must know the problem task and domain well before performing knowledge acquisition.

Another lesson the novice KE quickly learned was to start coding as soon as possible, especially to show the expert the results to date. The expert was interested in seeing the expert system operating in an interactive fashion. By doing this, the expert was pleased to see substantive results, and it helped convince her that her valuable time was being well spent. Also, the expert could easily identify weaknesses in the knowledge base by working through sample sessions on the computer instead of merely looking at a "paper knowledge base."

A fourth obstacle that occurred was not having test cases that used standardized language. The KE should have plenty of test cases available, and all the test cases should use the same terms. In testing the expert system prototype, the wording of two functional requirements might be dissimilar, but they might have exactly the same meaning. Different contractors developed functional requirements for different satellites. As a consequence, the contractors used different wording for the functional requirements, even though some requirements from one satellite to another might have the same meaning. In testing the expert system–generated requirements against the documented, historical requirements for a given satellite, a third person had to act as an interpreter to translate if an expert system–generated requirement was the same as a particular documented requirement, even though the wording was different. Fortunately, the expert system prototype tested well, but the testing procedures were complicated by the need to have a person act as a translator. A valuable lesson learned in this study was that test cases should be available and use standardized language. Also, through rapid prototyping, problems in the testing procedure can be realized early on in the development of the expert system.

The last major lesson learned by the novice KE from the expert system prototyping was to have patience. When interviewing the expert, the expert sometimes went off on tangents, reminiscing about events of the past. Some of these "war stories" were relevant; others did not pertain to the knowledge base development. The novice KE had to diplomatically steer the expert back on course and realign the expert's thinking for answering the questions at hand.

Overall, this expert system prototype, called READ (Requirements Engineering Automated Development) (Liebowitz, 1986, 1988), was successful in terms of quality of decisions reached and advice obtained, correctness of reasoning approach used, and user friendliness. It was a valuable learning experience for the novice KE. Other important lessons learned were as follows:

- Match the tool to the problem, not the problem to the tool;
- Tape record each session (if the expert allows), as well as taking notes;
- Beware of feeling expert;
- Beware of human biases in judgment, such as causality (assigning cause where none exists) and recency (people being influenced most by the most recent events);
- Make sure the problem is well scoped (take a few minutes to a few hours to solve it);
- Try not to create overexpectations; be cognizant of the limitations of today's expert systems technology.

The next case study takes a look at the procedures used by an experienced knowledge engineer.

Case Study 2: *The Experienced Knowledge Engineer*

This case study involves the same knowledge engineer as in the previous case, but after a few more years of knowledge engineering experience. This time, the expert system prototype development effort focused on training satellite analyst-operators on how to solve satellite contingency problems. Specifically, TOPSCO (Liebowitz and Lightfoot, 1987) was developed for training on power subsystem contingency operations for ERBS (Earth Radiation Budget Satellite).

An expert system was useful in this domain for various reasons. First, there were few experts (actually only two persons) knowledgeable about the ERBS command and control operations, and it was beneficial to capture their expertise in a system for training neophytes and for solving ERBS power subsystem problems in the operational mode. Second, because of the demanding schedule of an ERBS analyst-operator, there is a large turnover, and thus a need is created for a tool for quickly training the new analyst-operators. Third, most of the analyst-operators have only a high school education, and they are dealing with complex subjects such as thermodynamics, engineering, and physics. Again, this creates a need for some tool to help train these individuals and to help them solve contingency problems if and when they occur. Last, if some problem occurs within the power subsystem module of ERBS (or any satellite, for that matter), then the analyst-operator needs to react quickly and correctly in order not to damage the satellite. An aid such as an expert system would help identify the power contingency problem and would lead the analyst-operator through the steps necessary to correct this action.

The first major step of the knowledge engineer's duties was to select the problem task and make sure it was adequately scoped (i.e., narrowly defined) for expert system prototype development. Several problem selection criteria were used (Liebowitz, 1989):

Type of problem criteria

- Task involves mostly symbolic processing;
- Test cases are available;
- Problem task is well bounded;
- Task is required to be performed frequently;
- Written materials exist explaining the task;
- Task requires only cognitive skills;
- Experts agree on the solution.

Expert criteria

- An expert exists;
- The expert is cooperative;
- The expert is articulate;
- The expert's knowledge is based on experience, facts, and judgment;
- Other experts in the task exist.

Domain area personnel criteria

- A need exists for developing an expert system for that task;
- The task would be provided with the necessary financial support;
- Top management supports the project;
- The domain area personnel have realistic expectations on the use of an expert system;
- Users would welcome the expert system;
- The knowledge is not politically sensitive or controversial.

Upon selecting the problem task and domain expert, the KE sought and obtained the support and commitment from NASA management. The next step involved the familiarization of the problem domain.

The KE obtained and read various manuals and spoke to numerous individuals to better familiarize himself with ERBS command and control operations. The manuals were most helpful in that they provided background information on the subject as well as elaborate flow charts on how to solve different power subsystem contingency operations. The flow charts served as a framework on which to structure the knowledge base. Also, by reviewing the manuals, the KE could see how best to modularize the knowledge base.

There were eight major power subsystem contingency problems, and procedures to solve these contingencies could be decomposed according to these categories. This was later confirmed by the domain expert during the knowledge-acquisition sessions.

For prototyping purposes, an expert system shell could be useful, if appropriate, for rapidly building the prototype. According to the expert and NASA management, the prototype should be developed and implemented on a microcomputer and should be easy to use by the satellite analyst-operator and easy to maintain. Also, through analyzing the problem requirements, interviewing the expert, and observing the satellite analyst-operator perform his duties, it appeared that the problem was mostly goal-driven (i.e., backward chaining), it involved some uncertainty, and the knowledge appeared or could be easily expressed in "if-then" rules. After reviewing some of the expert system shells on the market to see whether their characteristics matched the problem requirements, Exsys (1985) was selected as the shell to help develop the expert system prototype.

After performing knowledge acquisition, knowledge representation, knowledge encoding, and knowledge testing and evaluation over a ten-week period, several valuable points were learned. These include the following:

- The expert may not be right all the time;
- Throw-away versions of even the prototype may be needed;
- The user-machine interface is a crucial element in the acceptance of an expert system;
- Convincing the users to accept the system is just as important as, or even more important than, obtaining the expert's approval;
- The expert is eager to see workable versions of the system early on;
- Document the system;
- Use systems analysis-software engineering techniques and methods (e.g., decision tables, functional requirements analysis) wherever possible to enhance the expert system development.

These are helpful points to remember when constructing expert systems. The next case study involves a systems analyst becoming a knowledge engineer, and the adaptation process that was needed.

Case Study 3: *The Systems Analyst As the Knowledge Engineer*

This last case study involves the development of an expert system prototype called EVIDENT (Liebowitz, 1986; Liebowitz and Zeide, 1987) and the experiences of a systems analyst acting as a knowledge engineer. EVIDENT, which is under development, is an expert system prototype aimed at helping the law student or young attorney determine whether a piece of evidence is admissible under the federal rules of evidence.

Evidence is the subject of one of the most difficult law school courses (Liebowitz, 1986). This area presents hardships for the law student primarily because of the numerous rules of evidence to remember, as well as the need to recall their countless exceptions. EVIDENT could serve as a learning aid to help the law student determine admissibility of evidence under the federal rules.

The knowledge engineer for the development of EVIDENT had a systems analysis background but also had some experience in knowledge engineering. From a systems analyst's perspective, several areas of difficulty had to be overcome. The first area dealt with the sometimes "spongy and subjective" nature of the problem domain—evidence law. Even though evidence is a subject that is probably more concrete than other areas of law, there is still room for interpretation of the law. A systems analyst is accustomed to working on objective problems for which a decision can be reached by objective means and standards. In law, many gray areas are open to interpretation by the judge or attorney. The law can be interpreted differently, depending upon how "good" the attorney is. Thus, there is a strong element of subjectivity in law, which is a different kind of thinking for the systems analyst. A systems analyst usually has measurable, objective, and specific goals and constraints and usually does not create information systems (such as a management information system, or MIS) which handle an element of judgment or uncertainty. With expert systems development, however, uncertainty and judgment are usually an important part of the expert system, and ways for handling uncertainty typically should be encoded into the expert system. Understanding and encoding this element of uncertainty is something that the systems analyst is not accustomed to doing when developing MISs.

Another area where traditional systems analysis differed from knowledge engineering practices involved the lack of structured methodologies for expert systems development. In systems analysis, many techniques and methodologies have been developed and used for designing, building, testing, and implementing MISs. In the expert systems area, however, there is not a proliferation of structured approaches developed and used for expert systems building. This might be because the field of expert systems is relatively new, and standards and structured methodologies are just beginning to be formulated. The handcrafting of a knowledge base through interviewing techniques took some time for the systems analyst to get acclimated versus having some structured approach, like an automated knowledge acquisition tool, for developing the knowledge base.

The systems analyst also needed good interpersonal communication skills. This is probably one of the most important traits a knowledge engineer can possess. Usually, the systems analyst is involved in the technical development of a system (i.e., an MIS) and does not have the opportunity to become involved in the managerial, and usually more vocal, aspects of the system's development. As such, the systems analyst does not have the chance to enhance his or her interpersonal communication skills. For the systems analyst to adapt to a knowledge engineer's role, it is crucial that the systems analyst be a proficient speaker, interviewer, and communicator. Without developing this skill, the systems analyst will have difficulty becoming a good knowledge engineer.

The last major adjustment the systems analyst must make to become a knowledge engineer is understanding the principles of artificial intelligence, the tools for expert systems development, the expert system design issues that need to be examined, problem selection criteria, and the expert system building process. The knowledge engineer is well versed in these areas, and it takes many years of experience and education to become proficient in these subjects. The transformation of a systems analyst to a knowledge engineer is not an overnight process, and the systems analyst should not be fooled into thinking that it is.

CONCLUSIONS

Becoming a knowledge engineer is a rewarding experience in that one is able to combine the interpersonal skills with the technical knowledge. The job is a challenging position in that the KE needs to understand not only the fundamentals, principles, and building process of expert systems, but also the expert system problem domain itself. In the years ahead, there will be tools available, such as automated knowledge-acquisition aids and improved expert system shells, that will help the KE better and more easily perform the job. If one is interested in becoming a KE, now is the time to get started because the age of artificial intelligence is upon us. Through some formal training and experience on expert systems development projects, you too can start becoming a knowledge engineer!

REFERENCES

BADIRU, A. B. "Expert Systems and Industrial Engineers: A Practical Guide to a Successful Partnership." *Computers & Industrial Engineering,* Vol. 14, No. 1, Pergamon Press, Oxford, England, 1988.

EXSYS, INC. *Exsys: Expert System Development Package,* Albuquerque, NM, 1985.

FADEN, M. "What You Want in a Knowledge Engineer," *Expert Systems User,* England, September 1986.

FREILING, M., J. ALEXANDER, S. MESSICK, S. REHFUSS, and S. SHULMAN. "Starting a Knowledge Engineering Project: A Step-by-Step Approach, " *AI Magazine,* Vol. 6, No. 3, American Association for Artificial Intelligence, Menlo Park, CA, Fall 1985.

HARMON, P. "Smart Buys in AI." *Datamation,* The Cahners Publishing Co., Newton, MA, August 1, 1987.

HART, A. *Knowledge Acquisition for Expert Systems,* McGraw-Hill, New York, 1986.

KAPLAN, S. J. "The Industrialization of Artificial Intelligence," *AI Magazine,* Vol. 5, No. 2, American Association for Artificial Intelligence, Menlo Park, CA, Summer 1984.

KAY, S. "MIS Managers Feel the Growing Need for AI Experts," *Digital News,* Digital Equipment Corporation, Hudson, MA, December 14, 1987.

LIEBOWITZ, J. "Development of an Expert System Prototype for Determining Software Functional Requirements for Command Management Activities at NASA Goddard," *Telematics and Informatics,* Vol. 3, No. 1, Pergamon Press, Oxford, England, 1986.

LIEBOWITZ, J. "Expert Systems in Law: A Survey and Case Study." *Telematics and Informatics,* Vol. 3, No. 4, Pergamon Press, Oxford, England, 1986.

LIEBOWITZ, J. *Introduction to Expert Systems*, Mitchell Publishing, Santa Cruz, CA, 1988.

LIEBOWITZ, J. "Problem Selection for Expert Systems Development." *Structuring Expert Systems: Domain, Design, and Development,* J. Liebowitz and D. A. DeSalvo, eds. Prentice Hall, New Jersey, 1989.

LIEBOWITZ, J. and P. LIGHTFOOT. "Training NASA Satellite Operators: An Expert System Consultant Approach," *Educational Technology,* Educational Technology Publications, Englewood Cliffs, NJ, November 1987.

LIEBOWITZ, J. and J. S. ZEIDE. "EVIDENT: An Expert System Prototype for Helping the Law Student Learn Admissibility of Evidence Under the Federal Rules." *Computers and Education,* Vol. 11, No. 2, Pergamon Press, Oxford, England, 1987.

MCCULLOUGH, T. "Six Steps to Selling AI." *AI Expert,* Vol. 2, No. 12, Miller Freeman Publications, San Francisco, CA, December 1987.

SMITH, R. "On the Development of Commercial Expert Systems," *AI Magazine,* Vol. 5, No. 3, American Association for Artificial Intelligence, Menlo Park, CA, Fall 1984.

TAYLOR, E. "Developing a Knowledge Engineering Capability," *AI Magazine,* Vol. 6, No. 2, American Association for Artificial Intelligence, Menlo Park, CA, Summer 1985.

WEISMAN, R. "Six Steps to AI-Based Functional Prototyping," *Datamation,* The Cahners Publishing Co., Newton, MA, August 1, 1987.

WIELINGA, B. J. and J. A. BREUKER. "Training of Knowledge Engineers Using a Structured Methodology," *Expert Systems and Knowledge Engineering,* T. Bernold, ed. Elsevier Science Publishers, Amsterdam, 1986.

WINSTON, P. H. "The Commercial Debut of Artificial Intelligence." *Applications of Expert Systems,* J. R. Quinlan, ed., Addison-Wesley, Reading, MA, 1987.

4

The Archivist's Assistant: From The Expert's Perspective

RENEE M. JAUSSAUD, Archival Consultant

INTRODUCTION

In the summer of 1985, I had the opportunity to serve as the domain expert for the development of a prototype expert system. The National Archives and Records Administration (NARA) contracted with American Management Systems (AMS) to build a prototype expert information-retrieval system to test the feasibility of using such a system to replicate the processes by which an archivist responds to reference inquiries. This chapter describes my experience on the project.

When the prototype project started, another project was already under way to develop an automated information storage and retrieval system (ISAR) for the National Archives. The purpose of an ISAR is to allow the integrated storage and retrieval of administrative records and information. National Archives management and American

Management Systems knowledge engineers agreed that the development of a prototype expert system would provide valuable insight into the design of the ISAR. They also recognized that the building of a prototype would identify what elements of the new information-retrieval system should be designed to interact with expert systems.

The National Archives began operation in 1935 with the primary mission of preserving the permanently valuable records of the federal government. The archives has accessioned more than 1,400,000 cubic feet of records. *Accession* refers to the transfer of legal title and physical custody of records from the agency that created or maintained them to the National Archives. The records were received from the executive, legislative, and judicial agencies of the federal government. The records include textual materials, maps, photographs, motion pictures, and sound recordings.

The National Archives accessions records that have been appraised by knowledgeable archivists and determined to have historic, legal, or intrinsic value. A major function of the National Archives is to provide public access to records that are not subject to restrictions on access because of national security or privacy regulations.

A *reference archivist* is a National Archives staff member who meets with the researcher, a member of the public, and ascertains, through dialogue, his or her research interest. Based on the information gathered, the archivist suggests the records that are most likely to yield the information desired.

The reference archivist usually works in a *custodial unit,* an organizational unit that has physical custody of records. Figure 4.1 shows the custodial units that are part of the Office of the National Archives. The reference archivist serves as a bridge between the researcher and the records, and has developed substantive expertise in using a variety of reference tools, such as administrative histories and finding aids to assist researchers in gaining access to records.

I served on an advisory committee composed of five knowledgeable reference archivists from the Office of the National Archives who met with the AMS knowledge engineers. The committee represented a wide diversity of backgrounds, training, and professional attainments. Four archivists, all of whom worked in custodial units, had developed expertise in nineteenth-century military records, modern military records, audio-visual materials (photographs, films, and sound recordings), and Interior Department records.

The other archivist represented the consultant's office, part of the Central Information Division shown in Figure 4.1, where new researchers are interviewed during their initial visit to the National Archives. The consultant directs researchers to the custodial units that have responsibility for records pertinent to the researcher's area of interest.

The committee met twice as a group. The first time, we heard and discussed a presentation by AMS knowledge engineers on the proposed prototype system. The second time, we observed a demonstration of the completed prototype. All five archivists worked on the prototype development in one-on-one meetings with the knowledge engineers.

The development of the prototype did not always flow smoothly. The major stumbling blocks I faced were

1. establishing a basis for communication between the archivist and the knowledge engineer;

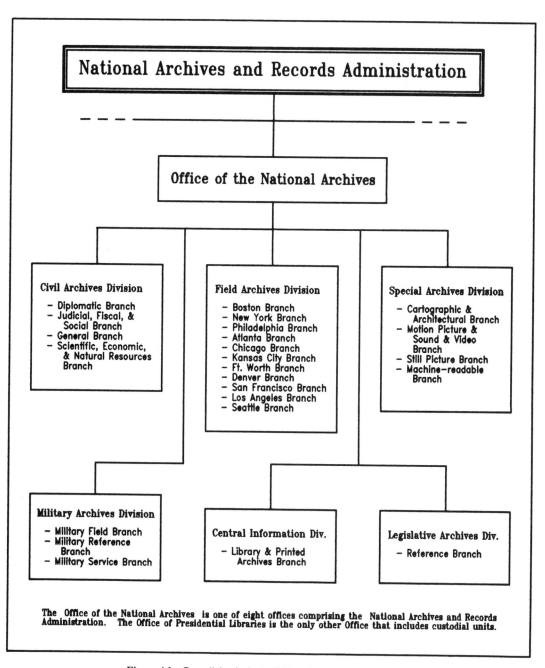

Figure 4.1 Custodial units in the Office of the National Archives.

2. resolving apparent inconsistencies in how I went about my job as reference archivist;

3. assigning certainty factors to units of information in the knowledge base.

SELECTION AS DOMAIN EXPERT

When I was selected to be a member of the advisory committee, I had been employed at the National Archives for fifteen years. I worked for the Scientific, Economic, and Natural Resources Branch of the Civil Archives Division. As Figure 4.1 shows, that division is part of the Office of the National Archives.

In addition to assisting researchers, I performed duties relating to the appraisal and accessioning of records. My qualifications as a domain expert included familiarity with the administrative procedures and policies that govern these functions and that determine the allocation of accessioned records to custodial units. I am also conversant with the organizational structure of this institution and the administrative relationship between the central office of the National Archives and our regional archives branches, which are also custodial units.

Guides and inventories to the records are the primary devices that the National Archives uses to disseminate information about its holdings to the public. Part of my work as an archivist includes the compilation of administrative histories and series descriptions for guides and inventories.

Just before the prototype project began, I had taught the section of the archivist's training course that dealt with National Archives descriptive practices. The experience of compiling written descriptions of records and the discipline of teaching descriptive techniques contributed to my ability to find and elucidate significant facts about an agency and its records.

My expertise includes a knowledge of materials documenting the exploration, settlement, and economic development of the United States west of the Mississippi River. This comprises specialized historical knowledge about the functions of the agencies that have constituted the Department of the Interior.

Certain areas of the knowledge may be very deep. For example, in the case of some major departmental functions, such as water resources management, I make it a point to learn about the administrative history of every government agency, in addition to the Interior Department, that has dealt with water resources. The selection of a domain expert was based in part on the need for expertise extensive enough to support a substantial knowledge base.

While I was intrigued by the potential of an expert system like the one proposed by AMS, I had reason to be skeptical about the feasibility of developing it. I began this project with no computer systems experience. Nor was I conversant with the computer industry's language and technical terms.

The National Archives staff had been attempting to come to terms with a computer-based statistical control and description storage system that was introduced in the mid-1970s. The early system failed to adequately support descriptive work and the production of published guides and inventories. Its poor performance and inflexibility had caused many staff members, including me, to conclude that automated systems are more trouble than they are worth.

I agreed to participate in the prototype development because the National Archives and Records Administration needed to enter the technological age. I also believed that the knowledge engineers were willing and able to put forth the necessary effort to understand how the National Archives works and to aid us in developing a computer system that was fitted to our needs.

PROJECT OVERVIEW

My participation in the project covered three phases: knowledge acquisition, knowledge base development, and prototype testing. My time on the project totaled about 150 hours, of which about 110 hours over a span of six weeks were spent on knowledge acquisition. Most of that time was spent in meetings with an AMS knowledge engineer.

The second stage of the project, knowledge base development, took about forty hours of my time over about eight weeks. During this time, I compiled information about selected records for the prototype knowledge base. The knowledge engineer and I worked independently during this stage but met periodically to apprise each other of our progress and to compare notes.

The testing phase of the project involved a comparison between my responses and the responses generated by the prototype to identical queries. It took me about one hour to consider the queries and provide my answers.

I worked chiefly with one knowledge engineer, Amy Glamm, throughout the project. This arrangement was very beneficial. We were able to maintain continuity from session to session in the resolution of questions and the development of ideas. We found that meeting in a room equipped with a blackboard allowed each of us and the observers who attended our working sessions to easily see our ideas and participate effectively.

The first, and probably most serious, hurdle we confronted was finding common ground in our professional areas. We made an effort to accomplish this task because the success of the prototype project depended on our ability to exchange information effectively. We understood that some concepts were going to take time and patience to communicate. Instead of letting this obvious difficulty delay our work, we went ahead with the knowledge-acquisition phase of the project, trusting that our comprehension levels would build with experience.

The specialized archival terms that appear in this chapter are the ones I used during discussions with the knowledge engineer and the same ones I often use when talking with researchers. I avoided using archival terms during the project, just as I avoid such terms when dealing with researchers. I did use certain inescapable concepts such as record group, series, and hierarchy, to convey a sense of how I went about my job as a reference archivist. (See the Glossary of Archival Terms.)

As the development of the prototype progressed, I came to realize my need to learn some basic computer terminology and assimilate certain technical concepts. I became acquainted with the concepts of heuristic searching, rules, backward chaining, and certainty factors. The knowledge engineer demonstrated how the concepts were used in the development of the prototype. I acquired a working understanding of the concepts by giving examples of their use.

KNOWLEDGE-ACQUISITION PROCESS

The knowledge engineer and I began the knowledge-acquisition process by conducting an exhaustive review of thirty-five to forty typical reference requests that I had handled previously. The requests included both written and oral queries. Most were very complicated, involving several subject areas. We analyzed each query to ascertain precisely how I sought information, what information I gathered, and how I used it.

The knowledge-acquisition sessions required me to be intensely introspective about how I went about doing my job. During my career at the National Archives, I have accumulated a considerable amount of information about the records I work with and have gained valuable experience dealing with the public. However, I had never given much thought to how I manipulated the information about the records nor what attributes of my approach to researchers enabled me to be a successful reference archivist. I was often more worn out after a three-hour knowledge-acquisition session than after a full day at the office.

The knowledge engineer and I kept in mind that the actual consultation process is not highly structured. The length and complexity of a consultation depends on the nature of the inquiry, the researcher's knowledge of the subject area, and the researcher's experience in working with primary source material. If the query is complex, many subject areas could be discussed in my initial meeting with the researcher. After the researcher has examined some files, I am available to answer questions and suggest additional areas to search. Follow-up consultations are routine for complex research projects.

Our analysis of the reference queries did reveal a pattern for evaluating and answering reference questions. The first step is to determine whether a researcher's subject of inquiry is an area of federal responsibility. This step is customary but not necessarily obvious to the researcher. For example, if a researcher is studying the administration of public land laws in western states, and the specific laws under consideration were enacted by Congress, then the subject is an area of federal responsibility. If we determine that a researcher's subject area is not a federal responsibility, and therefore is not likely to be documented in federal records, then we make an attempt to assist the researcher in identifying the state, county, or local government that has jurisdiction.

We also determined that once the federal area criteria has been satisfied, I always seek at least two elements of information: (1) subject and (2) time frame or exact date (the latter is necessary for some searches).

We initially considered the researcher's geographic area of interest to be a third major element. This is always an essential point of information when the research interest concerns a specific location (town, state, or region) or when the files to be examined are arranged by geographic area, such as records relating to private land grants and land entry papers.

However, upon further review and consideration of the case studies, we realized that geographic area is not a significant information element in every case. Therefore, for the purposes of prototype development, we decided to treat geographic area as a minor information element. We did retain it in a minor capacity as a third element of information, because in my experience, consideration of geographic area helps some researchers organize and focus their thoughts.

In the early knowledge-acquisition sessions, my approach to some of the queries appeared muddled. When the knowledge engineer and I looked at the queries in depth, my methods seemed inconsistent. This development was a matter of mutual concern. The credibility of the inferences we were developing about the fundamental importance of the three information elements—subject, time frame, and geographic area—were in doubt. To resolve this problem, we identified and scrutinized those queries that caused us difficulty. We reviewed each query in detail and evaluated each point I raised. We were able to identify two query attributes that compelled me to adopt particular strategies, query complexity, and subject matter.

When I understand what the researcher is looking for and I know the information elements of the query, I am able to propose a more efficient search strategy. Because complex research areas usually involve several record groups and numerous series, I break down the main points of the queries into smaller segments. Usually each segment concerns one record group or, if necessary, one series. This ensures that all pertinent issues are addressed.

The knowledge engineer and I meticulously examined many complex queries and delineated the rules of a consistent strategy. We found that, after identifying the basic segments of a query, my strategy is to discuss each one with the researcher. The aggregate result of the discussion is the identification of the query subject, topics, time frame, and geographic area. Understanding what the researcher is looking for and knowing the information elements of his query, I am able to propose a more efficient search strategy.

We realized that subject specification occurred frequently during a consultation with a researcher and during the knowledge-acquisition sessions. Subject specification always occurs with complex queries. To incorporate this step into the prototype, the knowledge engineer and I defined a fourth information element, which we referred to as the *topic*. We exercised this tactic because it signified an important part of my approach to complicated reference queries.

In the prototype, the subject element was intended to help the researcher identify his or her general area of interest. The topic served to clarify the research area.

We also used topics in the prototype to equate to program areas, pointers to record groups, agency organizational units, and series. A detailed discussion on the relationship of topics to program areas and their function in the operation of the prototype is presented later in this chapter. The knowledge engineer and I made an intentional distinction between subject and topic to facilitate the development of the prototype knowledge base. In day-to-day use, the subject and topic terms are comparable.

The knowledge engineer and I solved the problem of how to deal with the first attribute, query complexity, by devising topics. The second attribute we identified when scrutinizing the complex queries was subject matter. We found that the subject information had to be organized into three query categories: subject, person, and document. We established this breakdown because I took a different approach depending on the query category. We examined the similarities and differences in how I handled document and person as distinct from subject.

When a reference request pertains to a person, the archivist will ascertain what relationship that person had with the government. For the purposes of this project, the knowledge engineer and I devised two broad categories for this relationship, which we termed *active* and *passive*.

We defined an active relationship to apply to persons who had been government employees, had served in one of the branches of the military, or had filed a claim that was adjudicated by the government or had received a land patent. By *passive,* we meant that the citing of an individual's name in government records was not necessarily the result of an action the individual took, but may have been the result of an action initiated by a government agency, such as the compilation of census records or ship passenger lists. We limited requests about persons in the prototype to individuals who had been employed by the federal government. The prototype has rules linking occupations to record groups and other rules to direct the user to employee records (Table 4.1).

TABLE 4.1 LIST OF OCCUPATION TITLES

Record group	Occupation title	Reliable matches of occupation[a]
RG 16	Secretary*[b]	Office of the Secretary
	Solicitor	Office of the Solicitor
RG 22	Biologist	Bureau of Biological Survey
	Fisheries warden	Bureau of Fisheries
	Refuge warden	Division of Wildlife Refuges
	Special agent*	
	Teacher*	
RG 48	Clerk	
	Inspector*	
	Secretary*	Office of the Secretary
	Territorial governor*	
RG 49	Receiver	
	Register	
	Special agent*	
	Surveyor	Division "E" Surveys
	Surveyor General	Division "E" Surveys
RG 57	Geologist	Geologic Division
	Hydrologist	
	Topographer	Topographic Division
RG 75	Indian agent	Bureau of Indian Affairs
	Inspector*	Inspection Division
	Special agent*	
	Teacher*	
RG 79	Park ranger	National Park Service
RG 95	Forester	Forest Service
	Engineer*	Division of Engineering

TABLE 4.1   LIST OF OCCUPATION TITLES *(cont'd.)*

Record group	Occupation title	Reliable matches of occupation[a]
RG 115	Engineer*	
RG 126	Territorial governor*	Office of Territories

[a]Based on keyword searches of record group and organizational unit titles.

[b]An asterisk (*) indicates an occupation title used by more than one agency.

If a researcher is interested in a document, I need to know the exact date of the document, the type of document (letter, report, executive order), the gist of the information conveyed in the document, or the action that was taken. These points helped determine the program area affected and, by association, what federal agency created the document or was responsible for acting upon it.

Once the federal agency is established, the researcher is well on the way to finding the document and related records. The prototype's knowledge base accessed documents by using a keyword search strategy on the series titles. Table 4.2 shows examples of documents that fulfill a specific need, and the agencies most likely to contain the document in its files.

TABLE 4.2   SELECT LIST OF DOCUMENT TYPES

Document type	Agency
Annuity payment roll	Bureau of Indian Affairs
Contract and bond file	Bureau of Land Management
Easement documents	
Geologist's notebook	U.S. Geological Survey
Legislative bill	
Letter received	
Letter sent	
License	Bureau of Indian Affairs
Log book	U.S. Fish and Wildlife Service
Map	
Master plan	National Park Service
Photograph	
Proclamation	Bureau of Land Management
Report	
Secretarial decision	Office of the Secretary (Interior and Agriculture)
Selection list	Bureau of Land Management
Survey field notes	Bureau of Land Management
Township plot	Bureau of Land Management

A recapitulation of the three subject categories and four information elements appears in Figure 4.2.

```
        Subject: Subject
                Topic
                Time Frame
                Geographic Area


       Subject: Person
                Topic (occupation)
                Time Frame
              . Geographic Area


        Subject: Document-Type
                Topic (information conveyed or action taken)
                Time Frame
                Geographic Area


The topic element serves the same basic function in each of
the three subject categories—to define the query and identify
records likely to contain useful information.
```

Figure 4.2   Subject categories and information elements.

AN ARCHIVIST'S SOURCES OF INFORMATION

To understand how the knowledge engineer and I approached the development of a knowledge base for the prototype, we will examine the basic sources of information that archivists typically rely on to navigate the records.

Archivists mentally manipulate two related, but distinct, areas of information. The first area concerns government organization and major program responsibilities. As archivists working with federal records, we have a working idea of the relationships between the three branches of government: the judicial, the legislative, and the executive. We also have a working understanding of the relationships between executive agencies with emphasis on the history of the allocation and reassignment of program areas.

The second area of information concerns the subject content and arrangement of the records in the custody of the National Archives. Archivists acquire their knowledge about government organization and record content from certain well-understood sources, and all archivists draw on the same sources to varying degrees. Those sources that specifically deal with records in the custody of the National Archives (i.e., guides, inventories, file title lists) are called finding aids.

Types of finding aids are defined by the record level they describe. The *Guide to the National Archives of the United States* is an example of a general guide that describes in condensed form the contents of all the record groups in the National Archives. An inventory provides a detailed description of the records comprising a single record group. Information about agency organizational units is found in inventories. Guides and inventories contain administrative histories. File title lists, file manuals, and indexes are collectively termed series level finding aids.

Administrative histories provide an overview of agency organizational structure and development and describe program areas. Three administrative history sources often consulted by archivists and knowledgeable researchers are the annually revised *Government Organization Manual,* the *Guide to the National Archives of the United States,* and the administrative history sections of inventories compiled by the National Archives staff.

With varying degrees of detail and explanation, these sources mention the titles of any predecessor and successor agencies, the date of and statutory authority for the establishment of agencies, organizational structure and pivotal reorganizations, titles and duties of major personnel, and the principal program areas. Carefully read, these sources can provide insight into the administrative relationships between organizational units of the federal government at the departmental and bureau levels.

Some administrative histories also examine organizational changes within agencies and the concomitant internal reallocations of program responsibilities. Inventories compiled by the National Archives staff contain brief administrative histories of an agency's subordinate organizational units (i.e., divisions and branches) that are represented by records in the National Archives. An understanding of the purport of an administrative history is essential when a research project is complex or covers a long time span.

Archivists assimilate three kinds of information about the records in the custody of the National Archives that constitute the second area of information mentioned above. These are

- what agencies and their subordinate organizational units does the archival repository have records for;
- what program areas are documented in those records;
- how the records are arranged.

Inventories are compiled by the National Archives staff to inform colleagues and the public about these three points of information. An *inventory* systematically describes the contents of a record group or a major physically segregable subgroup. A *record group* is usually defined as the collected records of a bureau, service, or other federal agency. A record group is comprised of one or more series. A *series* is defined as a set of files or documents that are organized according to a consistent file system. The contents of an inventory are organized hierarchically by subordinate organizational units or functional areas. (The latter is necessary when the records are fragmentary or when detailed information about internal agency organizational structure is not available.) The basic inventory entry, a *series description*, explains the arrangement and content of each series of records. A series description may also include cross-references to other series that document the same program areas.

For those records that are not described in inventories, the archivist relies on any file title lists and file manuals that may exist. Sometimes file title lists are prepared by the clerks who transfer the records to the National Archives. Frequently, lists are compiled by National Archives staff for records that are heavily requested.

There are finding aids that are also records, such as indexes created by the originating government agency. The National Archives staff does not routinely compile indexes.

I found that a very important source of information about the records is my accumulated knowledge, gathered during my fifteen years of experience in handling reference queries and examining the files. Because many series of records are not described in inventories or accompanied by file title lists or indexes, this indispensable knowledge enabled me to provide efficient and effective assistance to researchers. Most of my cumulative knowledge about the organization and content of record groups and series is cognitive. As time permitted, some information was jotted down in notebooks. The knowledge engineer and I referred to both collected sources of knowledge as the archivist's notebook.

HOW AN ARCHIVIST ASSISTS THE RESEARCHER

In addition to evaluating how I resolved reference queries, to add depth to the operation of the prototype the knowledge engineer and I also examined the other steps I took to assist a researcher. After determining the query category and obtaining the subject information elements, I briefly explain to a researcher how I arrived at my recommendations. Usually, this involves a concise overview of the pertinent agency administrative histories. My objective is to get the researcher directly involved in the decision-making process.

Because most researchers have limited experience in dealing with original records, I developed an approach to provide them with information about the records. I put series in context by presenting the information in an outline format. This format is based on the hierarchy model used for inventories. The sequence goes in descending order from the general to the specific: record group (agency), organizational unit or functional area, and series. To facilitate the use of the series, I also include a succinct explanation of the series arrangement and, if available, a finding aid citation.

While my primary aim was geared to making an understandable presentation, I also hoped that the presentation would help the researcher think about the program and organizational interrelationships between agencies. For complex research topics, I often wrote out or dictated a research guide tailored to the researcher's area of interest. I used the same outline format to compile the information for the prototype.

As part of this dialogue, I also suggested research strategies. Taking into consideration the research request, the researcher's experience with original records, time constraints on the researcher, and the complexity of the records, I would deal with the issue of what records have priority. Two factors usually determine priority. The series must contain a significant volume of documentation bearing on the research query (depending on the research area, this can be a one-inch file or five linear feet of files). Or, if the series is large (ten linear feet is an arbitrary but reasonable limit), then the contents must be accessible via a detailed finding aid such as an index, file manual, or file title list. If neither of these criteria is met by the available records, then it comes down to the archivist's best guess. The knowledge engineer and I made an attempt to integrate this part of the consultation into the prototype by assigning certainty factors to the records in the knowledge base.

I have often found it necessary to instruct researchers about how to use inventories. My aim is to help them learn to make independent and discerning research decisions. Researchers who understand the organization and content of inventories can rely more on their own judgment in selecting records for examination. It is a matter of great concern to the National Archives staff that one of our primary means of conveying information about the records to the public is so difficult for many people to understand and use.

Some filing systems are very trying to use. I explain complicated file schemes to researchers and reassure them that, with some experience, they can do effective research. It is necessary to understand the series arrangement in order to catch crucial cross-references to other files. I urge researchers to make the effort to become self-reliant, because ultimately they benefit.

KNOWLEDGE BASE DEVELOPMENT

From my vantage, it appeared that the knowledge engineer achieved a good awareness of how I gathered and handled information furnished by researchers, as the rules governing the manipulation of the prototype knowledge base clearly demonstrate. But the knowledge engineer could not acquire a strong understanding of how the records reflected the intricacies of government program implementation and management without more experience in working with archivists.

I recall a conversation in which the knowledge engineer assumed that if a division or branch was renamed, then the new name better described the unit's mission. I pointed out that this was not always the case. As an example, I cited the Division of Wildlife Services of the Fish and Wildlife Service. The previous name of this unit was the Division of Predator and Rodent Control. The new title was misleading and certainly not a reliable indicator of the mission of the unit. This incorrect presumption on the part of the knowledge engineer did not hinder the development of the prototype. However, these kinds of misconceptions would have to be found and corrected so as not to distort the operation of a full-scale expert system.

Throughout the knowledge-acquisition process, the knowledge engineer and I were alert to possible subject areas for the prototype knowledge base. The subject we selected is titled "Trans-Mississippi West, 1880–1940." This area has many potential series of records with a rich diversity of related subject areas that fit into the time frame. The records are relatively recent and heavily used by researchers.

The knowledge engineer and I agreed that the prototype would appear to be more substantive if we could include references to a great number of finding aids. Many of the record groups containing records for this general subject area are described in published or draft inventories. A large number of series are accompanied by file title lists or indexes.

The prototype knowledge base comprised 184 series. Many of the series were cited by me during the knowledge-acquisition phase of the project. The series are taken from fifteen record groups: eight Interior Department agencies, five Agriculture Department agencies, one independent agency, and one National Archives Gift Collection. The Scientific, Economic, and Natural Resources Branch is the custodial unit for textual materials in these record groups. The record groups contain documentation about similar program areas, and many of the series could serve for more than one research topic (see Table 4.3).

TABLE 4.3   LIST OF RECORD GROUPS

Department of the Interior	
RG 22	United States Fish and Wildlife Service
RG 48	Office of the Secretary of the Interior
RG 49	Bureau of Land Management
RG 57	United States Geological Survey
RG 75	Bureau of Indian Affairs
RG 79	National Park Service
RG 115	Bureau of Reclamation
RG 126	Office of Territories
Department of Agriculture	
RG 16	Office of the Secretary of Agriculture
RG 83	Bureau of Agricultural Economics
RG 95	Forest Service
RG 114	Soil Conservation Service
RG 164	Office of Experiment Stations
Independent Agency	
RG 187	National Resources Planning Board
National Archives Gift Collection	
RG 200	Ethan Allen Hitchcock Papers (Ethan Allen Hitchcock served as Secretary of the Interior, 1898–1907.)

Series of maps and photographs with references to the specialized custodial units (cartographic and audio-visual) that maintain them were included to provide greater depth to the knowledge base. The project team felt it desirable to cross as many organizational boundaries as possible.

The record groups, organizational units, and series were arrayed in the same hierarchy order that is used in inventories. This is similar to the outline I use when compiling research guides for researchers. Figure 4.3a shows the components comprising the series format. Figure 4.3b shows an example of a series using the same components. The series is always presented with the titles of the organizational unit and record group that define its context.

```
        Record Group
            Organizational unit or functional area
                Series: Title
                        Bulk dates
                        Arrangement statement
                        Finding aid citation
                        Finding aid arrangement
                        Custodial unit—for nontextual records
                        Microfilm publication

The record group, organizational unit, series title, bulk
dates, and arrangement statement are the basic series format
components and are always stated. The four additional
components appear when they pertain to a series.
```

Figure 4.3a   Series format components.

```
        Record Group 57, Records of the U.S. Geological Survey
            Geologic Division
                Geologists' Field Notebooks
                1867-1939
                Arranged by assigned number
                Index
                Alphabetically by compiler

No custodial unit is given because all the textual records
cited in the knowledge base are in the custody of the
Scientific, Economic, and Natural Resources Branch. The field
notebooks have not been published as a microfilm publication.
```

Figure 4.3b   Example of series components.

At the same time I was contemplating potential series and record groups, I was drafting the list of general subject areas and related topics. The knowledge engineer and I made extensive revisions in the subject and topic lists until we were satisfied that the options were sensible and reflected the diversity of the records I worked with. We selected nine general subjects, with a total of forty-two subordinate topics. The subjects were Alaska, economic development, environment and conservation, Indians, land resources, national resources, territories, transportation, and water resources. Each subject had at least three subordinate topics. For example, under transportation we listed canal, highway, railroad, and wagon road. The vocabulary sources we relied on for subjects and topics were the indexes to the 1985 *Government Organization Manual* and the *Guide to the National Archives of the United States.* The choice of subjects and topics was based on my knowledge of research areas selected by researchers.

LIST OF SUBJECTS AND TOPICS

1. Alaska
      Fisheries
      Fur seals
      Matanuska Valley Colony
      Metlakahtla
      Native school
      Reindeer
2. Economic Development
      Agricultural college
      Geologic survey
      Topographic survey
      Township survey
      Townsite
3. Environment and Conservation
      Drainage
      Flood control
      Predator control
      Soil erosion
      Timber trespass
4. Indians
      Census
      Industry
      Inspection
      Irrigation
      Reservation

5. Land Resources
    Grazing
    Homestead
    Soil conservation
    Timber
    Wildlife
6. National Resources
    National Forest
    National Park
    Wildlife refuge
7. Water Resources
    Aquifer
    Fish hatchery
    Hydrology
    Irrigation
    Watershed
8. Territory
    Fort
    Prison
    Territorial government
    Territorial official
9. Transportation
    Canal
    Highway
    Railroad
    Wagon road

Agencies administer a wide variety of programs. Not all major program areas are reflected in the names of agencies (titles of record groups), titles of organizational units, or series. To avoid limiting the identification of records containing information about a program area to a keyword search of the hierarchy titles in the prototype knowledge base, the knowledge engineer and I developed topic associations for each level of the hierarchy. The topic correlations are based on information found in administrative histories of the agencies and series level finding aids. This procedure made important series with uninformative titles such as *central files* and *letters received* serviceable. The prototype was designed to treat each topic as a keyword for a search of the knowledge base and also use the rules to identify likely series (Table 4.4).

The knowledge engineer and I formulated a rule to incorporate a fallback position I routinely used during consultations with researchers. If a topic term or keyword fails to point

TABLE 4.4   EXAMPLE OF A RECORD GROUP WITH ASSIGNED TOPICS

Record Group 95, Records of the Forest Service	Assigned Topics
95.1 General Records	
95.1.1 (1)[a,b] Letters received, 1888–1899 (alphabetized by name of correspondent)	National Forest Timber
95.1.2 (2) Letters sent, 1886–1899 (chronologically) index	National Forest Timber
95.1.3 (27) Records of the National Forest[c] Reservation Commission, 1911–1958 (chronologically by date of meeting)	
95.2 Division of Engineering	
95.2.1 (57) Correspondence and related records, 1932–1952 (subject)	National Forest
95.3 Division of Range Management	
95.3.1 (63) General correspondence, 1905–1952 (subject)	Grazing, wildlife National Forest
95.4 Division of Timber Management	
95.4.1 (64) General correspondence, 1905–1952 (alphabetized by subject)	Timber
95.4.2 (72) Records regarding timber surveys, 1908–1930 (region and thereunder by national forest)	
95.5 Division of Wildlife Management	
95.5.1 (73) General correspondence, 1914–1950 (subject)	Wildlife Wildlife refuge
95.6 Division of Land Acquisition	
95.6.1 (75) General correspondence, 1901–1940 (subject)	Wildlife refuge
95.7 Division of Watershed Management Research	
95.7.1 (135) Reports and Studies, 1925–1951 (subject and thereunder station)	Flood control Soil erosion
95.8 Photographs	
95.8.1 (151) Photographs showing Forest Reserve Areas, 1895–1945 (by reserve area) Still Pictures Branch	

Note: Topics are cumulative upward at levels of the hierarchy.

[a]Inventory entry number for the series is in parentheses.

[b]Assigned decimal numbers expedited identification of hierarchy levels in the knowledge base.

[c]Series with underlined terms are accessible via keyword search.

to a series of records that was likely to contain documentation about a program area, I usually recommend that the researcher examine the agency's central files, if they exist for the necessary time period. The rule was designed to instruct the prototype to make the same suggestion.

We also built into the prototype a technique I use to mentally translate researcher's language into terms that I know agencies use to characterize their programs and that archivists use as descriptive terms in finding aids. I compiled a thesaurus of some of the same translations for the knowledge base, thus enabling the prototype to conduct keyword searches on the titles of record groups, organizational units, and series. Figure 4.4 gives examples of translations used by the prototype.

```
irrigation—reclamation
fish hatchery—fish culture station
Bureau of Land Management—General Land Office
aquifer—groundwater
employee file—application and appointment file
township survey—cadastral survey
Army Corps of Engineers—Topographical Engineers
fort—military reservation
Indian reservation—Indian reserve
National Forest—forest reserve

The word or phrase on the left is the term likely to be used
by a researcher. The equivalent word or phrase is the term
frequently  found  in  administrative  histories,  hierarchy
titles, and series level finding aids (i.e., file title lists,
file manuals, and indexes).
```

Figure 4.4   Thesaurus incorporated into prototype.

The knowledge engineer and I developed and revised several formulas to assign certainty factors to the three levels of the hierarchy that were references by the knowledge base. The part of the formulas that caused us constant difficulty was how to determine the relative weight to give each hierarchy level. I will explain two formulas. With each, we assigned certainty factors to the record group, organizational unit, and series based on keyword match and assigned topic match. Both formulas were based on records hierarchy. The certainty factor was intended to reflect the likelihood that a level (record group, organizational unit) would indicate a series containing information on a particular research area.

According to the first formula we devised, the certainty factor for keyword match was revised to close and exact matches, with the certainty factor going up if the match holds or improves as levels become more specific (record group 60, organizational unit 80, and series 90 or 100). If the topic matched at the record group level, we assigned a certainty factor of 60, a match at the organizational unit level was 80, and a match at series title level was 90 or 100.

We had begun apportioning certainty factors in this procedure with the intention of including terms found in indexes and file title lists. A match at the finding aid level was 100 for both keyword and topic. We adjusted the formula when there was not enough space in the knowledge base to include entries from series level finding aids. We assigned a certainty factor of 100 at the series level if I knew that the cited finding aid included an exact match for the keyword or topic. We retained a certainty factor of 90 at the series level if there was an exact match but no finding aid was available.

The second formula option we considered was making the certainty factor 100 if the subjects or topics were exact matches at any level of the hierarchy. This procedure left us with the problem of how to handle hierarchy levels that might contain pertinent information but did not exhibit exact matches.

When the knowledge engineer and I strictly followed this formula, we got false readings. A keyword or topic could match at the record group and organizational unit levels and not identify any records to examine because the National Archives had not yet accessioned records from that agency documenting that program area. Another error could occur when a high certainty factor was assigned to a series because of an exact match, while a lower factor appeared with another series that did not exhibit a close match. The lower ranked series could contain the largest concentration of pertinent information.

Ranking the records in the prototype seemed unnecessary. By defining the topic relationships, I had already identified those records that contained particular information. Developing certainty factors for this prototype was a frustrating exercise. However, certainty factors gave the knowledge engineer a method for accumulating evidence that one set of records contained more information about a topic than another.

There were three other approaches I took in handling reference queries that the knowledge engineer and I discussed in detail but could not include within the scope of the prototype. One tactic, which I call end runs, occurs when a reference specialist or researcher must examine the index for one series to gain access to another series that contains the information he or she is seeking. End runs are possible only when there is a close relationship between the file systems of multiple organizational units within an agency. I often use end runs to help answer reference requests. A second approach includes referrals to records held in archives branches, the Library of Congress, and state historical societies. I often refer researchers to other repositories that hold records related to their research interest. Third, we also considered including references to major printed sources such as the *Congressional Serial Set*. This is a series of volumes containing annual and other reports of executive agencies and transcripts of hearings and reports generated by congressional committees.

PROTOTYPE OPERATION

In this part of the chapter, I discuss the operation of the prototype as seen from the viewpoint of a prospective user such as a researcher. The prototype search method is by keyword association and rules matching topics to series. The user is introduced to the prototype with an explanation of the purpose of the system and an overview of the content of the knowledge base.

To illustrate the steps involved in the use and operation of the prototype, I use as an example a research area that might be selected by a researcher—a history of the reindeer industry in Alaska from 1890 to 1940. The steps are illustrated in Figures 4.5 through 4.9.

The options for subject categories, topics, and geographic areas are numbered. The user selects a number, and the prototype provides the appropriate word or phrase. In each illustration the user selection is underlined.

To begin a search, the user is asked to select from one of the three subject categories— subject, person, or document. At this point, as shown in Figure 4.5, the screen would show a list of the nine subject areas plus the categories person and document.

```
 1.  Alaska
 2.  Economic Development
 3.  Environment and Conservation
 4.  Indians
 5.  Land Resources
 6.  National Resources
 7.  Water Resources
 8.  Territory
 9.  Transportation
10.  Person
11.  Document

User Selection: 1. Alaska
```

Figure 4.5 Subject selection.

If a subject is selected, the screen will show the topics associated with that subject. The user identifies a topic that is the nearest match to the research interest, as shown in Figure 4.6.

```
Alaska: 1. Fisheries
        2. Fur Seals
        3. Matanuska Valley Colony
        4. Metlakahtla
        5. Native School
        6. Reindeer

User Selection: 6. Reindeer
```

Figure 4.6 Alaska topic selection.

Next, the user is asked to give the time frame or date, as shown in Figure 4.7.

```
The prototype instructs the user to indicate the year or time
frame of the inquiry.

User selection: 1890-1940
```

Figure 4.7 Time frame selection.

Then the user is asked to indicate the word or phrase that best describes the geographic area of the research topic. The selections are shown in Figure 4.8.

```
              1. state or territory
              2. states or territories (regions)
              3. mountain or mountain system
              4. lake or reservoir
              5. island or island system
              6. none of the above

         User selection: 1.

   A prompt on the screen requests a specific word or phrase if
   a number from 1 to 5 is selected.

         User selection: 1. Alaska
```

Figure 4.8 Geographic area selection.

In this situation, the selection of Alaska as the geographic area does not add any information for the prototype to use for a search of the knowledge base.

Context information is essential in order to establish an agency's place in the scheme of government organization. Its relationships to other agencies become apparent and provide an opportunity for the researcher to consider the records of other agencies as potential sources of information.

Because most basic research is done at the series level, the prototype was developed to always list the series linked to the topics selected by the researcher. The series should be presented in context as part of an organizational unit that in turn is part of a record group.

Therefore, the information on the screen includes the record group number, organizational or functional area title, series title (with bulk dates of series contents), series arrangement, and a finding aid citation if a finding aid is available. When no finding aid is available, the prototype is instructed to include a statement to that effect. This is done to eliminate any question regarding the availability of a series level finding aid. Figure 4.9 illustrates what the screen would show if the topic were reindeer, 1890–1940.

```
RG 22   General Records,
        General Correspondence, 1890-1956
        (file classification scheme)
        appendix in manuscript inventory

RG 48   Post 1907 Records
        Records of Ernest Walker Sawyer concerning
        Alaskan Reindeer, 1929-1933
        (alpha. by subject)
        no finding aid is available

RG 48   Post 1907 Records
        Office Files of Ernest Walker Sawyer, 1929-1933
        (alpha. by subject)
        no finding aid is available

RG 75   Alaska Division
        Letters Received, 1884-1907
        (by year, thereunder by assigned number)
        no finding aid is available

RG 75   Alaska Division
        General Correspondence, 1908-1935
        (by year, thereunder by subject)
        file title list

RG 126  General Records
        Central Classified Files, 1907-1951
        (by area, thereunder by subject)
        appendix in inventory

RG 126  Office Files
        Office Files of Ernest Walker Sawyer, 1929-1931
        (by subject)
        no finding aid is available
```

The first series listed, RG 22 General Correspondence, is an example of an outcome of the rule that said that, if the topic selected by the user is recognized as an agency program area (the necessary clue linking reindeer to RG 22 is in the knowledge base), and if no series in that record group is found in the knowledge base by topic association or keyword search, then the prototype will cite the agency's central files.

Figure 4.9   For research area—Alaska, reindeer, 1890–1940.

A researcher could approach these records in several ways. Each researcher defines his or her own requirements. I might recommend that one researcher start with the series that has *reindeer* in the title followed by those series that are accompanied by finding aids. The remaining series would be considered last. Another researcher might be chiefly interested in Ernest Walker Sawyer's role in administering the reindeer industry. This researcher would give priority to the three series that cite his name in the title and, as time permitted, look at the other records for background information.

If the user selects the person category, then the prototype requests the name of the person, the occupation, and the dates of government service. The dates must be within the framework of the prototype knowledge base for the query to continue. The prototype first checks whether the name matches a name at any level of the hierarchy. If that fails to give a positive result, then the prototype uses rules to match an occupation to a record group and within the record group identifies any available employee files. If that process does not reveal any information, the prototype searches the two remaining levels of the hierarchy for an exact or close match to the occupation. For instance, if the occupation is geologist, the prototype will tag all words that start with "geolog." The query is over if no match is possible.

LIST OF INDIVIDUALS NAMED IN HIERARCHY TITLES

Ansel Adams (Record Group 79, National Park Service)

Horace M. Albright (Record Group 79, National Park Service)

John Collier (Record Group 75, Bureau of Indian Affairs)

Ferdinand V. Hayden (Record Group 79, National Park Service)

Ethan Allen Hitchcock (Record Group 48, Office of the Secretary of the Interior & Record Group 200, National Archives Gift Collection)

Harold L. Ickes (Record Group 48, Office of the Secretary of the Interior)

Clarence King (Record Group 57, U.S. Geological Survey)

Ernest Walker Sawyer (Record Group 48, Office of the Secretary of the Interior & Record Group 126, Office of Territories)

Roger B. Toll (Record Group 79, National Park Service)

When a document is requested, the prototype requires the type of document and date. The prototype conducts a keyword search for documents. If the search fails, the query is ended. The document search strategy was never fully developed.

TEST OF THE PROTOTYPE

The knowledge engineer ran a test comparing the responses the prototype and I made to eight identical queries. In some cases, the prototype recommended more series than I did. A comparison of our answers showed that the prototype found pertinent series that I had not listed. Our evaluation revealed that I had simply forgotten some of my knowledge. The prototype did not omit any information that was available to it for recall.

However, unlike the archivist, the prototype could not consider "researcher over-load." When dealing with complicated queries, sometimes I purposely limit the amount of information I give a researcher at one time. I watch for signs that a researcher has reached the saturation point. To overcome this problem, I meet several times with researchers who have complex research topics. This gives us the opportunity to review the information they have gained from the records to that point in their visit. On the basis of the new information, the researcher and I can reevaluate the research strategy. In this respect, the prototype did not begin to approximate my processes as a reference archivist. The prototype was not prepared to limit the responses to a query based on the researcher's comprehension level.

The members of the advisory committee conducted a cursory review of the proto-type. Should the National Archives decide to build an expert system, the prototype should be subjected to a detailed critical analysis. Unfortunately, other reference archivists were not offered an opportunity to work with the completed prototype.

CONCLUSIONS

The experience of building the prototype carried over to a committee I served on following the project. The Advisory Committee on Archival Issues was charged with formulating descriptive input forms that broke down information about records into specifically defined data elements. Some of the data elements were identified during development of the prototype. Consistent records descriptions are more amenable to use in and retrieve from a computer knowledge base. Some of the data elements were designed to be governed by a controlled vocabulary. The recommendations made by this committee will affect the development of the planned NARA automated information storage and retrieval system (ISAR).

The development of an expert system for an institution with holdings as complex and voluminous as those at the National Archives would require a substantial, long-term commitment of staff energy and funds. The development and operation of a full-scale expert system would require dedicated effort at every stage of the undertaking and periodic reassessment thereafter.

However, there would be substantial benefits. As a supplement to published guides and inventories, an expert system would be a means by which staff members and the public could quickly acquire information about the records.

An expert system could permit a researcher to begin laying the groundwork for a visit to the National Archives before leaving home. For example, a researcher could work with the system online at a nearby research institution. In some cases, the information gathered by a researcher in this phase could answer his or her questions or enable the researcher to order copies of documents by mail. Such a system would also permit a researcher who had arrived at the National Archives to get started with the research without waiting for a reference archivist to become available. The data about the records would have to be provided in a form that reassured the researcher that he or she was getting enough information to make informed decisions about research strategy.

An expert system could be an excellent tool for training new reference archivists. If further investigation of archivists' methods of responding to reference queries reveal substantial differences in their techniques based on the type or origins of records, then the expert system could make that information available to all reference archivists.

The knowledge-acquisition stage of the project made me more aware of how I deal with researchers. I also became more systematic and efficient in gathering and processing query information. I have a sense that I probably also presented information to researchers in a more straightforward and organized manner.

ABRIDGED GLOSSARY OF ARCHIVAL TERMS

accession   The transfer of legal title to and physical custody of records to an archival repository.

administrative history   A narrative history of an organizational unit (i.e., agency, division, branch, section) that includes names of predecessors and successors, the date and statutory authority for its establishment, organizational structure and pivotal reorganizations, titles and duties of major personnel, and major program responsibilities.

appraisal   A process to determine the historic, legal, and intrinsic value of records.

archivist   A person who engages in activities associated with an archival repository, such as appraisal, accessioning, arrangement, description, preservation, reference service, and exhibits.

custodial unit   The branch, or organizational unit, of an archival repository that has physical custody of records. The unit also provides reference service for researchers seeking access to those records.

description   The process of compiling finding aids.

file manual   A detailed explanation of a file classification system.

file title list   A series level finding aid. A list of file folder headings appearing in the same order as the files comprising the series.

finding aids   Descriptive materials compiled by originating office or archival repository to establish intellectual control over records. Finding aids include guides, inventories, file manuals, file title lists, and indexes.

guides   Descriptive works that can be general guides that describe all the holdings of a repository such as the *Guide to the National Archives of the United States;* or specialized subject guides that draw together references to all the records in a repository that include information about a particular subject, such as the work *Documenting Alaskan History: Guide to Federal Archives Relating to Alaska.*

hierarchy   A means of establishing intellectual control over a record group by imposing a systematic framework on its contents. A hierarchy has three basic levels: record group, organizational unit, and series. There usually are multiple subordinate organizational unit levels (i.e., office, division, branch, section).

index A series level finding aid that provides specific pointers to documents or files containing information about a particular subject.

inventory A record group level finding aid. A descriptive work compiled by archivists to establish intellectual and administrative control over a record group. An inventory includes an administrative history of the agency, administrative histories of the agency's major organizational units, and series descriptions.

record group The collected records of a bureau, service, or some other government entity.

reference archivist An archival repository staff member who assists researchers in identifying and gaining access to records bearing on their research area.

series Files or documents organized according to a consistent file system.

series description An explanatory statement that always includes the series title, bulk dates, linear footage, arrangement, and content (types of documents and subject matter). It may also include cross-references to related series and any available index or file title list.

PART TWO: STRATEGIES

5

Evolution of the Knowledge Systems Marketplace: The Intellicorp Experience

DAVID J. MISHELEVICH, IntelliCorp

INTRODUCTION

Whenever a new technology is introduced into a field such as computing, the results are
unpredictable. The rate and form of introduction depends on many factors, not all of which
are technological. The purpose of this chapter is to review the evolution of the development of knowledge-based systems from IntelliCorp's perspective. Changing customer
and client desires combined with the rapid change in hardware and software continually
play a major role in the environment in which a vendor must operate. The capabilities of
hardware and operating-system software affects which platforms are practical foundations for the building of knowledge systems. The ongoing development, sale, maintenance, and enhancement of tools for building knowledge systems is not an easy task. The
field has seen firms de-emphasize the selling of tools in favor of providing relatively more

knowledge system contracting and consulting services, or only providing the tools in connection with the delivery of such services. We present a case study from the view of one firm, IntelliCorp, Inc. which stands as one example of what has happened in the industry as a whole. IntelliCorp has used an approach in which contracting and consulting services are becoming an increasingly important part of the business, but the primary emphasis remains the provision of the product. One consequence of this approach is that further product improvement (as well as ongoing maintenance) is amortized across a large customer base than just those who are purchasing contract and consulting services.

DIFFERENCE BETWEEN KNOWLEDGE SYSTEMS AND EXPERT SYSTEMS

The term *knowledge system* is used rather than *expert system* in this chapter to emphasize the greater scope and depth of intelligence that can be incorporated in systems when model-based reasoning (supported by frame-based knowledge representation and object-oriented programming) is used in addition to rule-based reasoning (Mishelevich, 1987). Building models based on first principles means that the knowledge and its processing are much more readily visible and understood than when privately held knowledge incorporated in rules is involved. In addition, maintenance of the knowledge system is much simplified, particularly with respect to systems that would require large numbers of rules to represent the knowledge. Of course, a mixture of model-based reasoning and rule-based reasoning can be used in a hybrid approach. One strategy is to use rule-based reasoning to provide the control structure for when and how model-based reasoning is applied. Even when building diagnostic systems, it is both possible and efficient to use an object-oriented, model-based approach even though rules are usually first considered as the mechanism to be used in such systems.

One strength of model-based reasoning is that once a model is established, it can form the basis for several different applications. For example, the same model of a factory can be used to deal with scheduling, capacity planning, diagnosis, simulation, and training. In addition, the users can be of various types depending on the level of abstraction presented to a specific individual or category of individual. Thus, the same system and model can be used by domain experts, executives, operational staff, students, and supervisory personnel. The same system can effectively serve the needs of multiple uses and multiple users.

Model-based reasoning is an evolutionary step that has been effectively used during the time the Knowledge Engineering Environment KEE has been continually developed and applied.

HISTORICAL DEVELOPMENT

IntelliCorp was formed as IntelliGenetics in the fall of 1980 by four faculty and staff members from Stanford University. It began with the goal of providing tools to support the work of molecular biologists. One component of the company became dedicated to the development of general-purpose tools for the development of knowledge systems, whether such systems were in the arena of the biomedical sciences or not. This component became the Knowledge Systems Division and was responsible for the release of the first commercial product for building knowledge systems, the Knowledge Engineering Environment (Kunz et al., 1984; Fikes and Kehler, 1985), the first copy of which was sold in the summer of 1983. In the fall of 1983, the initial public offering was made, with a second public offering occurring in November of 1985. In May of 1986, IntelliGenetics became a joint venture with Amoco (which has full operational control) with a 40 percent interest retained by IntelliCorp, which carried on the activities previously the responsibility of the Knowledge Systems Division. Amoco's interest in the concept was fueled by the development for them by the applications group at IntelliCorp of the Strain Management System, which has been further developed and released by IntelliGenetics as Strategene. IntelliCorp remains a leader in the business of providing knowledge system tools, with KEE now becoming available on a variety of platforms, including the 80386 environment, the MicroExplorer, UNIX-Based workstations, Lisp machines, and the IBM mainframe. The IBM mainframe implementation is IBM-logo KEE sold by both IBM and IntelliCorp.

In the mid-1980s, the primary artificial intelligence (AI) software firms were called the "Big Four." They included the Carnegie Group, Inference, and Teknowledge in addition to IntelliCorp. The evolution has brought about a change in which Paul Harmon (Harmon, 1988) designates the "New Big Four" as IBM, DEC, IntelliCorp, and Texas Instruments.

REVENUE GROWTH

From fiscal 1984 to fiscal 1986, IntelliCorp's revenues grew rapidly—from $2.1 to $18.6 million. Since 1986, revenues have stabilized at slightly over $20 million per year. Comparisons with other original major organizations are incomplete, since both Carnegie Group and Inference are privately held. Both companies, however, have de-emphasized the sale of tools relative to service—Inference less than Carnegie Group. Teknowledge, a public company, had $2.9 million in revenues in fiscal 1984, had up to $20.5 million in fiscal 1987, and dropped back down to $14.4 million in fiscal 1988. That firm announced early in 1988 that the product development and sales staffs were being radically reduced. This decrease was reported to be due to concentrating on the provision of services and only selling of 200 products in connection with those services. Teknowledge decreased its staff by somewhat over 60 at that time. Early in 1989, Teknowledge merged with American Cimflex in Pittsburgh, Pennsylvania with the resultant company called Cimflex Teknowledge. Other AI software companies have had staff decreases as well, including IntelliCorp, with a decrease slightly over 20 (10 percent) in July of 1987.

APPROACHES TO SALES

Early in KEE's history, Sperry (since merged with Burroughs to form UNISYS) showed strong interest in artificial intelligence and IntelliCorp. Sperry not only applied KEE technology internally, but obtained a nonexclusive arrangement to sell KEE and later other IntelliCorp products. Since IntelliCorp had only a small sales force located at IntelliCorp headquarters, it was hoped that large sales would be built up through Sperry. That occurrence would have obviated the need for IntelliCorp to establish a geographically distributed sales in the United States. Unfortunately, that approach was not successful, so IntelliCorp established its own sales offices (in Mountain View, California; Denver; Chicago; Dallas; Washington, D.C.; Philadelphia; New York; and Boston). The company serves Europe through sales offices in Munich and London. In addition, a distributor network is also being expanded in Europe. Sales in Japan are covered through CSK as the distributor. Sales in other areas of the Pacific Rim are covered from corporate headquarters or a distributor.

A new type of relationship has been created, one in which an IntelliCorp development appears under another vendor's logo. This is the situation with IBM KEE. In October of 1987, the relationship was announced with KEE on the IBM mainframe to be developed under a joint arrangement between IBM and IntelliCorp. The strategy is to have the IBM version of KEE as a high-end tool sold by IBM to complement its two other knowledge-system products, ESE and Knowledge Tool. The IBM product announcement of KEE was made in August of 1988 with product release in December of 1988.

SHIFT IN PRESENTATIONS

Potential customers were informed about KEE early in its history through the American Association for Artificial Intelligence (AAAI) Conference and other exhibits; relatively little advertising was done. Recently, more emphasis has been placed on specialty shows, and a significant seminar series concentrating in the manufacturing and finance domains has been developed. Attendance at the AAAI was at its height in Philadelphia in 1986 and has been decreasing ever since. The primary reason for this is that AAAI has been returning to an academic focus and is less likely to be a vehicle for early potential buyers of tools and services.

THE KEE PRODUCT

IntelliCorp's primary product, KEE, is a high-end tool of which more than 2,500 development copies have been sold. KEE is a hybrid tool, meaning that it has frame-based knowledge representation in addition to supporting knowledge to be incorporated in rules. Conservatively, over one-half of high-end tool sales have been of KEE. Some 400 copies have been sold in Europe (both by IntelliCorp's direct sales force and distributors) and over 150 copies in Japan (through IntelliCorp's distributor there, CSK). The system provides an object-oriented environment with knowledge representation in frames (KEE units). Rules, methods, and active values (demons) are used for reasoning. Common windows, ActiveImages, and KEEpictures allow portable graphics interfaces. Programming can be done in Lisp, TellandAsk (a more English-like language), and C. Triggering events can occur in KEE in several ways, including through the interface, programmatically, via rules, and through the active value mechanisms. The rule system supports forward chaining, backward chaining, and mixed modes with a single rule syntax. For development, rules can be used interpretively, while for improved performance for delivery, they may be compiled. In the Symbolics environment, J-KEE is available, which provides a Japanese language facility.

INTEGRATED PRODUCT STRUCTURE

KEE was designed to support a layered architecture such that the use of intermediate-level tools (ILTs) on top of KEE gets one closer to the user solution. Addition of intermediate-level tools has been catalyzed primarily by feedback from the customer base on desired improvements in functionality. Frequently, such needs were identified as IntelliCorp performed applications work with clients and certain capabilities of more general interest were being constructed. In Figure 5.1, two ILTs are shown that are built as layers on top of KEE, SimKit, and KEEconnection.

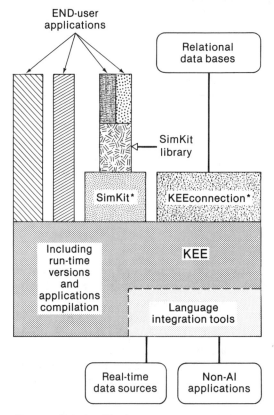

Figure 5.1 Integrated layered approach to KEE and related products.

*Intermediate-level tool

SimKit: The Simulation PowerPak

As an example of responding to customer needs, simulation applications were being developed that took advantage of the object-orientation of KEE combined with the ability to do significant graphics work. SimKit is a tool that incorporates functions for laying out icons (representing machines in a factory, for instance) on a canvas and functionally connecting them to simulate an operating entity, clock and calendar facilities, data collectors with various displays, and other features to support knowledge-based simulation. Libraries (e.g., QLIB, the queueing library used for discrete simulation) are built on top of SimKit, and user-problem-related models can be built on top of either a library or a sublibrary. This brings one even closer to the user solution and decreases the relative amount of effort to create the end-user application.

KEEconnection: Data-Base Connection PowerPak

As applications destined for production use developed, it was clear that customers did not want their knowledge-system applications to be isolated from the rest of their information system environment. Thus came the genesis of another intermediate-level tool, KEE-connection, which permits the interfacing of KEE-based knowledge systems to relational data bases such as Oracle and Ingres. Mappings from the data base to the knowledge base are supported. The connection allows the formulation of set queries (i.e., retrieving all the items in the data base possessing a given logical set of attributes) through the generation of SQL, where the appropriate SQL is generated by KEEconnection. The data base need not be resident on the same machine, and multiple data bases can be included.

In situations where the given relational data base is not yet supported in the product version of KEEconnection, or a connection to a data base that is not in a relational format is desired, custom work from IntelliCorp's Applications and Research Division through its Data Access Applications Business Unit can come into play. For example, connections have been made or are under way connecting to DB2, SQL/DS, ADABAS, COMETS, and flat files, and discussions have been held on approaches to provide connections to IMS/DL-I data bases. The KEEconnection DB2 interface is configured with the knowledge system and KEEconnection running on a Symbolics Lisp machine, with connection using IBM's Systems Network Architecture (SNA) using Logical Unit 6.2 (LU 6.2) peer-to-peer communications using a VAX as an SNA gateway. Other configurations are planned, including (1) UNIX-based workstations running KEE and KEEconnection interfaced to the mainframe, and (2) having KEE, the run-time component of KEE-connection, and DB2 all running on the same mainframe.

Other Connections

There are other ways in which knowledge systems are not isolated. In addition to connections to data bases, it may be desirable to produce interfaces to either real-time data streams or non-AI applications running on the same platform (Fig. 5.1). For example, using IntelliCorp's C-Integration Tool Kit, one can (currently in the SUN UNIX environment) provide paths to data being filtered by a C program running as another task under UNIX or interface to a spreadsheet. In addition, it is possible to use methods written in C in KEE slots and to have KEE function calls within those methods.

EVOLUTION OF PLATFORMS

The hardware and systems software platforms on which knowledge systems of various combinations of complexity and scale can be built have changed radically over the past five years. Increases in the capabilities of workstations, including personal computers, have occurred nonlinearly, fueled in part by the ever-widening popularity of the micro-computer. There also has been an impetus for improved performance resulting from the ability of those in the business and engineering communities to cost effectively absorb additional capabilities. Thus, expenditures for improvements in hardware and systems software have been amortized over a very large customer base. Power is now available at the user's desk that was rare even in mainframes only a decade ago. Thus, the potential vehicles to support tools for the development of knowledge systems have greatly broad-ened; so have the expectations of the marketplace.

Early in the development of commercial tools, knowledge systems were done on Lisp machines because that class of machines was the only category of sufficient power to support Lisp adequately and deal effectively with the problem of garbage collection although OPS rule-based systems were also offered in the VAX environment. KEE, for example, was offered on four Lisp machines (LMI, Symbolics, Texas Instruments Ex-plorer, and Xerox), first being shown on the Xerox 1108 D Machine in 1983. As the Lisp machine market has evolved, however, LMI is no longer in the business and overall KEE sales on Lisp machines has relatively decreased).

In the mid-1980s, UNIX-based workstations began to become available with sufficient power to be able to support adequate implementations of Lisp. Fortunately, Common Lisp became a recognized standard and, thus, the implementations of the language on workstations from various manufacturers were quite close. In response to market desires, IntelliCorp began offering KEE on UNIX-based workstations in 1986, beginning with the SUN 3. In the fall of 1988, the system became available not only on the SUN 3 and SUN 4, but also on Apollo systems, the IBM RT PC, and the DEC MicroVAX; porting to HP workstations is also underway. The original versions of Common Lisp on UNIX-based machines supported only stop-and-copy garbage collection, although now implementations with incremental garbage collection are beginning to appear. KEE has also been released on the Texas Instruments Micro-Explorer (an Apple MAC II with a TI Lisp board installed). Both the central-process-ing unit in the MAC II and that on the Lisp board can be active concurrently, allowing multiprocessing in addition to multitasking. The various processes can be observed through multiple windows on the MAC II monitor screen. Typical configurations include four megabytes of RAM in the MAC II and eight or twelve megabytes on the TI Lisp board. The system running on the Lisp board provides for incremental garbage collection.

KEE is also available now on the Compaq 386 (and is to be released on the IBM PS/2) in a UNIX environment. The interface is supported under a DOS-equivalent system running as a UNIX task, under which Microsoft Windows runs. Another type of platform is forthcoming in that KEE is being ported to the IBM mainframe, based on IBM Common Lisp starting with the MVS operating system. Other mainframe implementations have been developed by other vendors, including those from Aion, Inference, and the Artificial Intelligence Corporation which has developed its KBMS tool. KEE runs on IBM Common Lisp in a TSO environment. The implementation of IBM Common Lisp (and thus KEE) involves a distributed architecture because the KEE interface runs on a personal computer communicating with Lisp and KEE running on the mainframe. It is highly likely that many KEE systems in delivery mode will be embedded and not have a graphics interface. Instead, the systems will be accessed by applications with their own 327X text interfaces. Of course, KEE in many cases will be directly accessed through text interfaces as well.

PORTABILITY IN ADDITION TO FUNCTIONALITY

The reason that KEE can be made available rather efficiently on various platforms is that, when going from KEE 2 to KEE 3, not only was functionality added (e.g., Multiple Worlds and the Assumption-based Truth Maintenance System, or ATMS) (Nardi and Paulson, 1986; Filman 1988), but standardization was added as well. The product became based on Common Lisp and a windowing standard called Common Windows was developed by IntelliCorp. This has been looked at as a "virtual-workstation approach" (Mishelevich and Fine, 1987). Thus, if one stayed within KEE, Common Windows, and Common Lisp, one could move applications easily from one platform type to another. From the systems standpoint, if Common Lisp is available on a given platform and Common Windows is ported (the difficult part), then KEE should run with little added. In practice, this has turned out to be the case. In some cases, embedded systems without the KEE interface are of interest and KEE can operate in a text-only mode if the given Common Lisp can support it.

THRUST IN DELIVERED SYSTEMS

Delivered systems represent the maturation of the field, and many more are forthcoming. While some applications will be delivered on the same class of workstations on which the development occurred, there frequently is a need to provide for lower-cost delivery vehicles. There are multiple ways in which these might be provided.

RunTime KEE

Once the application has been developed, it can run without KEE's development interface. A user-tailored interface may be "locked down" such that only the intended functions are available. In some cases, it will be desirable to embed the application such that a graphic interface is not needed at all. In some such cases, one or more components of KEE may not be needed at the multiple-world facility. Only loading what one needs can decrease the memory space and processing required. Thus, delivery may be practical on a smaller machine. Of course, as the relative power and cost effectiveness of hardware increase, the situation will be aided by trends already in motion; the availability of KEE on 80386-class machines as well as relatively inexpensive SUN workstations has already opened up more practical delivery alternatives.

Use of Distributed Architectures

IntelliCorp offers PC-Host, which provides for a run-time system in which the knowledge-processing component of KEE runs on a mainframe computer (currently the VAX) and the interface operates on IBM PCs (or compatibles). Because of this separation, the situation is one of a distributed architecture. The personal computers are usually AT (or equivalent) machines. If only text interactions are required, then terminals or microcomputer can be used to support the interface. Each of the users gets a personal copy of the knowledge base and KEE, and in those situations in which updating of the knowledge based on user interactions will occur, suitable strategies for integrating the feedback from multiple sources must be developed. The IBM mainframe will provide a delivery environment on a distributed basis as well.

Compilation Technology

For flexibility and to facilitate rapid development, KEE runs (primarily) interpretively in the development environment. Lisp methods in slots may well be compiled, but not other components. Once the application (or an appropriate part of it) is completed, the backward- and forward-chaining rule compilers can be utilized. In the former case, speed improvements on the order of forty times are typical, while in the latter case, improvements on the order of fifteen times are most likely to be the case. These figures are application dependent, however. Fortunately, systems with compiled rules can also include interpreted rules (although the latter need to be in separate rule classes). Having the availability of both interpreted and compiled rules in the same application means that efficient incremental growth can occur. In tools that provide for compiled rules only, one must bear significant time delays every time a change is made.

   Some components of graphic interfaces can be compiled as well. One approach is to compile hierarchical KEEpicture graphics into composite bit maps and is known as the "polyhotspot" facility. One can also compile and optimize ActiveImages (e.g., thermometers, dials, bar charts) each time they are shaped and placed on the screen.

   Another process being considered is to not only compile methods, rules, and graphics, but to also compile the knowledge base itself. This approach, called applications compilation, involves the removal of KEE functionality not required for that specific application. It would not be necessary that the target language be Lisp. Because of the support of C methods in KEE now when the C-Integration Tool Kit is used, parts of the system may already have been written in the target language. Early in the development of this approach, it is highly likely that the use of facilities such as multiple worlds or the Assumption-based Truth Maintenance System will not be included. In any case, the applications compilation process is by no means an automated process and must be considered on an application-by-application basis.

LISP VERSUS C

In 1986–1987, there was a lot of interest in exploring the implementation of the major Lisp-based tools in the C language. Much was made by some vendors of the necessity for doing so in order to fit more into the mainstream of both the engineering computing and the business data processing worlds. IntelliCorp, while examining the situation, determined that the functionality of C at that time combined with Lisp being made available on "conventional" workstations (by vendors such as Lucid and Franz) as opposed to Lisp machines did not make the Lisp-to-C change for KEE appropriate. As noted above, a C-Integration tool kit has been provided. The subsequent experiences of the other vendors validated the IntelliCorp approach. What will happen in the future, of course, is difficult to say. Other vendors have brought out both Lisp-based and C-based tools for microcomputers, although they have been ported to other platforms as well.

EVOLUTION IN TRAINING

As the functionality of the KEE product increased, the number of days of training increased as well. For example, in going from KEE 2 to KEE 3, the number of days went from five to seven. In 1987, two days of applications-methodology training were additionally made available to students. At the time of the transition from KEE 2 to KEE 3, a videotape-based update training was offered covering the additional functionality that came with KEE 3. With the cost of development systems coming down, particularly evident with KEE being ported to the 80386-based environment, it was desirable to offer stand-alone training in addition to the classroom offering. In 1988, the KEEtutor package was released that includes exercises to be loaded onto the student's machine as well as videotape and hard copy materials. Thus, it is possible to effectively train those individuals who for economic or other reasons will not be participating in the classroom.

CHANGES IN THE MARKETPLACE: EXPLORATIONS
TO SOLUTIONS

Over the past two years, we have seen a distinct difference in the market as articulated by customers and potential customers. Prior to that time, many of those pursuing the purchase of knowledge-systems tools have changed from exploring the technology in the research and development sense to wanting solutions to their problems in which the people involved do not care whether those solutions involve traditional data processing, artificial intelligence, or any other vehicle. Of course, in many cases, there will be a middle ground. An example of this middle position was the experience at Morton Thiokol, in which the technology was being explored, but with the view of having a pilot project that could eventually be deployed and be a model for other work in knowledge systems within the company. The process has been described in terms of the exploration of the potential, the selection of candidate problems, the training of staff, management of the project, and the technology-transfer process (Cupello and Mishelevich, 1988).

In consulting and contract services, we have seen a resulting transition from the majority of the work being short-term effort, primarily technology transfer, to the majority of work being medium- to long-term contracts.

DEVELOPMENT OF THE CONTRACT/CONSULTING-SERVICES PRACTICE

As product customers worked with KEE, SimKit, and KEEconnection, there was expressed need for assistance, and work in customized programming began with early product release. As IntelliCorp developed, more applications products were brought into being and now include:

- Short-term consulting
- Medium- to long-term contracts
- Turnkey systems
- Demonstration Prototype Program
- Apprenticeships
- Custom ports
- Reusable applications modules

With respect to the case study in this chapter, the importance is that as the business grew, different requirements needed to be served. Those organizations getting started early in knowledge systems were almost uniformly exploring the technology and were getting into the field without having to justify the investment on the basis of a specific solution being sought. There was still interest in getting started efficiently, however, and, thus, within IntelliCorp, the apprenticeship was born to give clients a power start with a given application. The apprenticeship is an intensive four-week experience at IntelliCorp broken into two two-week periods, usually with two weeks in between during which the apprentices work at their home location with telephone support from IntelliCorp. At the end of the six-week period, the apprentices have usually completed a demonstration prototype and have learned by working on something very useful. The apprenticeship experience and the technology-transfer process is described in Chapter 2. Clients have reported that they have accomplished more in that six-week period than would have been true working on their own for six months to a year. Thus, the apprenticeship has been an effective, successful, and satisfying mechanism for helping to enable client success in constructing knowledge systems through use of a technology-transfer vehicle as embodied in the apprenticeship.

Another example of evolution in contract and consulting services was the demonstration prototype, which came about because some potential customers for KEE were not interested in exploring the technology, but wanted to solve a specific problem. These potential buyers wanted to see proof of the concept without having to invest in setting an in-house knowledge systems operation prior to seeing a short-term result on their particular problem. Thus, the Demonstration Prototype Program is now being offered.

As certain applications-related functions were repeated in the development of more than one project, reusable segments of code were developed that sometimes are packaged into a reusable applications module. Examples are a connection to a given data base and a knowledge-base browser. In addition to the above, protoproducts are also being evolved. In some cases, a selected set of reusable applications modules may be put together to form most of a given protoproduct.

Evolution of the Applications and Research Division

With the increasing volume of contract and consultation services, there came the need to develop an effective infrastructure. The structure evolved from having separate applications and contract-research units in a single Applications and Research Division with four business units, three in the applications arena and one in research. The applications business units are focused in specific areas reflecting the way IntelliCorp's business has developed; they are likely to change over time. The four units are the Data-Access Applications Business Unit, the Knowledge-Processing Applications Business Unit (which concentrates in the financial and government sectors), the Manufacturing-Applications Business Unit, and the Research Business Unit. Work ranges from single consulting days through multiple-year contracts and turnkey systems. In terms of client profile, nine of the Fortune 10, seventeen of the Fortune 25, and twenty-four of the Fortune 50 Industrials have used Applications and Research Division services.

One of the most successful and satisfying mechanisms for aiding client success in constructing knowledge systems has been the technology-transfer vehicle as embodied in the apprenticeship.

CONCLUSION

It is particularly difficult to accurately predict the future in a rapidly changing field with respect to the users of a given technology or its vendors. Clearly, the movement to more powerful hardware and software platforms available at lower cost will positively affect the development and fielding of knowledge-system applications. Improvements in the understanding of human factors as to what techniques most effectively facilitate high-bandwidth communications between the user and the system will aid utilization as well.

A critical need for a vendor of products and services is to remain responsive. One important strategic decision made by IntelliCorp was going to Common Lisp and Common Windows at the time of change from KEE 2 to KEE 3. This approach allowed efficient porting not only to a variety of UNIX-based workstations, but also to the 80386 and the IBM mainframe. Another was the architectural decision to use a layered approach with the Intermediate-Level Tools SimKit and KEEconnection effectively adding functionality to KEE and getting the vendor-provided tools closer to the user solution. While it was not appropriate in this case study to examine approaches and decisions on future strategic directions of IntelliCorp, a review of the past can be of value. Of course, keeping that which has been successful and can serve well in the future is important; remaining responsive to the realities of an ever-evolving marketplace is mandatory.

REFERENCES

CUPELLO, J. M., and D. J. MISHELEVICH. "Managing Prototype Knowledge/Expert System Projects," *Communications of the ACM,* 31:534–541, 550, 1988.

FIKES, R. E., and T. P. KEHLER. "The Role of Frame-Based Representation in Reasoning," *Communications of the ACM,* 28:904–920, 1985.

FILMAN, R. E. "Reasoning with Worlds and Truth Maintenance in a Knowledge-Based Programming Environment," *Communications of the ACM,* 31:382–401, 1988.

HARMON, PAUL. "How Fast the Market Is Changing," *Expert Systems Strategies,* 4(3):7, 1988.

KUNZ, J. C., KEHLER, T. P., and M. D. WILLIAMS. "Applications Development Using a Hybrid AI Development Environment," *AI Magazine,* 5:41–54, 1984.

MISHELEVICH, D. J. "Knowledge Systems for Competitive Advantage," *Proceedings of the Third Annual Artificial Intelligence and Advanced Computer Technology Conference,* 3:7–15, 1987.

MISHELEVICH, D. J., and G. FINE. "Delivery of KEE-Based Knowledge Systems including Integration into Existing/Conventional Environments," *Proceedings of the First Annual Artificial Intelligence and Advanced Computer Technology Conference/East,* 1:131–140, 1987.

NARDI, BONNIE A., and E. ANNE PAULSON. "Multiple Worlds with Truth Maintenance in AI Applications," *Proceedings of the Seventh European Conference on Artificial Intelligence,* 7:436–444, 1986.

KEE and IntelliCorp are registered trademarks of IntelliCorp, Inc. ActiveImages, J-KEE, KEE, KEEconnection, KEEpictures, KEEtutor, Knowledge Engineering Environment, PC-Host, Sim-Kit, and TellandAsk are trademarks of IntelliCorp, Inc. Strategene is a trademark of IntelliGenetics. Ingres is a trademark of Relational Technology, Inc. KBMS is a registered trademark of Artificial Intelligence Corp. MAC II is a trademark of Apple. MicroExplorer is a trademark of Texas Instruments. Oracle is a registered trademark of the Oracle Corporation. VAX is a trademark of the Digital Equipment Corporation, and SQL, ESE, and Knowledge Tool are trademarks of International Business Machines.

6

Cost Justifying Expert Systems

DONNA M. THOMPSON, ICF/Phase Linear Systems
JERALD L. FEINSTEIN, ICF/Phase Linear Systems

INTRODUCTION

Organizations around the world are exploring expert systems technology to gain a competitive advantage, to increase their profitability, and to improve their productivity. As these organizations seek to justify the costs of their expert systems, the framework must be laid in two key areas:

- **Application selection:** Is the application important to the organization?
- **Technology selection:** Is expert system technology the best approach?

The challenges of the cost-justification process are overcome most easily if these two areas are addressed at the outset.

While some research and development groups are exploring the capabilities and limitations of expert systems without the need for clear justification methods, other organizations find themselves in a strict cost-justification atmosphere. While this is not necessarily bad, an excessive reliance on hard dollar savings is seldom appropriate. Likewise, neither is investing heavily in technology for its own sake. How then can an organization find an appropriate method to successfully justify expert system projects?

This chapter explores these issues and builds the framework for successful introduction and dissemination of this powerful technology to assist organizations in capitalizing on the potential benefits that expert systems have to offer.

COST-JUSTIFICATION MOTIVATIONS

There are three major motivations for exploring expert systems projects: strategic, financial, and technology-based. These approaches are not mutually exclusive. Usually there are at least two motivating forces; the primary area of emphasis is a matter of degree.

Strategic Focus

The strategic focus emphasizes using advanced technologies to fulfill the organization's mission. While this approach is widely used, the major proponents are information-intensive organizations, particularly in the financial sector. Where improved timeliness and accuracy of information can turn into dollars and build barriers to the entry of competitors, innovative technologies are essential for survival and growth. The strategic focus is best illustrated by the following quote from *Modern Office Technology*[1]: "Not investing in the technology that is required to stay competitive in an intensely competitive environment can literally mean that a customer has made the unconscious choice to go out of business."

One of the best strategic uses of expert systems technology is to help an organization evolve toward its mission. Because information is a strategic resource, when expert systems are linked to the business strategy, clear long-term benefits can be reaped. To support this end, the method of analyzing investments has shifted from financial and organizational performance measures to market performance measures.

According to Ted Markowitz of American Express[2]:

> AMEX takes the view that each system is not cost justified based on sheer productivity increase alone. Using a more qualitative approach, we take into account that the expert system may change the way we do business. This strategic perspective provides us with service differentiation opportunities that are difficult to quantify and justify using conventional cost-justification techniques.
>
> If an expert system allows AMEX to provide a service that it could not provide in the past—that's worth something. As a premier customer service organization, we try to enhance customer services and provide customized products to better service our customers' needs.

---

[1]"New Dimensions in Cost Justification." *Modern Office Technology*, May 1986.

[2]Discussions with Ted Markowitz, Director, Technology Strategy. American Express Company, World Financial Center, New York, 1988.

The effects of this are difficult to anticipate and to quantify a priori, but are very valuable nonetheless. One of our expert systems, the Authorizer's Assistant, was able to be cost justified on productivity savings alone. But more importantly, the majority of the benefits derived from this expert system are from fraud and loss avoidance—far in excess of what we anticipated.

Howard Magnas of the Department of Energy tried several approaches before selecting an expert system to resolve edit flags on forms used by electric power plants to report power generated, fuel consumption, and fuel stockpiles. Magnas states: "When other approaches failed, expert systems were attempted—but not based on a pure cost-justification approach. The Energy Information Administration was looking for improved quality, accuracy, and consistency. The project was justified at the macro level in an effort to improve organizational effectiveness."

Expert systems can provide an information edge, a competitive advantage gained through improving the intelligence of an organization. This technological innovation is characterized by an ever-increasing rate of change and a significant capacity to affect business strategies. The strategic focus supports the theory that tomorrow's organizations will invest in knowledge workers or will lose their place in the international market.

While some organizations are exploring expert systems from largely a strategic focus, others are experiencing great success by focusing on financial benefits.

Financial Focus

Some organizations are looking for pure economic benefits as they pursue expert system investments. In a Delphi Study completed by the Automation Forum, respondents listed financial justification as the major obstacle in the advancement of industrial automation in the United States. While some installations have been technological successes, they often fall short of being financial successes. It is clear that technology for technology's sake does not work. But if technology is applied to solve a specific business problem, cost justification largely takes care of itself.

Well-selected, well-implemented expert system applications should have little difficulty in passing investment hurdle rates. In fact, expert systems should be one of the most lucrative capital investment opportunities available. Leveraging personnel resources to achieve increases in productivity is cited as a key benefit by many organizations.

Elizabeth Chase MaCrae, Associate Commissioner for Information Systems of the U.S. Immigration and Naturalization Service (INS), states that productivity is the major reason INS is implementing expert systems. MaCrae believes that substantial productivity benefits can be generated when expert systems are applied to routine and repetitive tasks in the organization. She states: "The technical implementation and the extent to which the system is 'really' an expert system are less important than bringing more powerful tools to automate routine, repetitive functions."

Jean-Claude Rault of EC2 in Nanterre, France, states that French firms are seeking quantifiable reductions in staff hours: "Productivity issues are very important in the manufacturing sector, while in the finance sector, French banks are thinking of ways to aid in customer services." In general, the focus is on attacking smaller, less sophisticated problems than those being attempted in the United Kingdom and in the United States in order to minimize risk and to successfully justify technology investments.

In most cases in which cost justification is an intractable problem (1) the application is not important to the organization; (2) the users do not support the approach; or (3) technology is being explored for its own sake. Only after these issues are resolved should the justification process estimate interest rate trends, inflation, sales, and productivity increases. In addition to financial benefits, expert systems can play a role in an organization's Management Information Systems (MIS) strategy by providing the framework for an advanced technology platform.

Technology Platform Focus

Organizations are seeking flexibility and responsiveness to a barrage of incoming data, increasingly dynamic markets, and increased competition from unanticipated sources. While the present limitations of automation are often unknown, the effects of future automation breakthroughs are even more uncertain. Expert systems can provide a technology platform to move toward these goals. Large organizations with R&D capabilities might choose a leading-edge approach. For those with limited technology resources, a follow-the-leader approach may be more appropriate. Most others are somewhere in between in the technology-adoption continuum.

The real value of many investments in technology is the potential to exercise options on future opportunities. Organizations that begin to disseminate expert systems technology will have a prepared staff with an up-to-date understanding of the issues. They will be more prepared for the next technology wave, including neural networks, parallel processing, other branches of AI, and expert data bases. Each forward step the organization takes allows it to capitalize on future developments. The framework for a long-term technology strategy should be in place. To do this, an organization must thoroughly understand its mission, its various "publics," and its users to fully map technologies to their needs.

Expert systems are a complementary technology such as office automation. They represent an incremental innovation leading to a steady improvement in the way in which decisions are made and tasks are performed. Taken as a total systems approach—not a subsystem-by-subsystem approach— expert systems can be viewed as a technology platform for the future. The technology platform focus toward expert systems enables organizations to incrementally implement new and sophisticated technologies as they evolve.

Cases in Point

The following cases are illustrative of innovative companies that have successfully exploited the power of expert systems technology.

- MUDMAN helps on-site engineers analyze drilling fluids for silt content, viscosity, and specific gravity, in some cases better than human experts, thus creating significant sales opportunities for N.L. Baroid.

- Westinghouse's PROCESS DIAGNOSTIC SYSTEM (PDS) provides an early warning device in monitoring steam turbines. Because the potential damage resulting from turbines releasing steel components involves tens of thousands of dollars in damage and in weeks of down time, detection of potential failures is extremely valuable.
- CORRECTIVE ACTION, by the U.S. Environmental Protection Agency, identifies alternative courses of action to take based on the level of urgency required to respond to leaks in underground storage tanks.
- APPLICATION ASSISTANT, by the U.S. Immigration and Naturalization Service, is designed to speed routine citizenship and student applications by aliens with legal resident status. Expected use of the system is 10,000 applications on peak days.
- CONSULTANT is used by IBM to help field service representatives improve consistency in pricing bids, improve customer service, and reduce marketing costs.
- MENTOR, by Honeywell, helps diagnose problems with commercial air conditioning, providing early fault detection and enabling preventive maintenance procedures to reduce machine down time.
- AUTHORIZER'S ASSISTANT, by American Express, provides quick charge approval for holders of the American Express Card while the merchant is still on the phone. The system raises authorizer's productivity by more than 20 percent while reducing losses from overextension of credit by an undisclosed amount.
- The Texas Instruments' CAPITAL BUDGETING system provides a consistent framework for engineers to submit capital requests. The system guides the user through the capital request forms and ensures that the information is complete and exceeds the minimum investment hurdle rate before forwarding it to the review committee.
- Digital's XCON system supports DEC's long-term strategy of offering customers precisely the equipment they need in spite of configuration and assembly complexity. It reduced the need for final assembly, testing, disassembly, and shipping of VAX computers for an estimated cost savings of $25 million.

These are but a few examples of how organizations are achieving real strategic, financial, and technology benefits with the judicious use of expert systems.

EXPERT SYSTEM JUSTIFICATION TECHNIQUES

Organizations can consider three possible approaches when justifying expert system investments: traditional financial techniques, new and evolving techniques, and a combination of these approaches. They are described in detail below.

Traditional Financial Techniques

The traditional cost-justification approaches of return-on-investment (ROI), net present value (NPV), internal rate of return (IRR), and the payback method can play a major role in justifying expert systems. These powerful tools can assist the financial analyst in the identification and quantification of tangible and intangible benefits. These time-tested techniques have three advantages:

- Management is familiar with them.
- Assumptions are dealt with explicitly.
- They blend objective and subjective analysis.

A wide range of expert system investments can be cost justified using these conventional techniques. Applications that involve concrete decision processes, procedure-oriented tasks, early fault detection and problem avoidance, and training are among the areas that handily lend themselves to financial justification techniques. The challenge is for business managers to assess where expert systems can have an impact and determine how to achieve economic results from their implementation.

Because we live in a world of scarce resources, organizations need to invest wisely and to consider new dimensions to investment analysis. One organization continually allocated funds to projects with high ROIs, including upgrading their copiers while rejecting other office automation technology applications. While these investments yielded excellent financial returns, over time the organization became increasingly out of touch with its markets. By investing in "safe" back-office activities, they were losing competitive advantage and market share. The competing technology projects were considered to be high risk compared to the copier upgrades. In reality, this short-sighted approach is much riskier. In the long run, strategic goals do support the survival of the organization, and thus, the long-term financial goals.

Adjustments in the investment hurdle rate should be viewed with caution. Expert systems are sometimes considered to be risky investments. However, if an expert system is going to improve consistency, reduce rework, anticipate errors, or improve customer service, the organization will be a stronger contender. Thus, the overall risk of the organization will be reduced when such an expert system is implemented.

When projects are ranked purely on tangible financial returns, the capital-allocation process may require rethinking. In some cases, projects with high ROIs are adopted over technology investments, to the detriment of the organization. The problem is not that expert systems cannot be justified in the capital budgeting process, but that the organization should consider strategic investments that may demonstrate lower ROIs but ensure the organization's place in the market.

If traditional financial techniques are applied narrowly in an increasingly competitive environment, these approaches may not fully consider the strategic aspects of future investments and the long-term effects of not investing. These justification techniques, when linked to a strict financial capital budgeting process, may fall short of the mark when investments in new technologies to support the organizational mission are considered. The pure financial approach is too rigid and should not be the main driver in selecting between competing investments. A graphic portrayal of a justification decision process in presented in Figure 6.1. This can be tailored to suit your organization's cost-justification process.

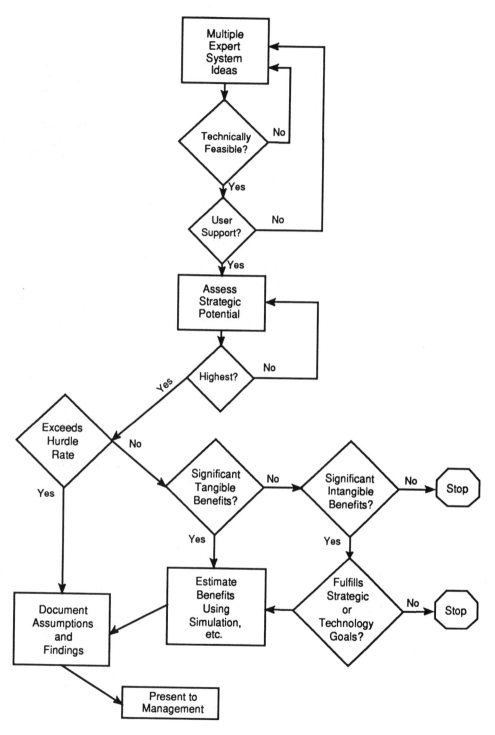

Figure 6.1 Expert systems justification flow chart.

Although properly structured expert system investments can be cost justified, there are cases in which investments in expert system technology cannot pass the rigorous tests met by other investments. This is true when organization-approved justification procedures do not accommodate establishing a competitive edge, changing for the sake of survival, creating barriers to market entry, and attacking niche markets. In some applications, the benefits cannot be fully anticipated or the project is experimental. One approach is to view these investments in the same vein as releasing a new product. Carefully scrutinize the potential projects, estimate potential costs and benefits, and then do what makes good business sense.

Additional Techniques

Several approaches can be used in expert systems justification methods that lend credibility to the analysis and quantification of benefits. One technique with significant potential is dynamic simulation. Using this technique, the justification team can model and evaluate potential changes in the internal and external environment of the organization and identify the possible effects, time savings, productivity improvements, revenue increases, and cost decreases in an easy-to-use, interactive dynamic automated environment. Because the assumptions are portrayed graphically, the evaluation board can question and change the underlying assumptions, the rates, and the flows in the justification model. The basic framework allows for a quick reanalysis under multiple scenarios. In this context, the process can withstand careful scrutiny while the assumptions are reviewed and revised.

Expert systems are designed to increase both efficiency and effectiveness. Some efficiency benefits can be tangible, whereas those for effectiveness can be elusive. Most executives do not produce measurable outputs, their inputs are unclear, and their jobs are not routine. Therefore, traditional productivity measures do not apply to expert systems aimed at these areas. One problem often encountered, for example, is the accurate assessment of the value of an improved decision. Does 20 percent more information improve the decision by 20 percent? Usually this is not a linear relationship, and it also varies from case to case. How, then, can we measure the marginal gains of improved judgments?

Expert systems may be a catalyst for rethinking and restructuring processes. Sometimes the solution could have been achieved with conventional technologies but were explored in the context of expert systems. Even if the approach is not a pure expert system solution, the organization still benefits by having a creative innovative solution to a business problem. Because expert systems affect the way people do their work and the actual work that they do, traditional before and after analysis is not sufficient to capture the underlying changes and the benefits.

Significant payoffs can result from getting a new product to market sooner, reducing business risk in major decisions, building greater cooperation, developing proactive strategic plans that account for many contingencies, improving organizational responsiveness, and delivering entirely new services via the technology. Measuring these types of benefits requires a greater degree of estimation and judgment.

Techniques that may be applied in specific situations depend on the available data.[3] They include :

- Direct output models
- Inferred output models
- Direct input models
- Inferred input models
- Work value analysis

Direct-output models analyze the flow of costs and revenues by explicitly and mechanistically representing how improvements in one area will have an effect on a bottom-line measure of financial performance such as profit. However, tracing productivity gains in white-collar or judgmental activities and linking these to the bottom line is usually difficult.

Due to the intangible nature of decision-making involved in many expert system applications, the output is often uncountable and not easily related to profits. Even when models are developed, others within the organization are sometimes skeptical, thus making it difficult to gain backing for the model in an organization.

Inferred-output models project benefits by seeking agreement among managers on the range of payoff expected from an expert system project using data such as profit per employee, sales figures, market research, and costs of operations. Upper and lower limits are set by consensus, but regardless of the bounding techniques, the estimates are highly subjective.

These models are best used when there is a limited quantitative basis for making value estimates. These can be used when expert systems require major organizational restructuring, operational changes, innovations, or new ways of conducting business. Thus, the more the benefits are derived from white-collar productivity, the more inferred-output models are of use.

Direct-input models are useful when inputs can be determined exactly but outputs cannot be measured. For example, if in the justification process, the expert system promises to improve productivity by 10 percent, the work hours required to perform the task can be tallied before and after the expert system investment. However, the hours must actually be reduced to achieve the benefits—a task not to be underestimated.

Inferred-input models use projected increases in efficiency and effectiveness among workers rather than actual verified cuts in labor or head count. This technique attempts to establish the reduced need for resources to maintain the same quality and volume of output.

Work value analysis is a hybrid model that recognizes that decision makers regularly engage in a wide variety of activities. Two types of benefits can be derived: (1) reducing the time each task takes and (2) shifting time to higher value activities. When junior managers perform senior management activities, the value of that time is increased.

---

[3]Perry A. Schwartz. :"When You're Asked to Cost-Justify Systems," *Computerworld*, August 3, 1987.

Combination Approaches

Because expert systems codify judgmental processes, the benefits derived tend to be more intangible than those generated by conventional systems. For example, in the cost-justification process we are often faced with questions such as: Can time savings be captured and turned into "think time"? Can the value of ideas generated during this time be estimated?

The size of the gap between the results from the old technique and the new is directly correlated with how much is known about the application area and how clearly the benefits can be defined and quantified. In some cases, much more information is needed and more teamwork is necessary to agree on the potential outcomes and their likelihood.

Techniques can be combined creatively, for example, by using dynamic simulation to estimate work flow analysis and then using it as an input to an ROI measure. This combination approach is useful in many situations to get the justification process moving and to augment traditional financial techniques.

> Bill Foskett of the U.S. EPA's Office of Underground Storage Tanks didn't focus on costs but concentrated on the productivity effects of expert systems. If we had a tool, how would it help? What would it do for us? At the outset, we ran a dynamic simulation model to identify the bottlenecks in our processes, made quick decisions, and began prototyping three applications. We started small and explored opportunities for knowledge sharing. The actual costs are small in comparison to the productivity improvements. EPA is inundated with work due to regulatory and compliance issues. We must think of ways to do more work with existing resources. Therefore, we use combinations of tools to solve our problems.

HOW TO SELECT AN APPROACH OR COMBINATION OF APPROACHES

There is a wide range of justification methodologies. The key is to develop meaningful measures of gains in business effectiveness in your organization. There is no one correct method for all expert system projects. The combination of effective techniques varies from organization to organization and from project to project. The best guideline is to use the technique or techniques that work, depending on the application and the cost-justification environment. A balanced approach is the most effective. Some factors below may provide guidance on selecting an approach. They are organizational mission, organizational culture, and market considerations. Many other factors might come into play in your organization, but these areas may be helpful in generating specific ideas that you can use.

Organizational Mission

It is clear that expert system investments should support the organizational mission. While some approaches are better than others, the likelihood of generating benefits depends on the centrality of the user. Because effectiveness can be defined only in the context of the organizational mission, context-specific valued-added metrics can lend a detailed understanding of the user's needs in the context of the organization.

As with other technology investments, the initial step in exploring expert systems investments is to define the requirements from the user's perspective. Next, the application and potential payoffs are defined. Then an appropriate technology is selected. If this process is not followed, the justification process may prove intractable (see Fig. 6.2.).

Top management's justification guidelines play an important role in setting organizational strategy and thus establishing the direction for funding technology projects. In the capital budgeting process, the framework for organizational investments and the future is set. The process involves

- Sifting through many competing project requests to optimally allocate scarce resources;
- Providing guidelines as to what direction the organization is trying to move in;
- Defining acceptable benefits.

If cost-justification guidelines emphasize labor savings, it is natural that labor-saving projects will receive more favorable attention than competing projects. If, on the other hand, improvements in quality are valid justification criteria, then more quality-related projects can be expected to be approved. Because organizational performance is more

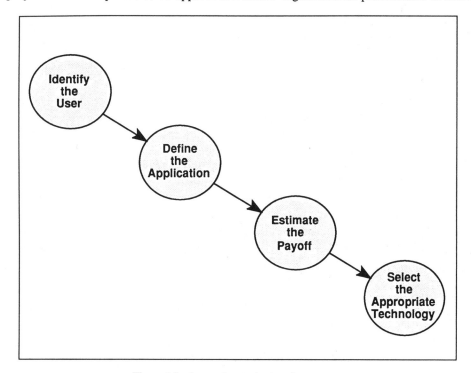

Figure 6.2 Approach to technology investments.

important than individual performance, this emphasis changes over time. It also may be different within each department, depending on the level at which expert system projects will be funded.

An understanding of the organization's allowable justification criteria is important at the outset. If these criteria are not established a priori, you could be facing a moving target. It is recommended that, as a first step, the project backer draft justification criteria before beginning the project to minimize conflicting objectives and unfortunate surprises as the project proceeds. If you are in a position to guide the organization, you should adopt an aggressive technology strategy while maintaining financial responsibility.

It should not be assumed, however, that investment in new technology is essential for survival in competitive marketplaces. Many organizations have sought technology solutions without refocusing their organizational missions. The results were often automated, but obsolete, processes. Clearly they were applying yesterday's solutions to tomorrow's challenges. Technology is powerful, but a strategic rethinking of what is to be automated is the clear path to generate significant benefits from technology investments.

The level of satisfaction with previous techniques, the strategic focus of the organization, and the view toward technology indicate that a blend of tried-and-true techniques and some new ones may be appropriate. Creativity is the byword. In the private sector, the survival of the organization may be at stake.

In each project, there are certain issues that are situation-specific and other issues that apply broadly to many expert system projects. The technique chosen must align with the organizational strategy, blend with the prevailing financial environment, and be compatible with the organizational culture.

Organizational Culture

When an organization focuses on human and organizational implementation issues, the benefits of expert system (ES) technology are more likely to accrue than when the organization focuses on the technical hardware and software issues. Clearly the selected approach must be palatable to the organization. Many organizations find that a blend of several techniques can help triangulate the results and more accurately predict the outcomes.

Benefits are achieved by enthusiastic users who use the system with the right skills, clear role descriptions, and good departmental organization. The type of user who should be selected is highly motivated and interested in expert systems technology, values personal growth, challenge, and opportunity, and has a healthy curiosity toward the technology.

Market Consideration

Prevailing market conditions can play a key role in the selection of justification techniques. In cases of contracting or declining markets, technology that helps to make the firm a low-cost producer might be easily justified. In mature markets, technology that helps revamp a service and breathe new life into a product might be easily justified.

In expanding markets, investments in new technologies can be more easily justified because as volume is increasing, costs can be spread across more units, decreasing the cost per unit. In niche markets, innovation is rewarded; customers will pay a premium for more value in their products and service offerings.

Each market condition implies a specific set of benefits the organization is seeking to achieve. The justification process should support this specific focus.

Balancing the Factors

Because expert systems can range from simple advisory systems containing accurate but common knowledge to a system to be used by the experts themselves, different cost-justification assumptions and approaches can be used in each case. Each of these systems offers benefits; some increase junior staff productivity, while others improve expert productivity. Both are key leverage areas in the organization.

The differences between organizations, their cultures, their leadership, their people, their talents, their market position, and their long-term strategies cannot be overemphasized. Each company's technology platform should support its needs. The selected justification approach should help fulfill this goal. Countless organizations adopt expert systems to match what their competitors are doing—not to support what they are doing.

At the completion of the process, after careful evaluation and review of techniques and approaches, it is helpful to build a library of justification techniques and guidelines for their use to assist with future technology projects.

THE COST-JUSTIFICATION PROCESS

The cost-justification process involves several key steps, including describing the project, estimating the costs, measuring the benefits, and bringing it all together. Consistent with that approach, before we can cost justify, we need to know the desired output from the expert system, how it will be used, how strong its recommendations will be, and how the task is currently performed. If the task is not currently performed, it is likely that a wider array of intangible and forecasted tangible benefits will be required.

The cost-justification process focuses on improved quality, decreased response time, enhanced flexibility, more custom approaches, reduced rework, more efficient flow of information and integration, and time savings. Many more strategic benefits can be derived if a broad perspective is adopted to capture as many of these benefits as possible. Extensive planning, coordination, and training are all necessary to achieve these potential benefits and to ensure continued management support for ongoing benefit generation.

Describing the Project

The first step in the justification process is to carefully and accurately describe the project. This includes identification of:

- What you are trying to accomplish with the expert system
- Why you are using expert systems
- What the project scope is
- Who the users are
- What benefits will be generated
- What assumptions have been made
- Where the decision points are to stop or to continue
- Whether the project can be divided
- Whether the project can lay the groundwork for other projects

The project description step helps to clarify the nature of the project and to help gain consensus within the organization. The description statement should be reduced to writing for careful scrutiny by the entire project team, from the expert to management.

Measuring the Benefits

Before benefits can be measured, we need to determine what functions the expert system will perform, how they were performed in the past, if at all, and how the service level will be changed. Figure 6.3 shows areas of potential benefit issues for a task that is being performed now, and Figure 6.4 shows one that is a new task. The following are some additional guidelines and information sources to identify and quantify benefits:

1. Ask management what benefits they will accept. Often a forty-minute time savings that occurs in five-minute increments eight times a day will not be accepted, because it does not alter organizational effectiveness.
2. Ask the users to help you define benefits. They can precisely define the gaps in their current data processing solutions.
3. Find similar applications and ask the users or developers what benefits they derived. Many firms will tell you the method used, although many will not disclose the exact return-on-investment figures.
4. Ask your vendor. Vendors are in a position to help you implement expert systems technology and can present cases of other users or put you in touch with other users of their software or systems.
5. Ask your consultant. Having been through the process many times before, consultants can draw upon their experience and provide an objective perspective.

The old adage "If you want to improve something, measure it," seems to apply here. By carefully scrutinizing processes and decision making, improved understanding of causes and effects can greatly improve the effectiveness of the organization's response. In measuring the benefits, it is helpful to evaluate expert system applications under different probabilities of success to capture a realistic view of the future costs and opportunities.

Time

- ❏ How is the function performed?
- ❏ How long does it take on the average?
- ❏ What is the longest time for the task? Shortest?
- ❏ What is the distribution of times for the task?
- ❏ What resources are currently applied?

Accuracy

- ❏ What is the current rate of success on the first pass?
- ❏ What inaccuracies are possible?
- ❏ How often does each of these happen?
- ❏ What are the consequences of these inaccuracies?

Consistency

- ❏ Are similar tasks currently performed with dissimilar results?
- ❏ What are the internal consequences of inconsistency?
- ❏ How is this viewed by those external to the organization?
- ❏ Has the organization been advised of inconsistent treatment of similar cases in the past?

Training

- ❏ How long does it currently take to become proficient?
- ❏ What is the cost of initial training per employee?
- ❏ How well do candidates perform after training?
- ❏ What on-going training efforts are necessary?
- ❏ How often is retraining required?
- ❏ What are the training implications in the future?

Improved Information

- ❏ What is the current output of the department per time period?
- ❏ How are incomplete cases handled?
- ❏ Are suboptimal tactics employed because consistent reliable information is not available?
- ❏ Is access to an expert a constraining factor in organizational performance?

Downtime Prevention/Fault Detection

- ❏ What are the costs of downtime?
- ❏ What are the costs of damaged equipment?
- ❏ Can the effects of lost customers be measured? Can they be regained?

Figure 6.3 Task being done now.

Product or Service Differentiation

❏ Will the system yield significant competitive advantages?
❏ Can additional services be provided because of more timely results?
❏ Can more products be offered because of improved information access?
❏ Can customer needs be more closely matched with flexible products with higher margins?
❏ Will customer loyalty be improved?
❏ What are the potential new markets? Sales volume?
❏ What is a realistic market share?
❏ What are the barriers to entry?
❏ Will the competitive profile change?
❏ How long can the leadership position be maintained?

Improved Information

❏ What are the benefits of improved information?
❏ Can more work be processed?
❏ Can new tasks be attempted?
❏ Will overall quality be improved?
❏ What are the ramifications of improved quality?
❏ Of static or deteriorating quality?

Time

❏ Will the function replace a series of processes?
❏ How long do they take now?
❏ What resources are currently applied?
❏ What other areas will the new application improve? Affect?

Figure 6.4 Task not being done now.

The multiplier effect can be achieved whenever improved effectiveness in one area results in improved productivity in other areas. If better information can increase the probability of success from 35 to 65 percent, then the information is valuable. Over enough cases, this difference will manifest itself in improved "win" records. But specific outcomes still cannot be guaranteed. Because human experts do not win all the time, neither will their expert systems. Systematic risk can neither be eliminated from business nor hedged away.

Questions that may help in identifying intangible benefits include

- What is the effect of doing nothing?
- What benefits can be attributed to "survival"?
- What is a 1 percent increase in market share worth?
- How do you measure the benefits of a satisfied customer?

- What is the benefit of flexibility?
- What is the value of more rapid-order processing of customer orders?
- What is the dollar value of information?

Other issues include: Is it possible to assess the timing and extent of a competitor's response to our investment in expert systems technology? How long will our benefits be derived? Can our system be matched, which would effectively neutralize our strategic benefits? Would we have been even farther behind without the investment?

The benefits of the expert system will vary based on user receptivity and acceptance. Will the system be used as projected to generate the planned benefits? Does the user feel secure in relying on the system? What methods can be used to ensure that the user reaps the benefits?

Can the benefits be recouped before technological obsolescence sets in? Will expert systems provide the technology platform for an evolving scenario of technologies such as natural language and neural networks?

Many successful end-user computing projects actually raise direct costs and do not decrease the labor force at all. White-collar productivity measurements require different models than those used in the past. Because executive output is difficult to categorize and more difficult to assign value to task by task, expert systems in these areas face significant cost-justification challenges. The outputs of managers are usually not measurable. Will a few minutes saved have an impact on corporate profits?

Reduced maintenance is also a benefit of some expert systems over conventional data processing technologies. In addition, end-user maintenance is sometimes an effective way to transfer this function closer to the decision makers. The benefits of reduced maintenance can be quantified when compared to current levels and types of software-maintenance activities in the organization.

Intangible benefits, although somewhat elusive, should be quantified where possible. The first step is to put them on paper. Solicit input from the users, management, the vendor, and any other source that could lend meaningful insight into the benefit picture. People may question the assumptions, the scenarios, the techniques used, and the size of the benefits, but not the existence of the benefits. Research the value of intangible benefits and adapt your tools accordingly. Because each project is different, it is unwise to rely unwaveringly on an old tool or, worse yet, on someone else's tool to perform the cost-justification process.

Be careful to measure expert system benefits under both prevailing and future market conditions. It is not accurate to assume a static marketplace over the life of the expert system. The benefits of a new approach to solving a problem may be difficult to quantify because there is no track record to follow. There is usually wide disagreement about what will happen in the future. Some will hold that the current situation can be maintained, while others will believe that the status quo will deteriorate if action is not taken.

Estimating the Costs

During the justification process, careful analysis and quantification of costs are performed. However, when estimating costs, use care. Do not imply precision in your estimates that you have no way of justifying; use round numbers and broad ranges such as $100,000–$150,000 instead of $112,000–$127,000. Some costs are relative, while others are direct out-of-pocket costs.

The cost analysis should include, at a minimum

- Software
- Hardware
- Licensing fees
- Design time
- Knowledge engineering
- Development
- Testing
- Validation
- Verification
- Evaluation
- Implementation and maintenance

As you do the analysis, consider what inflation will do to these costs. Document assumptions, such as price, sales, market forces, and competitor response. Use ranges to indicate imprecision in your estimates. Consider the timing of the benefits. Will significant benefits occur at the prototype stage, or will all major benefits accrue from the production system?

General Guidelines in the Justification Process

- Use objective rather than subjective data wherever possible.
- Use more than one method and compare results.
- Make sure that the methods used are comprehensible to the audience.
- Follow up on the project.
- Match estimates to actuals to refine the model.

It is easier to justify investments in activities that are being performed currently. The conceptual model of the task is clear: The benefits are easier to communicate. A thorough before-and-after analysis can be performed. The first step is to take a snapshot of current activities.

Bringing It All Together—A Sample Cost-Benefit Analysis

One effective method is a series of worksheets that assess one-time and ongoing costs and benefits. In the sample worksheet in Figure 6.5, costs are divided into two categories: out-of-pocket costs and labor costs. Two time factors—one-time costs and ongoing costs—are also given. The out-of-pocket costs are directly attributable to the expert system and would not have been incurred without the project. The risk factors on the out-of-pocket costs are fairly certain and are given a risk multiplier of 1. The labor costs, on the other hand, are somewhat less traceable to the system and are subject to considerably more variability. They are given risk multipliers between 1 and 1.6 to incorporate a conservative bias. A two-year time frame is assumed.

The benefits are also classified as one-time and ongoing. Conservative risk multiples, those less than 1, are applied to the benefits to capture the uncertainty and potential variabilty and interdependencies with other factors.

OUT OF POCKET	COSTS	RISK	NET	ONE-TIME	ONGOING	
Software	($2,000)	1.0	($2,000)	($2,000)		
Hardware	($12,000)	1.0	($12,000)	($12,000)		
Training	($3,000)	1.0	($3,000)	($3,000)		
Licensing	($1,200)	1.0	($1,200)	($1,200)		
Documentation	($800)	1.0	($800)	($800)		
Consulting	($6,000)	1.0	($6,000)	($6,000)		
Total out-of-pocket costs				($25,000)		

LABOR COSTS		RISK	NET	ONE-TIME	ONGOING	
Expert time	($2,000)	1.4	($2,800)	($2,800)	($750)	
Knowledge Eng.	($4,000)	1.6	($6,400)	($6,400)		
Programming	($6,000)	1.2	($7,200)	($7,200)	($1,250)	
Training	($2,000)	1.0	($2,000)	($2,000)	($500)	
Testing	($1,000)	1.1	($1,100)	($1,100)	($500)	
Validation	($1,500)	1.0	($1,500)	($1,500)	($500)	
QA	($1,500)	1.2	($1,800)	($1,800)	($500)	
Evaluation	($1,500)	1.0	($1,500)	($1,500)		
Maintenance	($3,000)	1.2	($3,600)		($3,600)	
Operation	($2,000)	1.1	($2,200)		($2,200)	
Total labor costs				($24,300)	($9,800) x 2	
COST GRAND TOTAL				($49,300)	($19,600)	($68,900)

BENEFITS		RISK	NET	ONE-TIME	ONGOING	
Time saved	$5,000	0.8		$4,000	$12,000	
Productivity	$4,000	0.9		$3,600	$7,000	
Loss reduction	$3,000	0.6		$1,800	$4,000	
Less rework	$1,500	0.6		$900	$1,500	
Accuracy	$1,000	0.9		$900	$12,000	
Total tangible benefits				$11,200	$36,500	
Strategic	$6,000	0.6		$3,600	$3,000	
Opportunities	$5,000	0.6		$3,000	$5,000	
Loyalty	$2,000	0.5		$1,000	$1,000	
Service	$2,000	0.7		$1,400	$1,000	
Knowledge	$6,000	0.8		$4,800	$2,000	
Total intangible benefits				$13,800	$12,000 x 2	
TOTAL BENEFITS				$25,000	$60,500	$85,500
NET BENEFITS						$16,600

Figure 6.5 Expert system justification worksheet.

WHEN TO JUSTIFY

While the cost-justification strategy is initially developed in the concept stage, the justification process occurs throughout the life of the expert system.

Concept Phase

In the concept stage, as the expert system begins to take shape, the level of advice, the task performed, potential benefits, users, scope, and benefits can be anticipated. From this information, the development process can be carefully guided to ensure that the benefits are delivered. The strength of the recommendations, the extent of distribution, the targeted users, and their characteristics all provide the framework for the cost-justification process.

Development Phase

The development phase can be subdivided into several steps to ensure multiple decision points during the process. They include

- Initial prototype
- Full prototype
- Production system

These phases are increasingly more sophisticated versions of the system as the design, functionality, and connectivity issues are explored. These phases provide multiple decision criteria and "go–no go" decision points and can be used to establish consensus and to gain management support.

Justification at the prototype stage is performed by demonstration of some of the potential benefits, such as improved decision time, improved quality, or more consistent output. This reinforces the project's objectives and helps retain the project's momentum, commitment, and funding.

Implementation and Maintenance Phase

During the system operation stage, the production system is being evaluated by the target users, and the real benefits can be measured. The projections can be turned into reality in terms of time savings, training benefits, codified institutional knowledge, and productivity improvements. The system can be thoroughly evaluated in an operational environment after the users have become proficient in the use of the system. Also at this stage, unanticipated benefits can be identified and quantified. In addition, data and knowledge base interrelationships and potential opportunities for reusing segments or modules of the knowledge base in other expert systems can be considered.

Another factor in measuring the overall impact of an expert system project is that it takes time to discover unanticipated benefits of ES. With training, learning curves, and lack of trust and confidence in the systems during the early stages, the full benefits do not manifest themselves for several months or more, depending on the complexity of the application and the implementation. After a project is completed, understanding the payoff is necessary to evaluating the results.

The justification team should consider full life-cycle costs. Figure 6.6 illustrates how life-cycle costs might be allocated to design, development, implementation, and maintenance based on the size of the knowledge base and its relative volatility. This can be used as a guide to ensure that full life-cycle costs are estimated.

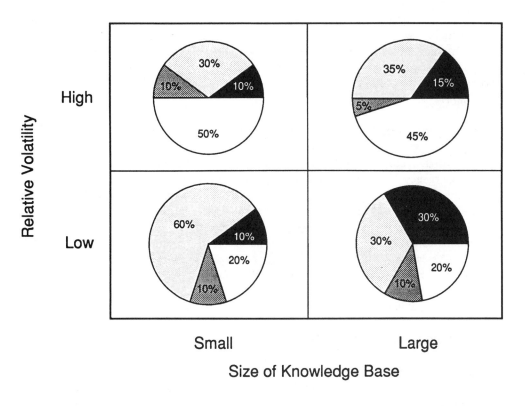

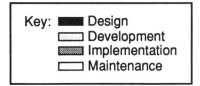

Figure 6.6   Assessing expert system life cycle costs.

CHALLENGES IN THE JUSTIFICATION PROCESS

Many challenges face expert systems users and developers when they attempt to justify expert system projects. For example, it is often difficult to attribute improved performance directly to the expert system, because usually procedures, work area layout, work flow, and other factors have also changed. Sometimes it is difficult to place a value on improved consistency of decisions. Other times, the benefits are long term. A cycle such as improved customer service and improved customer loyalty develops over time. Clearly this phenomenon is of value, but how much? How else can the organization get there?

The technology of expert systems is new and untested in many organizations. The path is new, the perils are unknown, and the benefits are difficult to predict. There is great uncertainty about the potential power of expert systems technology. Thus, a high risk factor is sometimes associated with it—in most cases, unnecessarily. Many organizations are reaping huge benefits from the technology. How can yours be one of them?

Limiting the Scope of the Expert System

Jack Frost, Director of the Information Management Staff of EPA's Office of Solid Waste and Emergency Response is looking for dramatic improvements in the consistency, timeliness, and reliability of decision making. As new engineers come on-line, expert systems can be used to supplement their training in the analysis of environmental problems. However, Frost cautions against excessive reliance on expert systems to make decisions for people. For the near term, he favors a conservative approach in which expert systems are limited in scope and advisory in nature. He also advocates the evaluation of the effects of potential liability issues in the justification process; the economics of the entire project will change if liability issues are involved from the misuse of an expert system.

Resolving Quantification Issues

What is the value of knowledge as a competitive weapon? The answer clearly depends on whether the specific piece of knowledge turns into a clear opportunity for the organization—something that is extremely difficult to predict in advance. There are no guarantees that innovation will move the organization ahead, but in many cases the lack of it could hold the organization back.

Maintaining Realistic Expectations

Oftentimes expert systems are introduced into an organization with such fervor that the benefits of the technology are oversold. This is unfortunate, because a properly applied expert system can usually stand on its own merits and surpass the established investment hurdle rates without embellishment. However, when this happens, the project team must deal with unrealistic expectations on the part of both user and management. The best solution is to establish communications early to dispel any myths regarding the capabilities of the expert system.

Training the Justification Team in Simple Finance

Is the justification team trained in simple financial analysis? Is it aware of opportunity costs? Many projects have floundered in this phase because of poor finance fundamentals. According to Hugh Evison Look, editor of the *Expert Systems—The International Journal of Knowledge Engineering* of Oxford, England[4] "Expert system developers may be technically competent but they are largely unprepared for the rigors of a financial justification process. Opportunity costs are rarely considered in their analyses. Investments are usually viewed in the most beneficial light with no analysis of sensitivity or variability in the extent and timing of costs and benefits." Look states that the justification process is approached with extreme naiveté. One problem is the relatively low entrance cost of the technology—a $500 shell. If the project reaches $50,000, the shell that began the exploration into the technology is totally insignificant in the decision process.

Gaining Funding

Expert systems can be evaluated against the potential of other technologies to solve problems. This powerful technique can reinforce the selection of expert systems as the appropriate technology, or it can identify alternative technologies. It should be remembered that this process is designed to assist organizations in implementing effective solutions, not to push through expert system projects. It furthers the progress of expert systems technology if projects can stand up to close and rigorous scrutiny. How else could the funding be used? What are the opportunity costs? The costs of doing nothing are usually very real. These should all be considered in the funding decision.

Differentiating among Multiple Expert System Opportunities

Oftentimes when expert system initiatives are begun on an organizationwide basis, multiple application areas are identified. While there are many alternative approaches to selecting and justifying the investment in expert systems, the matrix in Figure 6.7 below may prove helpful as a preliminary screen before a thorough justification process is begun on a more limited sample.

---

[4]Discussions with Hugh Evison Look, editor, *Expert Systems—The International Journal of Knowledge Engineering,* Learned Information Ltd., Oxford, England, 1988.

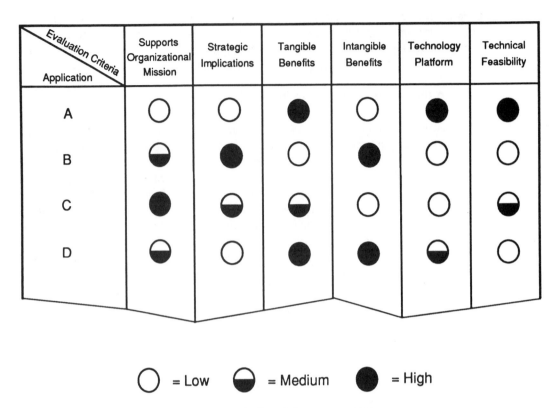

Figure 6.7   An example of differentiating among multiple expert systems.

RESPONSIBILITIES OF THE JUSTIFICATION TEAM

The responsibilities of the justification team are quite broad. First, their forecasts and assumptions must be realistic. The benefits can be measured only when the system becomes operational. If the benefits are not generated, the justification team loses credibility and is viewed as overly optimistic. The technology could stall in the organization if foresight and proper planning are lacking.

Even if the justification process proceeds smoothly, the system may not meet the user's needs, or the users may not be satisfied with the system. If rework is required, the economics of the project might change dramatically. If the system is not used at all, costs will be incurred and no benefits will accrue.

Minimize Project Risk

It is the responsibility of the developers to proceed incrementally, to start small, and to have a working system with limited functions and features before scaling up. The justification team can help to see that this happens. Properly managed expert system development efforts will assure that the organization derives some benefits from the project even if the overall scope or scale of the system must be revised.

Control Development Costs and Schedules

Prototypes can be seen as automated requirement-definition statements. Whereas in conventional development cycles, the design team spends significant time nailing down all functions, inputs, interactions, and outputs before coding begins, so does a prototyping effort lend insight into the project's functional requirements. At this point, the prototype may even be discarded as a system but retained as documentation of the requirements. From this point, actual development can begin in the same language or shell as the prototype or in a completely different software environment or hardware platform.

This prototype has also been referred to as "disposable" by Dan Yurman of the Information Management Staff at EPA's Office of Solid Waste and Emergency Response. Yurman states: "If the task is valuable enough to do a prototype and it is still valuable enough to move forward, then take the time to do the redesign, or you probably should not proceed anyway. Design the expert system to work effectively in its *delivery* platform—memory, storage, and processing requirements based on what you have learned in the prototyping process." Yurman also cautions organizations about migration plans across hardware environments. "The cost estimation and justification process should specifically include this redesign step. Failure at this level will send costs skyrocketing, and their migration may be technically infeasible. The benefits described during the cost justification process will never come to fruition."

Barry Boehm's[5] "build-it-twice approach" may be the best way to go. Boehm describes his method as a good approach for meeting the challenges of user satisfaction and application system efficiency in unfamiliar situations. Use the first effort to define the requirements. Use the second to efficiently develop the system based on new-found insights. This approach of building multiple decision points, starting the project in a small way, showing some benefits, and expanding is a very viable means for building expert systems.

Cost drivers in expert system development include size, complexity, required reliability, personnel attributes such as capability and experience, and project attributes such as schedule constraints and the use of software tools. Developing expert systems is a creative and cooperative enterprise that must be carefully managed to ensure full realization of potential benefits.

Builders of expert systems are beginning to develop extensive designs before any coding begins, similar to conventional data processing methodologies to address these cost drivers. What is appropriate is a middle-ground approach whereby a preliminary design is drafted during prototyping and is continually revisited; the prototype can then become the "design document." However, many projects lack the formality and structure that is necessary for complete design specifications.

---

[5]Barry V. Boehm, *Software Engineering Economics,* Prentice-Hall, Inc., Englewood Cliffs, N.J. 1981.

Gain and Maintain Commitment

Cooperation among all departments that will benefit by the expert system is an effective justification approach. Decision makers usually deal with open-ended problem-solving chains. That is, they rarely encounter a problem from the beginning. For example, an irate customer calls in. This could be the result of a problem resulting from one or several sources: improper design (Engineering), poor product quality (Manufacturing), late delivery (Shipping), or improper invoicing (Accounts Receivable). The combined efforts of these departments is the key to ultimate customer satisfaction. If an expert system potentially crosses organizational boundaries, cooperation among the teams involved will be quite persuasive in justifying the system with top management.

If a horizontal approach within the organization is not appropriate for the technology under evaluation, perhaps a vertical approach could be used. By assembling junior and mid-level management support, the expert system investment will present a stronger position when under the scrutiny of top management. Top management will be more confident if a balanced, thorough approach is taken.

Work with the Evaluation Team

The justification team should be available to work with the evaluation team to help identify areas in which benefits were expected, how they were quantified, and the basis of the assumptions made. Together, these teams can assess the actual and potential benefits of the expert system project.

Justification Guidelines

The following is a brief list of guidelines that may assist the justification team as they embark on quantifying costs and benefits:

- Estimate the cost of development software and expert system shells. These costs are usually a relatively minor cost in the overall expert systems life cycle.
- Accurately estimate the useful life of the software. Software life cycles are usually quite extensive, generating benefits throughout this entire time period.
- Consider hardware use as a cost, even if additional hardware is not acquired. Count in the hardware used; disk storage requirements and CPU use should be borne by the application.
- Base the justification on realistic assumptions. Do not
  - Underestimate costs
  - Overestimate revenues
  - Ignore variability
  - Assume linear benefits
- Capture costs and benefits over the full life cycle
  - Design

- Development
- Testing
- Validation
- Verification
- Operations
- Evaluation
- Implementation
- Maintenance
- Seek out and document hidden costs
  - Hardware add-ons
  - Software licensees
  - Staff resources
  - Peripherals
  - Memory expansion
  - Rework or revisions
  - Validation of changes

These justification steps are extremely important even if the project is not being carefully monitored or is exploratory in nature. Expert systems momentum is gained or lost by published success and failure throughout the organization. By removing barriers to progress, the entire organization can move forward into this and other high-technology areas.

Issues Involving Distribution

Many projects can withstand the rigors of justification in the development stages, only to find that distribution is impractical. Because of hardware migration difficulties, purchase of additional computers, add-on boards, math coprocessors, extended memory, software licenses, user training, and configuration management issues, the project economics change dramatically and could become prohibitive.

SUMMARY AND CONCLUSIONS

When properly applied, expert systems are a very powerful technology. Most organizations can achieve a combination of long-lasting strategic, financial, and technology benefits. The cost-justification process should present no barrier to investing in expert systems technology if systems are

- Directed toward high-payoff applications
- Designed to make people and processes more effective
- Built around highly trained staff
- Developed using incremental techniques

Later, as lower priority applications are attempted, risks and attendant costs for software and training will have been reduced, thus assisting in the dissemination of the technology throughout the organization.

Expert systems can and should be justified. However, the financial justification process should not be the main driver in the decision process. Healthy organizations pursue an aggressive technology strategy while maintaining financial responsibility.

FUTURE AREAS FOR JUSTIFICATION METHODOLOGIES

Three trends are meaningful in the context of justifying investments in expert systems:

- Increased availability of off-the-shelf software
- Expert system strategies that involve reusable knowledge bases
- Refinement and acceptance of advanced computing justification methods

As the industry moves toward more off-the-shelf expert system products, the cost-justification burden will decrease. These applications will embody standard business theory and practices in core knowledge bases. Users will be free to add custom rules and relationships that reflect individual expertise as well as specific regional or organization-wide guidelines. Depending on the application, the framework for up to three-quarters of the system can be delivered quickly and for a fixed price. Therefore, the costs addressed in the justification process will reflect only a one-time fee for the core, plus incremental development costs for the custom portion. Even though costs may be greatly reduced, the benefits reaped could match those of custom systems.

Another way to reduce both the cost and the risk of investments in expert systems is to plan a strategy of reusable knowledge bases. If several applications can be implemented in the same shell or software environment using compatible knowledge representations, modules can be reused or accessed by multiple systems. This will reduce the development cost of each system; each subsequent system will be easier and easier to justify because it builds on the existing technology infrastructure. Reusability of data, knowledge bases, rule libraries, subroutines, and modules should be explored.

While the cost of expert systems begins to fall, simultaneous developments in justification techniques will facilitate the dissemination of expert systems. The future directions of advanced technology justification practices include sophisticated combinations of modeling, simulation, and advanced statistical techniques with emerging technologies such as similarity networks and neural networks. Tracking past projects can be facilitated with similarity networks and other clustering techniques in the identification of common principles to guide future project-funding decisions. In addition, input-output pairs of past cases can be used to train neural networks in the cost-justification methodology. If these approaches are used, it will be possible to identify more causal phenomenon and more closely estimate elusive costs, benefits, and life-cycle issues.

REFERENCES

ARKES, HAL R., and KENNETH R. HAMMOND. *Judgment and Decision Making,* Cambridge University Press, Cambridge, MA, 1986.

BEATTY, CAROL A. "Tall Tales and Real Results: Implementing a New Technology for Productivity," *Business Quarterly,* November 1986.

BRIMSON, JAMES A. "How Advanced Manufacturing Technologies Are Reshaping Cost Management," *Management Accounting,* March 1986.

DORNAN, SANDRA B. "Justifying New Technologies," *Production,* July 1987.

DRUCKER, PETER. *Towards the Next Economics and Other Essays,* Heinemann, London, 1981.

FREEMAN, C. "The Economics of Innovation," IEEE Proceedings 132, Part A, No. 4, July 1985.

HILL, NEIL, and TONY DIMIK. "Cost Justifying New Technologies," *Business Quarterly,* Winter 1985.

FEINSTEIN, JERALD L. "EDAAS—A System to Protect Confidential Business Information," *Expert Systems—The International Journal of Knowledge Engineering,* Vol. 2, No. 2, Learned Information Ltd., April 1985.

LEONARD-BARTON, DOROTHY, and JOHN J. SVIOKLA. "Putting Expert Systems to Work," *Harvard Business Review,* March–April 1988.

ODGERS, JOHN F., and NORBERT NIMMERVOLL. "Accounting for Technological Innovation: An Overview," *Technovation,* Vol. 7, Elsevier Science Publishers Ltd., England, 1988.

SASSONE, PETER G., and A. PERRY SCHWARTZ. "Cost-Justifying OA—A Straightforward Method for Quantifying the Benefits of Automated Office Systems," *Datamation,* February 15, 1986, pp. 83–87.

THOMPSON, DONNA M. "Capturing User Requirements in Expert Systems." Presented at GIRICO Symposium 88, Quebec, Canada, April 1988.

THOMPSON, DONNA M., DAVID L. BAILEY, and JERALD L. FEINSTEIN. "Using Advanced Computing Technologies in the Analysis of Mergers and Acquisitions." Presented at the 8th International Expert Systems Conference, Avignon, France, 1988.

7

A Critical Review
of Legal Issues
in Artificial Intelligence

JANET S. ZEIDE, Attorney at Law
JAY LIEBOWITZ, George Washington University

INTRODUCTION

The legal field is steeped in history, with legal precedents deciding the outcome of each case. Even when new issues arise, traditional standards and principles are usually applied to determine the legal outcome.

A myriad of legal issues have arisen and continue to develop with the advent and proliferation of artificial intelligence (AI). However, computer technology poses a problem for jurists in that traditional standards and principles generally cannot be molded to apply to AI. Computer technology requires new legal analysis, interpretation, and theories because its nature is so different from other types of technology previously put before the courts. Artificial intelligence, with its ability to act like human experts, gives this technology a new role in society as machines are beginning to think like human beings.

Until now, although technology had eased the physical workload, human beings alone have held the ability to think and reason. If machines can think and reason like humans in narrowly defined areas of knowledge, then we will have to find a way to deal with the results of their actions and human interaction with them. This chapter considers some of the legal issues inferred by artificial intelligence.

THEORIES OF LIABILITY

One of the main problems that arises is how to attribute liability for computer programs and what theories of law should be applied, since the computer field is not one to which traditional legal principles can be summarily applied. Traditionally, manufacturers are held responsible under the theory of strict liability when their products cause injury (*San Diego Law Review,* 1983; Zeide and Liebowitz, 1987). However, when persons offering services cause harm in performing those services, they are charged with negligence.

The debate begins when one considers whether computer programs are products or services; they have qualities of both. The courts treat liability for injury from products differently than they treat liability for injury from services. Public policy considerations figure heavily into this debate.

Negligence

Negligence and *products liability* are legal terms that fit under the heading of torts (wrongful acts subject to civil action). Under negligence theory, given the circumstances of each case, the courts consider the reasonableness of the conduct or care used. Injured users of services, suing under theories of negligence, must prove that they were owed a duty of care—that is, that performance of the service fell below the standard of care (or that reasonable care could have prevented the injury and was not used), and that money damages provide appropriate compensation.

To compensate for loss or injury resulting from computer program error, a consumer would have to prove that a computer programmer was negligent in creating or copying programs. A plaintiff might have to specify the very mistake among thousands of information bits in the program, and then prove that the injury was reasonably foreseeable (*San Diego Law Review,* 1983).

Since proving such negligence could be difficult, a plaintiff might have a hard time recovering for injuries caused by computer program failures. Public policy considerations make strict products liability more desirable because it eliminates the need to prove fault.

Products Liability

Strict liability applies to unreasonably dangerous or hazardous products, regardless of conduct or care. The Restatement (Second) of Torts, Section 402 (1965), defines strict products liability as follows:

**SPECIAL LIABILITY OF SELLER OF PRODUCT FOR PHYSICAL HARM
TO USER OR CONSUMER**

1. One who sells any product in a defective condition unreasonably dangerous to the user or consumer or to his property is subject to liability for physical harm thereby caused to the ultimate user or consumer, or to his property if:
   a. the seller is engaged in the business of selling such a product;
   b. it is expected to and does reach the user or consumer without substantial change in the condition in which it is sold.
2. The rule stated in Subsection 1 applies although:
   a. the seller has exercised all possible care in the preparation and sale of his product;
   b. the user or consumer has not bought the product from or entered into any contractual relation with the seller.

Under strict products liability, manufacturers of unreasonably dangerous products are liable for injuries caused by their products regardless of reasonableness of care. Policy considerations for holding manufacturers to strict liability are partly based on manufacturers being in a better position than consumers to test for and identify problems, and to absorb or spread losses. The law expects assembly-line products to have uniform quality and design over which the user has no control, but over which the manufacturer does. If products are defective and unreasonably dangerous, then the court applies strict liability to manufacturers even if reasonable care was used in production and even if no amount of care in production could have prevented the injury.

Product versus Service

Strict liability applies only to defective products. Products are usually viewed as tangible items, with set monetary values, that can be owned (Corpus Juris Secundum, 1951). Computer programs have an intangible nature but are sold in physical (tangible) form.

Computer programs, consisting of electronic impulses, are not tangible; a program's single tangible aspect is the punch card, magnetic tape, or magnetic disk that stores and transports the program (Ducker, 1971). Furthermore, only the underlying ideas translated by a computer have real value (Brannigan and Dayhoff, 1981). It is interesting to note that ideas, not being concrete forms, cannot be copyrighted. But computer programs can be copyrighted (see "Protection").

Some courts, treating computer programs as intangibles, have scrutinized them under negligence theories in the few cases that have arisen. Tax courts facing the question of computer program tangibility have arrived at different findings: several have ruled that software is not taxable as personal property because of the program's intangible nature. Others have held that the tangible output is taxable even though the program itself may not be. One ruling maintained that a computer program should be taxable for its full value even though its nature is intangible and even though it is recorded on relatively inexpensive material (*Greyhound Computer Corp.* v. *State Dept. of Assessments and Taxation,* 1974).

Some intangible properties are not normally considered products capable of inflicting injury (licenses, for instance) (Brannigan and Dayhoff, 1981). However, strict liability has been applied to other intangible properties (such as leases of real and personal property, energy, and certain types of service transactions such as applying a defective hair treatment) (Prince, 1980). Manufacturers, realizing the enormous responsibility they bear for their computer programs, have attached disclaimers to products to reduce their liability. The legal effect of disclaimers—so far uncertain—centers on the product versus service question in terms of applying the Uniform Commercial Code.

Other Theories of Liability

Do computer programs merely provide information, as do books and magazines? Computer program manufacturers may wish to argue that this is the case in an effort to limit their liability. Computer programs contain a tremendous amount of data or information. They are designed to be consulted by experts and lay people as sources of information, confirmation of opinion, and training tools. There is usually no relationship between the producer and the user; they are anonymous to each other. Computer programs are bought. They are relied upon and usually considered accurate and up-to-date. These characteristics make computer programs sound very much like another popular type of reference tool—books. In fact, reference books are the primary source of information for professionals and laypersons alike. Sometimes it is possible to consult a human expert (who nevertheless trained with books and continues to review books and journals), but a human expert is not always available or accessible.

Because AI programs, particularly expert systems, take on an active role (that is, reasoning with and responding to the user), courts may be reluctant to simply apply established standards used for books and magazines, which are passive and do not allow for interaction of user and source. Again, the courts must balance the need to protect manufacturers (while not thwarting momentum and advances in the field) with the need to protect the public and provide for compensation when injury occurs.

It has been suggested (Gemignani, 1981) in post-trial memoranda in the *Chatlos Systems, Inc.* v. *National Cash Register Corp.* case that there should be a new theory of liability for computer programs. But a "computer malpractice" tort was rejected by the court because it would impose greater liability on computer sales and service providers and would hold the providers to professional standards. The court reasoned that there was no need to attach greater liability to the computer field, even though it is "technically complex and important to the business community" (Gemignani, 1981). Establishing computer malpractice as a new theory of liability would require standards for measuring the duty of care by which computer professionals are to be judged; no such standards currently exist. Commentators who argue in favor of this new tort say that recently adopted computer industry professional codes and standards are sufficient criteria by which to judge the conduct of computer program developers (Reece, 1987).

But there is a distinction to be made among those who provide computer sales and service and those who produce computer programs and AI programs themselves. Computer programs are designed and employed to act as the equivalent of a human being. In fact, in some areas, computers surpass human ability and "do better than we ourselves that which we believed sets us apart from the machines that serve us. Computers are no longer extensions of our bodies, but are limitations of our minds" (Gemignani, 1983).

When a person makes a mistake, and his or her actions are reviewed by a court for liability, a "reasonable person" standard is used. If computer programs, particularly expert systems designed to mimic the behavior of a human expert, are employed to replace, supplement, or act as a human, does an AI machine fall within the legal definition of personhood, and should there be a "reasonable computer" standard applied (or adopted)? According to one writer, "As computers behave increasingly like humans, the reasonableness of treating them like persons will increase" (Willick, 1983). Courts will most likely be reluctant to apply a human standard to a machine, but the problem of tracing blame to humans for computer program injuries remains. Of all those responsible for producing a computer program, it is almost impossible to attribute liability to particular individuals. This is an extremely delicate question with regard to expert systems, because they incorporate the knowledge of human experts and the technical work of human programmers. When a human expert is consulted, he or she then becomes open to malpractice suits. When this knowledge is incorporated into a computer program and the use of the program in some way causes injury, a straightforward malpractice claim cannot be made because of the many people and procedures involved. The courts will soon be faced with the task of tracing and applying liability where computer programs are involved. This is especially true now, with the expanded use of computer programs and the reliance we have on them.

RELIANCE

The crash of Northwest Flight 255 in Detroit in 1987 (Feaver, 1987) provides a good example of the reliance we are increasingly and routinely placing on AI programs and computers in today's automated society. Investigators are bemoaning the combination of human error, computer error, and—most importantly—complacency with an automated routine. For example, today's new airplanes apparently "are so automated that the only thing left for the pilots to do is to monitor systems" (Feaver, 1987). The legal issues raised by living in an automated society have to do primarily with our reliance on computers and our use, misuse, and even nonuse of them.

We are relying more and more on computers to aid us in highly technical and complex tasks to routine and "checklist" chores. In fact, computers touch our lives daily. And as their use becomes more prevalent, so does our reliance upon them.

Use and Misuse

Problems relating to the use and misuse of computer programs are popping up in courtrooms more frequently. This fact is not surprising, since AI applications are being used to teach, to aid the professional in making diagnoses and judgments, and to help laypeople (often to circumvent the services of a human professional).

A lawsuit could arise if computer programs—particularly expert systems—are consulted and fail to perform correctly, or give inaccurate or misleading answers that lead to injury (Brown, 1986). Such problems could be caused by hardware malfunction, knowledge base or program errors, misuse, unintended use, or undue reliance on the system (Nycum and Fong, 1985).

Nonexperts can misuse AI computer programs, and systems can be inaccurate in certain situations. For example, a family using a tax-preparation program may take a home-office deduction for which they are ineligible, and the expert system will not spot the oversight. Later, when the IRS discovers the mistake, the family will have to pay additional taxes, plus interest and penalties. A tax accountant would probably have found the error and alerted the family (Kutten, 1985). Indeed, an accountant who misjudged the situation and failed to warn a client of such an error would be negligent. But what if that same accountant was the expert whose knowledge was encaptured in the expert system?

Nonuse

The nonuse of computer programs—particularly expert systems—is the focus of much legal speculation about the future. As " 'computer literacy' becomes more and more a requirement for survival in any profession" (Gemignani, 1983), will it become standard practice to use AI applications in some fields where the technology is readily available? If so, a professional who consults an expert system as standard practice could be liable for the nonuse of an expert system; that is, it may be "just as bad not to use available technology as it is to rely on a system when you should have used your own brain" (Stanford University News Service, 1986). As one author asserts, for "certain sensitive, delicate or hazardous tasks (such as aircraft requiring fast and accurate response beyond human capability), it may be unreasonable not to rely upon an expert system" (Gemignani, 1984). This prediction, as it turns out, has proved not only true but also too conservative, because we are already relying on computers to aid us in relatively routine acts, including daily air flights. In fact, almost all of today's airplanes use some amount of computerized equipment; but when crashes or accidents occur, we often find, for example, that the computerized automatic warning device had been disarmed (Feaver, 1987). One news report tells of a voice-simulated automatic warning "Pull up, pull up." The (Spanish) pilot was heard on the black box recording to say "Shut up, Gringo" as he disarmed the computer and then crashed into the side of a mountain.

Expert systems such as Prospector (mineral exploration), ACE (telephone cable maintenance), and R1/XCON (computer configuration) are already used daily. These systems have succeeded, in some cases proving more accurate than human specialists. Moreover, they store more data and transmit that data faster than a human expert can (Nycum, 1985). Decision makers increasingly view expert systems as indispensable tools (Bequai, 1987).

In some fields, such as medicine, the nonuse of an available expert system gives rise to moral and ethical as well as legal issues. MYCIN, for example, is an expert system that is in daily use and readily available to some physicians as an aid in the diagnosis of meningitis. A scenario in which a physician does not consult MYCIN and fails to correctly diagnose and treat a patient is at issue when we talk about the nonuse of available computer technology. Some legal specialists believe that doctors eventually might risk malpractice suits for *not* consulting computer programs. In fact, a uniform medical code for software is being developed, possibly heralding the age of "automated medicine" (Gibson, 1987). Physicians' actions are reviewed by courts under a "state-of-the-art" theory—in other words, according to what is found to be standard practice in the medical community. Although many physicians are using computers in their offices today, few are using them for diagnostic purposes as yet. However, 25 percent of those responding to an AMA survey say that they intend to eventually use computers as diagnostic aids (Gibson, 1987). As more physicians use and rely on computer programs for diagnosis and treatment, the more likely the computers programs are to be viewed as standard practice. It should be noted, however, that courts looking to what is standard practice in an industry will consider the relative availability of resources. So although a high standard of care is uniformly required, the same methods may not be—for example, when examining standard practices in a large city versus a small town.

Our reliance on expert systems will, unfortunately, lead to injuries. This is inevitable because of the many people and interests involved. Injuries will take many forms, predominantly economic and physical.

INJURY

As AI applications gain acceptance and use, especially expert systems, the possibility of such programs causing serious injury also increases. When there are injuries, there are lawsuits. So far, few cases have come to court involving injuries from computer programs, but the potential exists, and some cases have been litigated involving injuries caused by robots.

Injury Involving Computer Programs

"The damage caused by a negligently driven car is usually quite localized. When computers across the country talk regularly to one another and major banks, utilities, industries, and government agencies, as well as private individuals, become heavily dependent on their computers, a major computer failure could cause billions of dollars in damages over a broad geographical area, and even widespread loss of life. On at least one occasion, a faulty computer almost started World War III" (Gemignani, 1983).

Injury Involving Robots

Consider the first patient who dies as a result of a bad diagnosis from a robotic doctor. Who will be held responsible? And how will that decision be made? We have a great many avenues for ascribing legal and ethical responsibility to people. Some of them extend to well-specified, well-understood machines. But even here there are problems when the decisions are highly consequential. For example, it is quite possible that we will never see commercial airlines flown entirely under computer control even if that technology becomes clearly superior—statistically—to human pilots. The reasons is that although human pilots crash the occasional plane when trying to land in poor weather, their failures are understandable and thus, though regrettable, can be tolerated. When the mechanical pilot fails, however, even though it might do so much less frequently, it's likely to be by flying a plane into the side of a mountain in broad daylight. And this kind of inhuman failure we are unlikely to tolerate, whatever the long-run statistics say. (Sheil, 1987)

What legal recourse does a worker have who is mistakenly injured by a robot? Or what would happen if an employee came back to the plant after closing time to pick up his jacket and a robot acting as a security guard apprehended and injured him?

These cases suggest the general issue of liability for injury caused by an AI machine. Strict liability holds manufacturers strictly liable for products causing harm even if they took reasonable steps to make those products safe (Stanford University News Service, 1986). The possibility of harm due to a malfunctioning AI machine exists. Nycum (1985) reports that, in one instance, a man was trapped by a manufacturing robot. Even though the manufacturer had made reasonable efforts to prevent such an occurrence, the robot did not have an easy-to-reach on-off switch. The man died of a heart attack. Human injuries resulting from a defective robot will most likely continue to be covered under strict liability. By usually having no human intermediaries involved in the application, it is easier for the courts to apply traditional tort analysis and remedy to the activity. However, according to Nycum (1985), manufacturers may argue that as robots become more intelligent, manufacturers should not be held responsible for acts beyond their foresight and control. As long as the courts continue to apply strict liability, workers injured by machinery would be covered under existing systems of workers' compensation.

Launch on Warning

AI applications, like expert systems, could cause irreparable harm and injury if mistakes in logic and knowledge are made. Having expert systems for determining and activating "launch on warning" situations could have fatal results. The effect of AI techniques on environments like the Strategic Defense Initiative (SDI) sheds light on injury issues.

Artificial intelligence techniques and supercomputer use will have to play influential roles in order for the SDI to succeed (Chien and Liebowitz, 1986). In particular, expert systems could have a major impact in meeting the objectives of the SDI project. However, there are several difficulties in designing expert systems for the SDI environment.

One important area is that the expert system must be "evolvable." Since new technologies, and SDI-related requirements will be discovered over the next fifteen years, the expert system must be able to easily handle the integration of this new knowledge into the old. Thus, a very modular approach to designing the knowledge base is needed, along with a fairly easy semiautomated (or fully automated) way of acquiring knowledge and integrating it into the knowledge base. A way of checking for consistency of information and possible conflicts of existing and new requirements must be incorporated into the expert system. Reliability of an SDI expert system is also a major concern, as expressed in Parnas' works (Parnas, 1985).

Another area of difficulty is in developing expert systems where there may be "no experts" who exist at the time of building the expert system. Experts may exist for developing parts of the knowledge base; however, the knowledge base may have to contain knowledge in areas in which no experts currently exist. For example, the effects of chemical lasers or neutral-particle beams on certain objects are areas that are not known now, since these weapons have not been built, tested, and used against ballistic missiles. Thus, the knowledge base may not yet be able to include such information, but as time goes on, this information may be obtained and encoded. This fact suggests that current expert system developments may either focus on a very narrow problem domain or concentrate on a larger domain, but the knowledge base should be "evolvable."

A problem associated with this is developing expert systems presently for the SDI environment, where there are great unknowns. Uncertainty exists such as in the Ballistic Missile Defense (BMD) system's architecture, the weapons selected for the BMD system, and the constraints on computing power. These uncertainties will be lessened as the years progress; however, it is not presently known with certainty what the weapons and actual BMD environment will look like in the years 1995–2000. Again, it is critically important for the expert systems built today for the SDI environment to be able to handle uncertainties and be modular in design for knowledge base evolvability.

Much work is needed to advance technology in order to meet the complexities and challenges posed by the SDI. Expert systems are one alternative that have the potential to contribute to SDI goals. There are, however, some interesting legal questions resulting from using expert systems in the SDI environment. What would be the repercussions if expert systems were to be used for "launch on warning" in the SDI environment? In other words, expert systems activate the U.S. response to launch U.S. missiles upon getting some warning that the Soviets have launched missiles toward the United States. But let us say that the information on which the warning was based turned out to be faulty. Or let us say that an expert system incorrectly identified something to be a warhead instead of space debris. And then another expert system is used to launch U.S. missiles based on this faulty warning. Anyone can guess the injuries resulting from this action. Is this a far-fetched situation? We hope that we will never be faced with these SDI scenarios. We also hope that an expert system will never be used to make the judgment and push the button for nuclear holocaust.

The immediate and certain consequences of injuries from AI applications have software developers concerned. Before cases get to court and before courts decide which theory or theories of liability apply, developers have begun trying to protect themselves.

LIMITING LIABILITY

While the legal explosion in the computer program arena is still only a potentiality, producers of computer programs have long been preparing for it. They are using several methods to try to limit their liability if their programs cause injury (Brown, 1986). Manufacturers have thus far had limited success at limiting their liability. Program producers are primarily trying to limit their liability before the fact by including various disclaimers in their sales contracts. They have also tried claiming First Amendment rights. On the other hand, program users have looked to tort theories for remedies; one factor that looms large over the situation is whether computer programs, particularly expert systems, are products or services.

CONTRACT THEORIES

Disclaimers and the Uniform Commercial Code

Computer program vendors have been routinely including strong and broad disclaimers in their software contracts. These carefully worded clauses have so far proven somewhat successful in court where an injured user has brought a breach of contract, breach of warranty suit or both. Four standard clauses are usually included in software contracts, which expert system manufacturers should be aware of.

Limitation of remedies.   When the contract contains a limitation of remedies clause, and software is defective, the user will only be entitled to have the software repaired or replaced by the seller. This precludes any other "remedies" such as damages. The program must be substantially free of defects for this clause to be an effective shield for the seller. If it is not substantially free of defects when sold, the seller must be able or willing to make the program fit the contractual description, or this clause will fail and remedies will not be limited to repair or replacement. Several cases have validated this disclaimer when it has been the subject of a computer contract case (Reece, 1987).

Limitation of liability.   A limitation of liability clause generally limits the seller's liability and excludes special or consequential damages. Consequential damages are those losses which are the result of special, unpredictable circumstances. According to *Black's Law Dictionary* (Black, 1979), consequential damages "resulting from a seller's breach of contract include any loss resulting from general or particular requirements and needs of which the seller at the time of contracting had reason to know and which could not reasonably be prevented by cover or otherwise, and injury to person or property proximately resulting from any breach of warranty." A user who sues a seller must show that this clause is "unconscionable" or unreasonable in order to overcome it. *Unconscionability* refers to the absence of meaningful choice on the part of one of the parties to the contract, so that the contract turns out to be unreasonably one-sided. Courts will look to the relative commercial sophistication and experience with contracts of the parties when considering a claim of unconscionability and have usually honored these clauses if the contract seems to have been fairly negotiated (Reece, 1987). Such a clause would typically read: "In no event will ABC Computer Company be liable for consequential damages even if ABC has been advised of the possibility of such damages."

Disclaimer of warranties.

ABC Computer Company does not make any express or implied warranties, including, but
not limited to the implied warranties of merchantability and fitness for a particular purpose.
(Gemignani, 1981)

With this disclaimer-of-warranties clause, vendors are stating that only those
warranties that are expressly stated in the contract are being made to the exclusion of all
other implied or oral warranties. This is another clause which, if sued upon, must be shown
to be unconscionable in order for it to be invalidated by a court. And a court would most
likely enforce such a clause where the user is a businessperson with experience in
commercial endeavors and would have dealt with contracts and disclaimers before.

Integration clause.   A typical integration clause will read (Gemignani, 1981):

There are no understandings, agreements, representations, or warranties, express or implied
(including any regarding the merchantability or fitness for a particular purpose), not specified
herein, respecting this contract or equipment hereunder. This contract states the entire obligation of the seller in connection with this transaction.

This states that the writing—the contract—is the entire agreement. What this means
is that even if the user relied on oral warranties, promises, or representations, or marketing
information such as brochures and ads, unless they are specifically written into the
contract, the user cannot claim them in a lawsuit against the seller. This type of clause is
widely accepted by courts and has been enforced in cases involving computer programs
(Gemignani, 1981).

The use of these disclaimers is based upon the theory of a contract for the sale of
goods, the software being the "goods." This again brings up the controversy of identifying
a computer program, like an expert system, as a product or a service. So far, the few courts
that have had to deal with this question have had varying results. Most likely, courts will
continue to look at the facts of each case rather than apply a general standard. Where a
computer program is specifically designed and created for a particular situation and user,
the software may be treated as a service (Gemignani, 1981). In addition, the courts may
look to the contract itself to identify whether it ultimately centered on the sale of a product
or the performance of a service. If the court finds that the basis or essence of the contract
was the performance of a service, a lawsuit based on breach of contract or breach of
warranty will not be successful. The Uniform Commercial Code (UCC) is the key to the
situation. It applies only to the sale of goods and will not apply if the software is
determined to be a service rather than "goods" or a product. In addition, in many instances,
software is leased or licensed, and no "sale" takes place. Without the "sale of goods," the
UCC will not apply.

It is also interesting to consider that, on one hand, courts will look for a "fairly
negotiated" contract to determine whether the disclaimers are unconscionable, while on
the other hand, these clauses have become so standard that it is unlikely, at the very least,

that a purchaser could buy computer programs (or hardware) without accepting the disclaimers as written. However, the law in computer cases is still being formed and the courts have many factors to consider in making their determinations. A major factor is public policy concerning the public interest and welfare.

Comparison to Books and Magazines

Books and magazines have traditionally been considered to be services and are therefore immune from products liability. Authors and publishers have often been protected by the First Amendment in suits brought by readers on the theory that free speech would be restrained if courts imposed liability for book or magazine content. In addition, courts usually hold that authors and publishers owe no obligation to readers, since there is no contract between reader and author or publisher. In attempting to defend themselves against lawsuits brought by users, producers of computer programs have argued that programs are providers of information, like books and magazines, and therefore should be protected in the same way.

However, courts have been unwilling to accept this analogy in the few cases that have come up. Instead of programs merely providing information, the information is seen as the product designed to aid the user (Bequai, 1987). In these cases, product liability has been applied.

Employers may also face the prospect of liability in an era of increasing use. In this case, tangential injury is possible—the displacement of human workers from jobs that AI programs are being produced to do.

WORK FORCE CONSIDERATIONS

Artificial intelligence introduces some interesting legal questions regarding work force considerations. Specifically, robots and expert systems are the AI applications that have the most potential for raising issues relating to work force considerations.

Robots

In many industrial plants, such as automobile and chemical plants, robots are part of the work force. Robots have been integrated into the mainstream of many industrial processes worldwide. Management might be pleased with using robots because: (1) they are reliable, (2) they perform accurate, standardized work, (3) they are not paid union wages and overtime, and (4) they do not waste time, get tired, or take coffee breaks. An important work force consideration, however, is what happens to the displaced worker whose job was taken over by a robot. Is the worker fired, or is he or she retrained to do other work?

It is management's responsibility to retrain these workers and gainfully employ them, instead of laying them off or firing them. Management should have on-the-job training programs to educate workers to perform jobs in other areas. Actually, many people believe that robots eliminate jobs by replacing workers, but the use of robots can

also create new jobs. People will be needed to provide preventive and corrective maintenance on robots. Other people will be needed to oversee the work of robots and manage
them. Perhaps, the displaced worker could fill these positions. If management does not
provide these opportunities for displaced workers and simply fires them—not for incom-
petence but for cost effectiveness—can these workers claim that they are being discriminated against? To protect workers, unions should have (if they do not already) clauses in
their labor contracts with management to either allow a certain percentage of the plant to
be automated or to make sure that management retrains the displaced worker without
firing him or her. As more robots become more capable and less costly and enter the
workplace, these issues will need to be addressed by management and labor.

Expert Systems

Like robots, expert systems can have profound effects on work force considerations.
Nycum (1985) points out that 99 percent of all clerical workers are women, and the
clerical field is the one most affected by computers. If expert systems are being developed
to replace clerical staff, can expert systems be considered a sexist threat? Can women sue
on the basis that they are being discriminated against by having these expert systems being
built and targeted toward their occupations? Already, expert systems, like INTELLIGENT
SECRETARY, are being developed to act as surrogate secretaries. Of course, since expert
systems are used in narrowly defined tasks, an expert system designed for secretarial
functions might be able to do only one or two functions, such as scheduling meetings or
routing calls. Can an expert system "screen" calls for the boss and provide certain answers
based upon knowledge of the situation, background of the caller, the mood of the boss
that day, and the boss's expected response to the caller? Can an expert system use
common-sense reasoning to solve this situation? These are research areas that have not
been resolved but will continue to be addressed in the coming years.

Already, however, with the proliferation of microcomputers, some of the secretary's
duties are being reduced. For example, it is much easier to use a word-processing package
on the personal computer for drafting a memo or report than writing it out longhand. Many
times, the boss will use the personal computer directly for these activities instead of giving
a longhand draft of a memo to the secretary to type. Also, there are systems available,
like VOICEWRITER, that will allow the boss to dictate, and a typewriter will spontane-
ously type out what is being dictated. If the vocabularies and the number of grammatical
rules in the system greatly increase over the coming years, this innovation could also
eliminate some of the functions of a secretary. Thus, a question to be asked in the coming
years is: Are expert systems and other AI technology taking away jobs from others, like
secretaries, or are they helping the affected individual perform his or her job better and
free up his or her time to do less mundane tasks?

Those involved in the production of computer programs have many concerns with
regard to defending themselves against potential lawsuits. But they are already finding
themselves in need of another type of protection—that of protecting what they produce
from any type of theft.

PROTECTION

The idea of "protection" in the computer arena has several different aspects. One area is the protection of those who produce programs that primarily involve a copyright patent analysis. Many hypothetical protection questions are also raised when a user and a computer program write poetry or music or generate other programs "together."

Ownership

The issue of protecting a program developer or producer is guided by the service versus product distinction already mentioned. If a program is a product, it is possible that it can be patented. However, this would require that it be deemed a novel invention, unique in the state of the art. It cannot be on the market for more than one year prior to the issuance of the patent. In addition, a patented product is usually a tangible item. But although programs are sold and transferred on physical discs, it is the content of the disc, not the disc itself, that is really the "product." For these reasons, developers usually go the copyright route for protection of their programs. This further substantiates the conflict of whether an expert system is a product or a service.

If a program is deemed a writing, it is possible that it can be copyrighted. A copyright will protect it for the life of the "author" plus fifty years. It must be a work of original (human) authorship. The "human" requirement presents a problem that may arise in the future. That is, who is the author when a user presents a problem or style, and with some guidance from the user, the program produces a poem, a musical composition, or a program? The examiners at the U.S. Copyright Office have the ultimate authority to make a decision on whether or not the author of the work is the human or the AI program. One writer asserts that courts "should track the ownership to the humans at the source of the resulting work" (Nycum, 1985). Besides deciding between user and program for ownership rights, courts may also have to assess claims to rights between user and the AI program developer—who will usually already have a copyright on the original poetry, music, or program-generating program. Courts will have to "determine which contending party owns how much, if any, of a given copyright" (Nycum, 1985) on the work produced by the user and the program.

An additional concern for protection involves the unauthorized entrance into and manipulation of an expert system's knowledge base. Knowledge engineers need to make provisions for ensuring that the knowledge does not get tampered with indiscriminately. Of course, there should be ways for updating an expert system's knowledge base, but only by those individuals authorized to do so. If unauthorized access leads to tampering with the knowledge base, users could rely on incorrect advice, which might detrimentally affect the outcome of a situation. Although this is not a current problem, the proliferation of expert systems may attract this type of "theft" or activity. Security laws to protect expert systems will have to be enacted as they have already been with regard to "unauthorized access" (Hoffman, 1980).

CONCLUSIONS

As AI applications continue to grow and penetrate the marketplace (Computer Law Association, 1988; Liebowitz and Zeide, 1987; Liebowitz, 1986; ACM SIGART, 1987) the likelihood of legal entanglements resulting from some AI applications increases (Frank, 1988a, b). At the present time, there have been very few cases as a result of AI-related issues. Since we live in a very litigious society, more AI-related legal cases will surely arise in the future. The doctor who did not consult an expert system or relied on the expert system's advice, the worker injured by a defective robot, and the secretary whose functions are being usurped by intelligent machines are likely candidates for legal action. Certainly, one person will always be the victor in these legal battles—the lawyer. But what will happen when an intelligent computer replaces the lawyer? Perhaps we'll never know!

REFERENCES

ACM SIGART, *Proceedings of the First International Conference on Artificial Intelligence and Law,* Northeastern University, Boston, MA, May 27–29, 1987.

BEQUAI, A. "Who's Liable: The Expert System or the User?" *Lotus Magazine,* March 1987.

BLACK, H. C. *Black's Law Dictionary,* West Publishing, 1979, p. 352.

BRANNIGAN, V. M., and R. E. DAYHOFF. "Liability for Personal Injuries Caused by Defective Medical Computer Programs," *American Journal of Law and Medicine,* Vol. 7, 1981, p. 123.

BROWN, M. "Expert Systems Pose Liability Problem in Courts," *Government Computer News,* August 15, 1986, p. 20.

CHIEN, Y. T., and J. LIEBOWITZ. "Expert Systems in the Strategic Defense Initiative Environment," *Computer,* IEEE, July 1986.

Discussions With Computer Law Association, Inc., 8303 Arlington Blvd., Suite 210, Fairfax, VA 22031, 1988.

Corpus Juris Secundum. Vol. 73, Property Section 1, 1951.

DUCKER, R. "Liability for Computer Software," *Business Law,* Vol. 26, 1971, p. 1081.

FEAVER, D. B. "Automation, Routine Can Produce Cockpit Inattentiveness," *The Washington Post,* August 23, 1987, p. A-1.

———. "Computer Failed to Warn Jet Crew," *The Washington Post,* August 21, 1987, p. A-1.

FRANK, S. J. "What AI Practitioners Should Know About the Law, Part 1," *AI Magazine,* American Association for Artificial Intelligence, Vol. 9, No. 1, Menlo Park, CA, Spring 1988.

———. "What AI Practitioners Should Know About the Law, Part 2," *AI Magazine,* American Association for Artificial Intelligence, Vol. 9, No. 2, Menlo Park, CA, Summer 1988.

GEMIGNANI, M. C. "Product Liability and Software," *Rutgers Computer and Technology Law Journal,* Vol. 8, 1981.

GEMIGNANI, M. C. "The Case for Computer Law," *Case & Comment,* May–June 1983, p. 3.

———. "Laying Down the Law to Robots," *San Diego Law Review,* Vol. 21, 1984, p. 180.

GIBSON, R. "The Computer Is In: More Doctors Use High-Tech Help for Diagnoses," *The Wall Street Journal,* July 8, 1987, p. 21.

Greyhound Computer Corp. v. *State Dept. of Assessments and Taxation. Atlantic Reporter,* Vol. 320, 1974, p. 52.

HOFFMAN, L. J., ed. *Computers and Privacy in the Next Decade,* Academic Press, New York, 1980.

KUTTEN, L. J. "Are Expert Systems More Trouble Than They Are Worth?" *Computerworld,* May 20, 1985, p. 72.

LIEBOWITZ, J. "Expert Systems in Law: A Survey and Case Study," *Telematics and Informatics,* Vol. 3, No. 4, Pergamon Press, Oxford, 1986.

LIEBOWITZ, J. and J. S. ZEIDE. "EVIDENT: An Expert System Prototype for Helping the Law Student Learn Admissibility of Evidence Under the Federal Rules," *Computers and Education,* Vol. 11, No. 2, Pergamon Press, Oxford, 1987.

NYCUM, S. H., and I. K. FONG. "Artificial Intelligence and Certain Resulting Legal Issues," *The Computer Lawyer,* May 1985, pp. 1–10.

PARNAS, D. L. "Software Aspects of Strategic Defense Systems," *American Scientist,* Vol. 73, No. 5, September–October 1985.

PRINCE, J. "Negligence: Liability for Defective Software," *Oklahoma Law Review,* Vol. 33, 1980, p. 848.

REECE, L. H. "Litigation over Faulty Software: Complex and Full of Difficulties," *National Law Journal,* April 20, 1987, p. 22.

San Diego Law Review. "Computer Software and Strict Liability," Vol. 20, No. 2, March 1983, p. 439.

SHEIL, B. *Thinking About Artificial Intelligence,* quote on cover *ACM Computing Reviews,* Association for Computing Machinery, Vol. 28, No. 8, August 1987.

Stanford University News Service. "Artificial Intelligence Goes to Court," *IEEE Expert,* IEEE, Vol. 1, No. 2, Summer 1986, p. 101.

WILLICK, D. J. "Artificial Intelligence: Some Legal Approaches and Implications," *AI Magazine,* American Association for Artificial Intelligence, Summer 1983.

ZEIDE, J. S. and J. LIEBOWITZ. "Using Expert Systems: The Legal Perspective," *IEEE Expert,* IEEE, Spring 1987.

8

AICorp
Enters the Market

LARRY R. HARRIS, AICorp

In September 1986, AICorp embarked on an ambitious project that would launch the company into the dramatic new market of mainframe expert system tools. This chapter presents an inside look at the technological, competitive, and personnel issues involved in the decision to enter this market as a vendor. Because AICorp's decision to enter the expert systems market was contingent on finding several corporate customers willing to participate with us in a development consortium, we include brief case histories of two of our consortium members that played an active role in providing feedback throughout the entire product development process.

We will start by looking at the status of the company and the AI industry in early 1986. The rather unique confluence of maturity of the expert systems technology and AICorp's INTELLECT natural language product line, the status of existing and potential competitors, and the personal careers of Bob Goldman (AICorp's president and CEO) and myself all played an important role in our decision to enter the expert systems market.

Next we will look at the early design ideas of the Knowledge Base Management System (KBMS), our mainframe expert system product, and what we decided would make the eventual product attractive to potential KBMS Development Consortium members. Finally we'll discuss the actual formation of the consortium and the process by which consortium members themselves decided to begin using this technology.

INTELLECT has led the natural language market since its introduction in 1981. In fact, AlCorp created the natural language market by introducing INTELLECT. By 1986, the product was well entrenched, with more than 500 copies installed. Although other products had been introduced in the PC environment, there was, and still is, little competition for INTELLECT in the mainframe natural language marketplace. This was gratifying, but we wanted to move AlCorp into another important AI market—that of expert systems.

Although there were many marketing challenges communicating the very real benefits of natural language processing, the product was mature, stable and continued to sell. This gave us a stable environment from which to launch an effort into a new product arena. The top-flight development organization assembled for INTELLECT could be directed toward designing and implementing a new product without having a significant impact on the evolution of INTELLECT. In the meantime, INTELLECT could continue to be sold, thereby generating revenue during and after the development period.

From 1981 to 1986, I was president and CEO of AlCorp. For some time, I had been thinking about what we could do in the expert systems area. The choices were by no means clear, because we were uncertain about how expert systems could be married with the natural language technology of INTELLECT. But we did believe that the company had an opportunity to sell expert systems in the mainframe arena, and we believed that our expertise in building INTELLECT in the IBM world was unique among AI companies. The major factor holding us back was our thin management. The development of a product from scratch would require an all-consuming effort on my part, and I did not feel I could do both jobs adequately. So the idea for a mainframe expert systems tool remained dormant for some time.

In March of 1986, Bob Goldman, then president and COO of Cullinet Software, decided to leave the company after ten years and after having led Cullinet from $20 million to nearly $200 million in sales. Bob's first decision was to determine the area of technology that would be most likely to become the next data base—the technology that would define a market large enough to grow a company as he had done at Cullinet. Within a couple of months, Bob concluded that this new technology was expert systems.

Once Bob made this determination, he investigated the opportunities at the leading vendors of expert systems products. Although Bob was offered the presidency of nearly all of these companies, he was concerned about their commitment and ability to move into the IBM world, which would best leverage his skill and experience.

Bob and I had known each other since 1979, when Cullinet first licensed the INTELLECT product. When I first heard of his interest in entering the expert systems market, we discussed the possibility of his joining AlCorp. Bob felt that, even though we had no expert system product at the time, we were better positioned to move into the mainframe market than anyone else. It was a perfect match, combining Bob's skills in managing growth and selling into the DP establishment with AICorp's existing technology and ability to create an expert systems product.

Expert systems products in the mainframe market were scarce in 1986. IBM had introduced Expert Systems Environment (ESE), and AION had introduced Application Development System (ADS). Our assessment of these products was that they were weak both in the sophistication of the AI component and in their level of integration with the rest of the IBM environment. We saw a clear opportunity if we could build a more sophisticated AI engine, seamlessly integrated with the IBM operating system. A major challenge would be delivering the full AI functionality we desired in a form that could easily be taught to IBM application programmers.

The design of KBMS revolved around two areas: AI functionality and integration into the IBM environment. In both areas we believed that we could deliver a product that offered substantially more than existing products.

On the AI side, the existing products offered only backward chaining as an inferencing strategy. We felt that it was important to include all of the major AI paradigms that had been recognized by the AI research community. These included backward chaining, but more importantly, forward chaining, hypothetical reasoning, and object-oriented programming.

We also decided to leave certain features out, such as rule induction, certainty factors, and multivalued variables. Rule induction simply did not fit into our tight development schedule. We are likely to add it in a future release. Certainty factors were rejected because they offer very little and have not been associated with a major AI success story as the other paradigms have. We decided to take the road of high-end Lisp machine languages, Knowledge Engineering Environment (KEE) and Automated Reasoning Tool (ART), and not implement certainty factors as a primitive in the language, since they could be added by the programmer so easily.

Initially, we did intend to support multivalued variables, but we got a surprisingly strong negative reaction when the idea was first presented to our KBMS development consortium members. They felt that the concept was too antirelational, and since they had just fought the battle of going relational, they did not want to take a step in the opposite direction. This is a clear case of how listening to your customers pays off. If we had included multivalued variables, it would have greatly increased both the complexity of using KBMS and the training process.

In the arena of integrating into the IBM environment, we knew from the INTELLECT product exactly what had to be done. We specified three major areas of systems integration: DBMS, application programs, and the operating system itself. There were also two areas of "people integration," referring to both the developers and users of KBMS applications.

We considered the data base integration to be the most fundamental, since accessing corporate data bases was the main reason people would run on the mainframe in the first place. KBMS makes its biggest statement in this area. By automatically mapping objects defined to KBMS as external database files, KBMS became the first programming language that could manipulate both internally and externally stored data objects with the same language. It actually makes the external data objects appear to be in memory. This is an extremely profound capability, because all other languages require an embedded data base sublanguage to manipulate external data objects. In the expert systems area, this means that the inference engine cannot be aware of external data until it is read in. Thus, the inference engine cannot directly reason over external data, which is a major flaw for a mainframe system.

We were forced into this type of object-oriented data base interface for the INTEL-LECT product because users could clearly not be expected to embed data base languages in their natural language request. INTELLECT's database interface had to first partition the request into the data objects referenced, then navigate among them and finally optimize the retrieval pattern. By applying this same data base interfacing technology to KBMS, we actually obtained deeper rewards. This object-oriented data base interface allows rules to be written at such a high level of abstraction that one business rule can be represented as one rule in the application. Without this type of data base interface, one business rule can easily become ten or fifteen rules that must be very carefully sequenced in the application. This, of course, not only slows development, but is a nightmare with respect to maintenance.

With regard to interfacing KBMS with procedural application programs, we came upon the idea of using SQL as a knowledge-manipulation language, much like relational data bases use SQL as a data-manipulation language. Jeff Hill, our senior vice-president of Research and Development, first came up with the idea in one of our early design meetings. It took me a while to fully appreciate the implications of the idea. It solved the two communication problems of how to specify a transaction to KBMS and precisely how the results would be passed back. The deeper implications of this are that a KBMS application becomes a much broader concept because it can respond to the entire range of manipulation requests expressible in SQL. This is quite different from the straight subroutine call type of interface that can perform only a single function.

Interfacing with the operating system and the various TeleProcessing (TP) monitors in the IBM environment was another important area. Bob Goldman's experience with making IDMS a high-throughput workhorse of a DBMS was invaluable in this area. INTELLECT never required the high level of transaction volume that we anticipated for KBMS. We were very fortunate to attract Tom Nelson, the chief architect of IDMS, to AICorp to design and implement the central server architecture for KBMS. This solves a wide variety of environmental problems of providing knowledge base services to applications running under CICS, IMS/DC, TSO, or even batch regions. It means that we could answer *yes* to nearly all environmental questions.

Interfacing with the people in any environment is always a serious undertaking. It is the primary function of INTELLECT. But integrating AI concepts into the mindset of IBM programmers and users presents its own unique problems. It was essential that the KBMS AI concepts be related to familiar concepts in the IBM world; for example, an object would be thought of as a data base file.

In this way, we could reduce the training time to an absolute minimum. We felt strongly that many features of the high-end AI tools were too esoteric for the IBM world. We believed that even though we wanted to deliver high AI functionality, we would not do so at the expense of complexity inappropriate for the IBM world.

In addition there were several features implemented specifically for the developer. First, we developed a full screen painter to easily generate menus and forms; second, we developed a full 4GL capability for generating reports. Third, we extended INTELLECT's screen editor to edit rules. This automatically provided an "intelligent editor" that guarantees knowledge base consistency at all times. For example, the screen editor will not allow a developer to delete a variable if any references to that variable exist anywhere in the program.

From the user perspective, we incorporated not only the normal interaction mechanisms such as menus and prompts, but also make natural language interactions possible through INTELLECT. The result is a wide range of choices for the user in interacting with the system.

THE OVERLAP OF INTELLECT AND KBMS

Merging the natural language technology of INTELLECT with the expert systems technology of KBMS was of particular significance to me. For many years, we had wondered exactly what role natural language could play in the context of expert systems. The solution went well beyond our expectations of simply being able to query the knowledge base. In fact, the terminology defined for query purposes plays an equally important role in rule definition, because the rules are always initially defined in user terminology. Thus, INTELLECT benefits KBMS development.

SELLING THE CONSORTIUM

With the design for KBMS in hand, we began looking for companies willing to sponsor the development of the product. At first, it would seem that asking a company to buy a product that would not be developed for two years is an insurmountable task. But, given the relationship we had with our INTELLECT customers, the unique attributes of the KBMS design, and the desire of many companies to move forward in the expert systems area, it was actually a relatively easy process.

In fact, the benefits of being a consortium member were quite significant. It offered a rare opportunity to participate in the development of what was likely to be an industry-leading offering in an important market segment. By joining the consortium, each company substantially increased the likelihood that KBMS would be an effective tool to solve their expert systems problems. In addition, any progress on the knowledge engineering of their applications would be of value, whether or not KBMS was a success.

From AICorp's viewpoint, the consortium provided much more than funding for the project. It ensured that we avoided the "ivory tower" syndrome by ensuring that we worked on real-world applications from the very start. It also gave us the opportunity to build up our customer support staff so that we could hit the ground running when the product was introduced. In addition, it gave us several references early in the product's life cycle.

THE KBMS DEVELOPMENT CONSORTIUM—TRANSAMERICA INSURANCE GROUP

Transamerica Insurance Group, headquartered in Los Angeles, California, is a leading U.S. property and casualty insurance company, with revenues of $1.5 billion and 4,000 employees nationwide. Transamerica is widely regarded as a pioneer in its use of new information technologies.

Donald J. Prado, vice-president and assistant director of Information Systems at Transamerica, cited his company's four years of positive experience with AICorp and the INTELLECT natural language product as having prompted Transamerica to join the KBMS Development Consortium. Mr. Prado said that he found AICorp receptive to ideas and changes from consortium members. From early in KBMS's development, the product met Transamerica's expectations in terms of flexibility and ease of use. Prado said, "We're pleased with the level of expertise and help we've received from AICorp. This combination of system reliability, ease of use, and assistance from AICorp has kept our AI project on schedule."

Before joining the KBMS Development Consortium, Transamerica had discovered that commercially available expert system products had both positive and negative points. No company or product seemed able to set a standard for commercial expert systems. Yet it was especially important to Transamerica to find an expert system for the IBM environment, in which most of its major business systems run. Working with AICorp enabled Transamerica to develop an expert system to meet its needs.

Transamerica's first KBMS application in insurance underwriting involved a critical aspect of the company's business. While they already had an underwriting application in place, which used conventional programming, they found the system extremely difficult to develop and very expensive to maintain. Transamerica took advantage of KBMS by implementing an upgraded version of the application within KBMS. Before using KBMS and expert systems technology, experienced underwriters decided whether policies met corporate standards. With KBMS, the company can use expert systems technology to review policy applications and recommend whether a policy should be written. This first level of processing helps Transamerica's underwriters be more efficient and effective in their jobs.

Don Prado commented that applying KBMS's advanced AI methodologies rather than conventional programming methods provides increased productivity and capability because of faster system implementation, more comprehensive knowledge-based functionality, flexibility to respond quickly and effectively to changes in the business environment, and reduced system maintenance.

Another KBMS application area is in claims processing, another very strategic area in which consistent adherence to specified criteria and streamlined processing can result in improved customer service and increased profits.

Transamerica views expert systems technology in general, and KBMS in particular, as a strategic tool for business management. Expert systems enable the company's operating management to exercise better control over all policy underwriting. KBMS, used in conjunction with existing systems, will provide nationwide consistency in underwriting.

KBMS DEVELOPMENT CONSORTIUM—SOUTHERN CALIFORNIA EDISON COMPANY

Southern California Edison is one of the largest electric utility companies in the United States, with $14 billion in assets and $5.4 billion in revenue. Its 17,000 employees serve 3.8 million accounts across 50,000 square miles, predominantly in southern California. Southern California Edison is regarded as a leader in developing and implementing innovations in utility operations.

Southern California Edison had several expert systems in place dedicated to solving highly specific problems. However, according to M. L. Mushet, manager of Technology Research at the company, they needed to address applications that relied on corporate data already in existence that affected multiple users. The ability to reason on corporate data would free the company to implement AI technology in new strategic areas. To accomplish that, Southern California Edison needed a facility for applying knowledge to mainframe-based corporate data in a multiuser environment.

"In searching for a commercially-viable system, we concluded that no acceptable AI-based system existed that would integrate IBM's DB2 and CICS, both of which are primary business system environments for us," Mushet said. AICorp and the INTELLECT natural language product had an ongoing record of quality performance at Southern California Edison, and the company therefore felt that the AICorp invitation to join the KBMS Development Consortium showed it had a solid understanding of the market, good business sense, and a significant technological understanding and capability.

Mushet believes that, as a member of the consortium, Southern California Edison was able to subtly mold the product to make it better for the company and for all other business users. They participated in many of the product design decisions that helped AICorp develop KBMS from a business perspective.

Without AI techniques, Southern California Edison programmers were required to understand both a problem and how to solve it before they could program the solution. With the AI-based KBMS system, they can now address problems whose solutions are not as well understood; this is opening up an entirely new class of applications for AI.

"It's important to have a range of representations of business problems. Sometimes it's an object representation, not strategic rules that is best, and KBMS allows that," Mushet explained. "Also, the product's integration with INTELLECT is really exciting. It allows us to go through ad hoc queries with INTELLECT and then automatically trigger KBMS."

Southern California Edison is a regulated monopoly and continually strives to improve service and reduce costs. The company continues to identify potential areas in which they can use KBMS to save time and money, particularly in their facilities operations. The company has several major electric generating facilities and is using KBMS to examine ways to improve operations at those sites. They believe that expert systems technology will help them evaluate current situations and recommend solutions that will reduce costs and improve services to their customers.

Mushet said that KBMS meets their expectations and provides a richness in modeling business problems. "We've seen the usability of the system. In fact, as an example, one of our early experiences showed that a KBMS model for predicting the weather temperatures was better than the National Weather Service and within half a degree of our own weather expert."

9

Managing the Development of Generic Expert System Products

WALTER REITMAN, Rensselaer Polytechnic Institute

INTRODUCTION

Expert systems are receiving increasing attention in the business world. One indication of this is the recent appearance of the first large-scale commercial expert system products intended for multiple business users and organizations. The generic products developed by Applied Expert Systems (Stansfield and Greenfield, 1987) Palladian Software (Bitran and Papageorge, 1987; Myers, 1988) and Syntelligence (Duda et al., 1987) are examples of such systems.

Such products are built on two premises: (1) There are certain bodies of generic expertise, such as financial knowledge, that are relevant over broad domains, cutting across organizations and specific applications; and (2), although generalizing and tailoring this expertise for multiple users entails technical problems and developmental expense, the benefits gained outweigh the costs.

146

Developing such commercial generic expert system products poses interesting issues for management. For example, these products require pragmatic knowledge as well as generic expertise. The development process must ensure that the knowledge makes its way into the product appropriately. Furthermore, development considerations may affect or be affected by other business decisions regarding the product.

None of these issues are new to commercial software development, but they have not been a part of expert system efforts in other contexts. Consequently, as we move from building individual applications to working on large-scale commercial generic products, we need to reexamine the organization and management of development. To build and field such large-scale products effectively, traditional organizational frameworks for expert system development may need to be reengineered to meet the technical and business requirements of this new context.

This chapter examines one such case, focusing on the management approach evolved at Palladian to support the development and deployment of its two generic expert system products, the Operations Advisor (OA) and the Management Advisor (MA). The OA does rough-cut modeling for operations planning. In manufacturing, it may be used to assess proposals involving new products or technologies in terms of their effects upon capacity, inventories, lead times, and unit costs. Thus it can help to improve manufacturing productivity. The OA also is being used to improve paper-processing productivity in the back-office operations of such nonmanufacturing organizations as insurance companies. The MA values new business opportunities. It can be used, for example, to ascertain the worth of building a new plant or developing a new product. It enables managers to assess the financial attractiveness of such proposals and their impact on existing business strategy.

The MA and the OA are built on a common AI core. We describe the main components of that core and how they bring the expert knowledge of the OA and the MA to bear on user problems. After discussing the functional and technical characteristics of the two systems, we will turn to the technical and business considerations constraining the choice of a framework for managing development. We will describe team staffing and functional organization and will then discuss evidence indicating that the organizational and management approach provides significant benefits, including substantial productivity improvement. This is followed by a discussion of the strengths and limitations of the approach and the conditions that might indicate or restrict its use in other organizations working on large-scale generic expert systems. The discussion concludes with remarks on the products' current status and future prospects.

THE PRODUCTS AND THEIR IMPLEMENTATION

Discussion of the management issues involved in developing and deploying these systems presumes a knowledge of what the products were designed to do. We will begin with descriptions of the two Palladian products and their implementation.

The MA and the OA are general knowledge-based application packages. They are intended for executives, managers, and other business end-users. Thus they differ from expert system tools, environments, and languages, in that they require no programming. They are general in that they deliver substantial amounts of relevant knowledge over broad business domains (finance in the one case, manufacturing and operations management in the other). Both Advisors are composite systems, using a collection of AI technologies.

THE OPERATIONS ADVISOR

The Operations Advisor is designed to link strategic corporate planning with operations (Bitran and Papageorge, 1987). Doing rough-cut modeling for operations planning, it makes explicit the relations among capacity, lead time, and work in process in a given facility. This lets managers balance resources or target specific performance measures. The OA also assesses proposals for strategic actions, such as new technology introduction, in terms of their effects on capacity utilization, inventories, lead times, and unit costs. Thus it helps evaluate and improve upon ideas intended to enhance a company's ability to compete.

Here are some examples of questions the OA is designed to help answer:

- What do I give up by introducing a new product into this plant?
- What impact would new process technology have on our specific operations?
- How can I achieve my target work-in-process and lead times with existing capacity?

Adapting the OA to the User

At the heart of the OA is a substantial body of broadly applicable analytic and heuristic information about the factors that affect operations management. Generic knowledge by itself is not necessarily very useful, however, unless it can be brought to bear on a manager's applications. There has to be some way to match general capabilities to the specifics of any given user's organization, situation, and goals.

In the OA, there are two components that do this. The first allows the organization, from corporate level on down to the specific user, to specify the significant features of the context and the problems the user must deal with. The second component enables the user to provide the OA with a high-level model both of a facility and also of the product families being produced in that facility.

At the most abstract level, the OA is designed to work with flows through networks of queues. This makes it capable of dealing with a broad range of plants and facilities. It also is useful for problems in managing back-room paperwork flows in nonmanufacturing organizations such as insurance companies. No doubt, there are operations problems that do not lend themselves to this conceptual approach. But for those that do, networks of queues provide an effective general framework for bringing the system's repertoire of analytic and expert heuristic methods to bear on the user's problems.

Working with the OA

The first step in using the OA is simplying the problem. Products are grouped into product families. Work areas are grouped into work centers. Then the system collects information from the user about his or her work centers and product families (Fig. 9.1). Next the OA analyzes the existing operations.

THE OPERATIONS ADVISOR ™

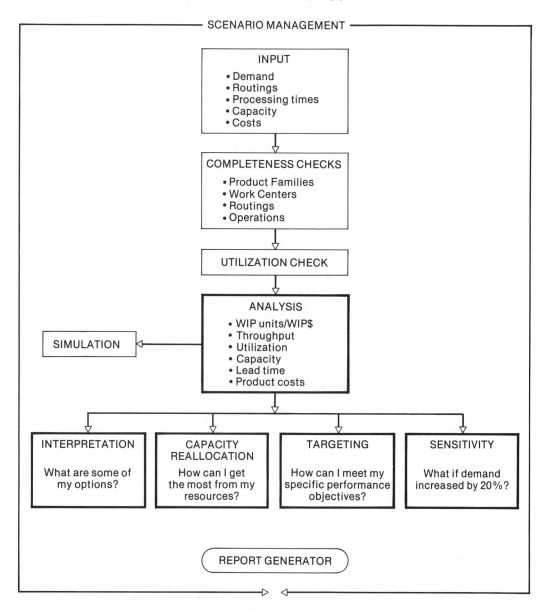

Figure 9.1

This analysis now provides the basis for more detailed explorations, evaluating current strategies against new opportunities and answering specific user strategy questions of the sorts illustrated above. Because the system is built upon an AI base, it can track where the user is in the process, and what he or she needs to do to achieve a given goal. Thus, the general analytic framework provides both an overall guide and a high degree of flexibility.

Using the Operations Advisor

To fix ideas, we will consider how the OA can help to relate corporate strategic planning with manufacturing management, by assessing the manufacturing feasibility and impact of proposed strategic corporate plans and policies. Let us assume that we have an OA user in a company that manufactures customized computer equipment. Because these products are expensive and are typically bought on special order, the company tries to avoid stockpiling. However, the company is losing business to competitors because of its long lead times. As a short-term solution, plant managers can always juggle schedules to speed up a particular order, but that is difficult, time consuming, and not generally cost effective.

At the strategic level, the company decides that it must meet competitive delivery schedules. To do this, the manufacturing managers must find more general ways of reducing lead times by half, thereby allowing them to commit to competitive delivery without constantly having to modify their schedules.

Assume that the OA already has a description of the company's workstations and product families. The user calls the targeting module, with the results shown in Figure 9.2. The "x" in the right hand graph indicates that, with somewhat more than 1,200 hours of productive capacity allocated to all printed circuit board production, the average lead time for these boards is approximately one week. The graph on the right also shows that by identifying production bottlenecks and reallocating capacity to these workstations from other work centers, the system can reduce overall lead time to slightly more than three days (0.7 of a week). But the user's target is to cut the current average lead time by half. Accordingly, the system also provides a curve showing how lead time can be reduced by adding capacity. In effect, the system not only deals with the user's explicit problem, but also offers a range of options. These are, in effect, descriptions of related possibilities, with their associated costs and benefits.

In sum, as this example illustrates, the OA links strategic planning with operations. It can help in developing and evaluating strategic proposals, and it can help to implement and effectively manage whatever plans are adopted.

THE MANAGEMENT ADVISOR

The Management Advisor (MA) (Myers, 1988) values business opportunities. It may be used, for example, to ascertain the worth to a company of building a new plant or developing a new product. In addition to financial value, the system looks at risk, timing, competition, and overall business impact. For each analysis, the MA also manages the relations among prices, market share, costs, depreciation, taxes, and the numerous other variables in a business decision that affect a company's bottom line. In addition to

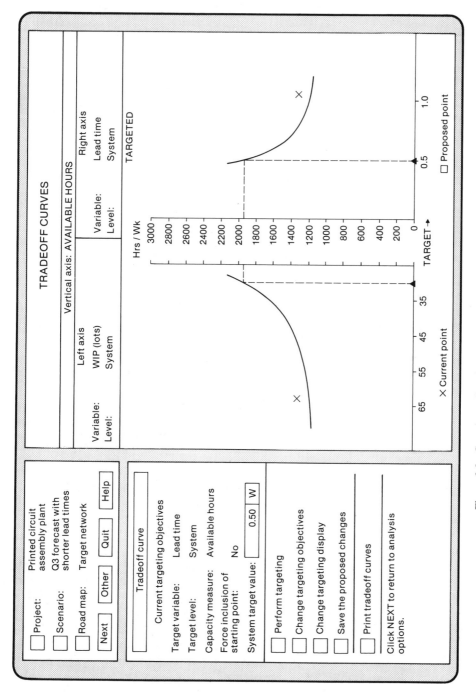

Figure 9.2 Capacity reallocation and targeting in the operations advisor.

providing internally error-free results, the MA is intended to enhance user productivity, to produce more accurate strategic projections, and to increase net project payoffs.

Here are some of the types of questions the MA is designed to help to answer:

- What are the best business areas for us to compete in?
- What are the most effective ways to obtain the necessary resources?
- What do we gain by closing a particular plant or consolidating a group of facilities?
- Where are the risks in this project?
- What should we do if things do not work out as we have anticipated?

Adapting the MA to the User

To match the MA's generic expert knowledge about business to the needs of a specific user and problem, the system includes a tailoring module. This gives the user control over income statement and balance sheet terminology, tax-depreciation treatment, inventory valuation methods, treatment of startup and R&D costs, and numerous other factors. In addition, it allows each corporate user to specify his or her valuation assumptions (hurdle rate), assumptions about accounts payable and receivable, cost of debt, and so on.

Accounting, financial, and modeling assumptions can be set at individual business unit levels. Users can deviate from the tailored assumptions, but all such deviations are flagged and must be justified. In sum, the tailoring options are intended to enable users to employ their usual ways of thinking about their individual business valuation problems, while at the same time ensuring a coherent analytic framework across the corporation as a whole.

At the most abstract level, the MA is designed to work with discounted cash flows. This is what enables it to value business opportunities of all sorts. Because organizations vary in their preferred valuation methods, the MA has the ability to present its results in other terms as well, including internal rate of return, undiscounted and discounted payback periods, profitability index, average returns on investments and assets, and average return on sales. Thus, users get the benefits both of a single coherent conceptual framework and a wide choice of measures matching their own ways of thinking about business opportunity valuation.

The MA's Analytic Strategy

Figure 9.3 shows the normal flow of work through the system. For a more intuitive understanding of why the MA does what it does, however, we will look at an example of how the expert it is modeled upon works.

An expert may be called in when a company is considering a major strategic move (such as developing a new product) and wants to be sure that the evaluation of the proposal is as good as it can be. Typically, the people in charge of the evaluation are perfectly capable of carrying out the mechanics of a net present value computation. What they are paying the expert for is help in improving their problem formulation and in applying the formal analytic methods in the most appropriate fashion.

THE MANAGEMENT ADVISOR™

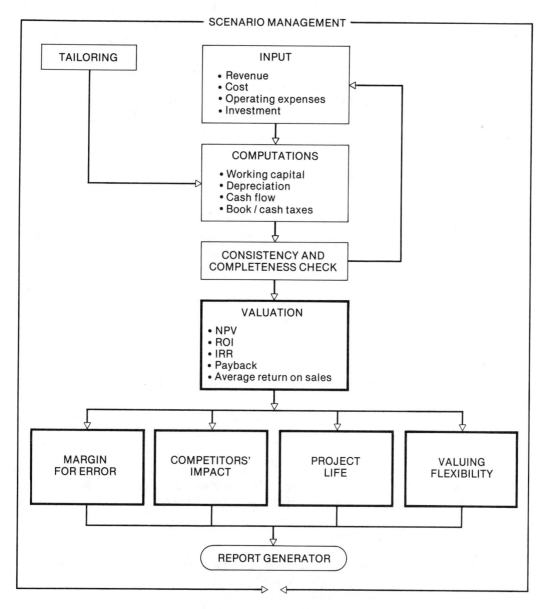

Figure 9.3

With this in mind, the expert sets about analyzing the initial formulation. The expert has perhaps fifteen groups of questions to ask the managers and analysts. For example, has the company taken adequate account of the competition? After all, if initial evaluation indicates that the project is going to be highly profitable, sooner or later the competition will pick that up and respond. What kind of response can the competition make? When can they make that response? How will that response affect the profitability of the project? As a result of the questions and the discussions they generate, the initial problem statement is iteratively refined and redefined, thereby sharpening up and improving the project evaluation. As we will see, the MA's competitive impact module goes through much the same process with the user of the MA.

In summary, the MA proceeds from the assumption that financial value and valuation are widely useful concepts, and it attempts to map the generic knowledge required for ascertaining value onto a broad range of specific business applications.

IMPLEMENTATION

The preceding discussion focused upon the intended business value of the Advisors to their users. Now we will turn to the technical implementation. Our purpose is to provide some feeling for how AI is used in the Advisors and the kinds of value it provides to Advisor users.

The OA and the MA are written in the Palladian Software Language (PSL), a Lisp-based AI language specifically designed for efficient implementation of management expert systems. Each Advisor consists of about 200,000 lines of code. Both run on high-end workstations and Lisp machines.

AI is used as the basis for these systems for three classes of reasons. To begin with, AI is used in the Advisors:

- to represent and deliver qualitative and quantitative expert knowledge of the business domain;
- to tailor the system to the specifics of the user's organization and application;
- to improve user productivity.

Now we want to describe the individual AI knowledge and control components that underlie the MA and the OA, and then show how they are integrated to achieve a high level of expert system capability, efficiency, and performance.

Composite AI Systems

The first expert systems used a single AI idea, the production rule concept. Knowledge was represented as a collection of "if-then" rules. As interest in expert systems developed, it soon became apparent that this pure rule-based approach was not a general solution. It is a useful methodology, but a limited one. To build more powerful knowledge-based systems, composite architectures making available additional AI concepts and methods have to be brought into play.

Composite systems combine several different AI approaches. Each approach is employed where it is most effective. Taken together, the collection of methods in a composite expert system provides far more power and efficiency than is obtainable using any single methodology. It is no accident that a number of today's large-scale commercial expert systems (e.g., those built by Syntelligence and Applied Expert Systems as well as those discussed here) although developed independently of one another, use composite architectures.

The decision to optimize Advisor performance with a proprietary composite architecture implies a highly skilled programming staff. As we will see, that is a significant consideration in constraining the choice of a management framework for this project.

The Palladian Software Language

The Palladian Software Language (PSL) composite architecture includes the following AI representation and control methods:

- contingent inheritance hierarchies
- object-oriented graphics
- production rules
- model-based reasoning
- goal-directed control
- constraint-based inference

Inheritance.   A contingent inheritance scheme is used to organize the basic assumptions underlying all analyses done by the Advisors. Inheritance ensures that these assumptions are incorporated in all analyses at all levels of the organization. The inheritance process is contingent in the sense that it can be modified by subunits, by individual users, and even for specific scenarios. When higher level assumptions are overridden, the system tracks these exceptions and their justifications, and the information is immediately available to anyone comparing or reviewing individual analyses.

Object-oriented representation.   This is used primarily in the MA and OA graphics interface. It makes it possible to create new screens by providing descriptions of what the images on the screen are to look like and how they are to be organized. The object-oriented graphics system knows about all the relevant graphic objects (panels, graphs, tables, etc.), and about how they break down into classes and subclasses. As subclasses inherit properties, new screens can be defined and rearranged very quickly, and they have exactly the desired properties.

Object-oriented programming is a well-accepted AI technology with a long history. In the MA and the OA, the idea is adapted to maximize its effectiveness for management software. Thus, the object-oriented graphics are fully integrated with the rest of the system. If, for example, you enter values by using the mouse to create or change a live graph, the results automatically become available not only to the relevant tables, but also to the entire network of financial or manufacturing relationships.

Production rules.   Although this is only one of the AI representations used in the Advisors, it plays several important roles. Most of the systems' reasonableness checks are implemented as rules. Thus, for example, if an MA scenario includes a year in which you have entered production costs but no revenue, the system will ask about the potential inconsistency. At that point, you have the option of either changing the data or leaving them as they are. As this illustration suggests, rules are a very useful way of representing real-world knowledge.

Model-based reasoning.   The expert knowledge encoded in the Advisors takes advantage of several different kinds of reasoning. Model-based reasoning is a way of representing highly integrated qualitative and quantitative thinking in an efficient parameterized fashion.

One very important application of this idea occurs in the MA's competitive impact module. Here, all of the experts' ideas about the options available to potential competitors, and about the ways in which those options interact with your own, are coordinated in a single integrated subsystem.

Parameterized models are widely used in conventional software. What is new in the Advisors, as shown in the following example, is the tight coupling of these models with the knowledge base and the other components of the composite Advisor systems.

Goal-based control.   This is another standard AI approach that has been adapted for use in the Advisors. Goals are packets of information about possible actions and the prerequisites they assume. Associated with suitable rules, goals can suggest themselves to the user at appropriate times. They make it possible to offer the user more responsive, context-sensitive choices.

The flexibility goal-based control affords the user is evident in the Advisors' roadmap mechanism. The roadmap is a graphic representation of all of the possible places in an analysis the user can go to at any given time. It also is a general navigational tool. All the user need do is point with the mouse to the place he or she wants to go. The Advisors automatically handle all the file management and other housekeeping.

The roadmap is always up to date, because the goal system works with the constraint system. The goal system specifies the prerequisites for a given alternative and then checks with the constraint system to determine whether the prerequisites are satisfied.

Constraint-based inference.   PSL's constraint-based knowledge representation and inference system is the newest AI methodology used in the Advisors. The most complete statement of the basic ideas can be found in dissertation by Steele (1980). The implementation in the Advisors is the first commercial application of these ideas.

Steele was concerned with developing a paradigm for efficient local inference from collections of facts. A constraint system can be considered a network of local computing devices interconnected by wires. A device always computes whenever and whatever it can. As Steele points out, the paradigm has the advantage that connections to a device are bidirectional: There is no distinction between inputs and outputs. Thus, in a network of such devices, computations are carried out in all directions just as soon as appropriate information appears in the network.

Constraint-based inference turns out to be a particularly powerful tool for dealing with the Advisors' complex system of interrelationships. In the MA, for example, no matter where or when the user enters or changes the financial data, the implications of the change are immediately and automatically taken into account, backwards, forwards, up and down. In addition to this immediate updating, the constraint-based inference system also makes possible automatic error detection and completeness checking. Finally, because the constraint system is specialized for dealing with a homogeneous body of knowledge, it achieves all of these results with a very high degree of efficiency. Thus, extremely complex analyses can be done many times faster than would be possible with a conventional rule-based tool.

Consider what happens in the MA, for example, should you decide to change your production cost figures. Costs affect revenues. Revenues may interact with tax rates and tax computations. If you are looking at margin for error, all of these interrelationships must be evaluated over and over again. The constraint system is the single most important factor enabling the Advisors to provide internally consistent complex results to the user in a real-time interactive mode. This capability produces a significant reduction in wasted effort and a corresponding increase in user productivity and useful end results.

Fitting It All Together: The MA's Competitive Impact Module

We mentioned earlier using the MA to assess the likely effect of competitive entry upon the expected value of a proposed project. The MA's competitive impact module is a good place to see how the several AI components in the Advisors work together to achieve a coordinated result. Conventional "if-then" rules are used to ascertain situations in which the module is appropriate. These rules operate only after the valuation component has completed its work. The "if" parts of the rules look for patterns having to do with absolute profitability, relative market share, growth rate of market share, and the like. Should the current situation match one of the entry condition patterns, the user is invited to call the module to determine the likely price effects of competitive entry into the market.

If the user decides to look into competitive impact, the module gains control through the goal system. First, the object-oriented presentation system creates a dialogue with the user to collect relevant information about the situation. Next, using the Advisor's inheritance mechanisms, the module constructs a new scenario that combines that information with its knowledge of the current situation and of how competitive entry is likely to affect price. This is achieved by means of model-based reasoning, working in conjunction with the constraint system. More specifically, the system uses its model of competitive impact to integrate situational knowledge with the information provided by the user. It then calls the constraint system to work through the network of financial relations, to determine equilibrium price under this particular combination of conditions. Finally, the results are presented to the user in an appropriate graph created by the object-oriented presentation system.

THE ADVISORS IN PERSPECTIVE

We have now considered both the intended business uses of the Advisors and also the benefits derived from implementing the systems on an AI core. In the next section, we turn our attention to some of the technical, business, and management issues associated with the development and deployment of the Advisors. Before we do so, however, it may help fix ideas about these systems if we briefly place them in context with respect to some other, more familiar, types of business software.

As we have indicated, both Advisors are modeled upon human experts consulting with intelligent managers knowledgeable about their businesses. Thus, although they begin with the problems these manager users start off with, the systems consistently behave as if these initial problems were just starting points for more detailed explorations. It is this capability as much as anything else that distinguishes these advanced expert systems from the straightforward spreadsheet or mathematical modeling approaches of conventional software. Being modeled on human experts, they are designed to help the user by taking on a substantial portion of the problem formulation and exploration process. They always follow the user wherever he or she chooses to go, but they are not passive systems. As the discussion of the MA's competitive impact module demonstrates, they transcend the limits of conventional decision support systems in a fundamental fashion. Such conventional systems, whether implemented as spreadsheets, or in modeling languages, or in custom-built software, require that the user explicitly specify all of the scenarios he or she wishes to evaluate. The Advisors, by contrast, not only evaluate explicitly specified scenarios, but they also actively collaborate with the user in defining, exploring, and evaluating other potentially interesting options.

TECHNICAL, BUSINESS, AND MANAGEMENT ISSUES

With the foregoing discussion of functionality and implementation in mind, we turn now to some of the management issues involved in developing and deploying the Advisors. Two groups of factors are involved: those having to do with the products' knowledge and technical requirements; and those stemming from overall business objectives.

Knowledge Requirements

Comprehensiveness of the knowledge base. Because it serves many users, the generic knowledge base at the core of each Advisor must be substantially more comprehensive than would be required for a single application.

Pragmatic knowledge. We have seen that, in common with many other expert systems, the OA and the MA each began as an effort to model an individual expert. Each of these two individuals is an outstanding professional contributor in his area. Each also has had substantial experience consulting for business on problems in this area. As we noted, however, any user must be able to employ the product in ways that are compatible with that user's normal thinking about his or her application. To ensure that the generic knowledge in each product can be applied effectively and correctly in all segments of its target market, the products also must contain substantial pragmatic knowledge, detailed information on the full range of user assumptions, procedures, and practices to be found in that market. Understandably, neither expert is able to provide all of this pragmatic knowledge solely from personal experience.

Modifications, enhancements, and major additions.   As commercial software products, generic expert systems go through a succession of releases. Some changes from one release to the next are bug fixes, but most are designed to adapt the product to new market segments, to enhance existing functionality, and to add new functionality. Almost all of these modifications and additions affect the products' knowledge bases.

Working on a comprehensive knowledge base for a generic expert system product, developing the pragmatic knowledge required to span its target market effectively, adapting and enhancing the existing functionality, and investigating new functionality for successive releases of the product all add up to a great deal more than can be expected of a single expert working within the schedule constraints of a commercial software development environment. Some form of team approach is required.

Technical Requirements

A number of technical alternatives were examined during the initial planning for the Advisors. These included conventional languages, expert system tools, and Lisp. Conventional languages were rejected because, at the time, they provided few of the conceptual, architectural, and environmental supports required for AI software development. Expert system tools were rejected because they were just coming onto the market. They lacked features that were likely to be required for the Advisors. Furthermore, there was a reluctance to be dependent upon another company's development strategy.

That left Lisp as the vehicle most likely to satisfy the Advisors' technical requirements. Based in Lisp, the Advisors could take full advantage of whatever technical features were needed to embed and deliver the requisite expertise. But this decision also meant that the technical staff would have to have outstanding design and programming competence, because it would be doing not only application development, but also fundamental system design as well. People of this caliber are very scarce. They are hard to attract even under the best of circumstances. It seemed advisable to bring the first-rate technical people into the project as fully as possible, thus giving them the opportunity to participate to the limits of their abilities in meeting the challenge of the product concept.

Business Requirements

The business factors motivating the use of an integrated design team approach for the Advisors fall under three heads: schedule constraints, human resource limitations, and market acceptance.

1. Given two equally good products that are equally well supported, a six-month head start may be all one of them needs to establish market dominance over the other. Schedules are tight, and there is no time to spare.

2. Given two development groups of the same size and technical competence, the one that makes better use of its people is likely to complete its product sooner, to come up with a more functional product, or both. Generic expert systems for management are new products. Funding is limited, and the technical and product management groups involved are small. Efficient use of knowledge and talent is critical. There is no room for duplicated effort.

3. Market acceptance depends upon many factors, including the effectiveness of sales and marketing efforts; product pricing, performance, functionality, and relevance to user problems; available delivery vehicle options; interfaces to other hardware and software; and the quality of training and support. In the environment we are considering, development interacts heavily with most of the factors determining market acceptance of the product.

Consider choosing a knowledge representation. Because it may constrain product functionality, delivery vehicles, and the price customers will have to pay for the system, it can determine the success or failure of the entire project. It is one thing to deliberately trade off functionality for affordability. It is quite another to arbitrarily designate a target delivery vehicle, or perhaps a price point, and then discover after many months of work that the product will not perform adequately as specified using any of the knowledge representations implementable on that vehicle or at that price.

All of the factors affecting market acceptance collectively define a multidimensional space of options. It is essential that the dimensional interactions and tradeoffs entailed in choices among the points in that space be well understood before decisions are made. This means that development must be organized and managed from the start in ways designed to maximize the likelihood of product acceptance. Because these choices will have to be evaluated and reevaluated many times during product planning and development, and because the factors involved transcend organization chart boundaries, some form of team approach again seems indicated.

STAFFING AND FUNCTIONAL RESPONSIBILITIES

The product planning and development issues previously discussed arise from combining two groups of objectives: those associated with building expert systems, and those connected with commercial software product development. The organizational framework constructed to deal with these issues builds upon both kinds of experience, combining elements of contemporary expert system development practice with a product management approach.

Each product development team consists of three components: the expert, the AI technical staff, and the product managers. The team meets regularly, and all members participate to some degree in all stages of product development.

The Expert

Each product is built under the conceptual guidance of a single expert, who commits a substantial block of time to the project on a long-term, high-priority basis. Other experts are called in as needed.

Technical Staff

As the products require a customized composite AI core and a highly efficient and generalizable implementation, the primary requirement for technical staff is design and programming competence in Lisp. In addition, since a large-scale commercial product on a tight time schedule is not something that can be created by single individuals working in isolation, technical staff members must be comfortable working as members of a highly interactive group. An interest in applications software is helpful, but not required. Some individuals will develop such an interest as they work on the project. Those who do not will have plenty of system design work to keep them busy. The key consideration is technical competence. If the technical staff has it, it usually is not difficult to match up individual interests with the various design and programming tasks to be accomplished.

Product Managers

Product managers typically have MBAs or Ph.D.s with a concentration in finance, operations, or a related discipline. In addition to solid knowledge of their domains, they also usually have several years of practical field experience—for instance, as consultants, financial managers, or manufacturing managers. In other words, product managers have management skills, significant domain expertise, and substantial experience working with the kinds of people who will be buying and using the products.

Matching Organizational Structure to Functional Responsibilities

There is at least one significant structural difference in organization between the product management and the technical groups. Product managers are members of either the MA or the OA product groups. Technical staff people are members of a single common group. Their responsibilities may involve the MA, the OA, the AI core, or any combination thereof. Here, as elsewhere in the Palladian team approach, structural organization closely reflects functional responsibilities. So far as their business functionality is concerned, the MA and the OA are almost totally disjoint products, so it makes sense for the MA and OA product management teams to be separate. On the other hand, there is substantial overlap in the implementation of the two products. They are, as we have indicated, designed around a common composite core. Thus, core changes in the interest of one product can affect the other positively or negatively, and this makes it especially important to minimize communication barriers among technical staff members, whatever their current assignments. Furthermore, having all of the technical staff in a single organization makes it easier to alter assignments across projects in response to unexpected problems.

The Product Manager's Job

To better understand the practical implications of the organizational arrangement under discussion, consider for example the detailed responsibilities of a product manager:

- working with sales to communicate the potential of the products to prospective customers, especially those with novel applications;
- working with customers and customer support to help make existing applications successful, and helping them develop new applications;
- participating in defining markets and marketing plans for the products;
- working with customers, potential customers, and the expert to develop the pragmatic knowledge necessary to adapt a product to a given market segment or class of applications, and embedding that pragmatic knowledge in proposals for rules, screens, and control flows;
- helping to evaluate tradeoffs among product pricing, functionality, delivery vehicle, and representation and implementation options;
- testing and evaluating releases before shipment to ensure that they perform to specification and meet customer requirements.

As we see, a product manager on a team is not just interacting with customers and developing product specifications. In particular, there is significant participation in the knowledge engineering process. It might appear organizationally cleaner to break this job up into several distinct organizational positions, but there are good business reasons not to. One reason is that customers usually prefer to build a good relationship with a single person. Still more important, all of these responsibilities are synergistic; they all draw upon and develop the same knowledge and skills—a deep understanding of the product and the business domain as they relate to specific customer applications, and the ability to work with the technical staff to engineer that pragmatic knowledge into the product.

HOW TEAMS EVOLVE AND FUNCTION

As product planning and implementation proceed, the workings of the design team become more streamlined and efficient. The expert, who may have had little or no prior software background, gradually becomes familiar with the language and concepts of the emerging implementation plan. Increasingly he casts his knowledge in terms of screen images, and sequences of screens, thereby bypassing some of the usual steps in the knowledge engineering process and, consequently, speeding up development. The same is true of the product managers. In addition, they develop close working relations with individual technical people. These also will expedite development once technical staff and product managers are paired and assigned to individual product modules. At the same time, through their interactions with the experts and prospective users, product managers continue to improve their knowledge of the domain, the product, and the various ways in which the product may be applied in solving users' problems.

As the meetings continue, the technical staff develops a working knowledge of the domain and the detailed objectives of the software. Taken together with their mastery of the implementation details, this knowledge enables them to work up improved ways of achieving functional objectives. In addition, owing to their detailed implementation knowledge, their suggestions will sometimes provide additional functional or technical benefits. A few technical staff members also eventually develop substantial domain competence, and given their intimate knowledge of the implementation details, they come to serve as reference sources and sanity checks with respect to new functionality proposals.

The team's evolving understanding of all aspects of the project also facilitates timely and informed decisions involving tradeoffs across organizational boundaries. Tight development schedules permit little room for setting up formal meetings or for circulating detailed written proposals up and down organizational channels. Team members are encouraged to take decisions expeditiously and at the lowest levels possible. Each team member knows or can quickly find out who needs to be involved in a particular decision, and the contextual understanding he or she has acquired on the team reduces errors and makes for better choices.

This is true not only during development, but also during the subsequent product testing and customer support phases. That is because contextual knowledge makes it easier to determine the persons required for diagnosing any given bug and defining and implementing corrections.

In other words, by investing the additional initial overhead required to establish the integrated design team as a functioning entity, the organization substantially improves productivity and turnaround time. From an AI perspective, better informed and integrated knowledge sources make for more effective search.

Balancing Flexibility and Responsibility

The integrated design team approach improves flexibility and reduces organizational barriers among the various elements of the commercial product development effort. But although the collaboration among team members may appear amorphous, it is not anarchic. Each component group retains its basic responsibilities. The expert must approve every major product design decision. The product managers must sign off on the detailed functional specifications. And the technical staff certifies the completeness of those specifications and retains sole responsibility for the adequacy of the technical design and implementation of the products.

Productivity Improvements

The impression of improved productivity is supported by some interesting quantitative data. Getting the first version of each product out on the market took about two years. Several times during this period, programmer productivity measurements were taken. The results consistently averaged forty-one lines of final code per programmer per day. These are gross figures. No adjustments have been made for such factors as time spent in meetings or machine down time.

Many factors enter into these results. All the design team members were highly talented and motivated. The technical staff was widely regarded as one of the top programming groups in the Lisp applications community. Many of them regularly put in sixty- or seventy-hour weeks, and each had his or her own Lisp machine and thus could take full advantage of the highly sophisticated development environments included with Symbolics and Texas Instruments software.

At a more subjective level, programmer morale was consistently high, and programmers believed that this was at least partly a result of minimal nonproductive requirements and distractions. They felt that the organizational environment encouraged them to make full use of their initiative and ability and to do whatever was necessary to get the job done. When combined with the productivity numbers, which exceed the results typically obtained in commercial software production by a factor of four times or more (Walston and Felix, 1977), these subjective observations certainly suggest that the management style and the team concept contributed significantly to the overall product development process.

ASSESSING THE APPROACH

Our discussion of this approach to the management of expert system product development is based upon a single case, so we cannot assess the approach in general. Within the context of this case, however, a brief summary of its advantages and limitations may be useful.

Advantages

Here are some of the principal advantages of the approach:

1. It addresses the problem of pragmatic knowledge. That knowledge is not "in" the expert. It is not really "in" the customers, either. It must be developed by the product manager, working with expert and customers, and then engineered with the technical staff into effective product functionality.

2. Customers have an advocate on the design team. Their needs and experiences have a direct effect on all aspects of product development.

3. It expedites development by using the expert's time where his comparative advantage lies: thinking about major enhancements and new functionality, and overseeing the conceptual coherence and integrity of the product.

4. In the standard knowledge engineering paradigm, primary responsibility for the process lies with the knowledge engineer. It is up to him or her to get the expert's knowledge out on the table, typically in the form of rules or frames. The expert is a relatively passive participant in the design process. By contrast, as the MA and OA projects evolved, and the domain experts and product managers became increasingly familiar with the software context and the product development process, they gradually became more and more directly involved in product design decisions.

This increased the level of involvement in and commitment to the projects, and it added a new dimension to the knowledge-acquisition process. Now the experts and product managers could communicate their knowledge not only in words, which required further mediation by other team members, but also quite directly, (e.g., in proposals for screen layouts, control flow diagrams, and other aspects of product design). In other words, the overall result is an expanded bandwidth that expedites knowledge transfer from expert and customers.

5. The contextual knowledge developed by team members makes for more efficient problem solving, with fewer false starts and dead ends. In AI terms, developing and using an integrated design team reduces backtracking and improves search. This is true for technical and knowledge engineering decisions, and especially for those complex business issues involving product development that cut across organizational boundaries.

Restrictions and Limitations

One of the primary lessons embedded in the Operations Advisor is that once you are working efficiently, every further advantage entails tradeoffs. Nothing comes for free. Accordingly, it should come as no surprise that the advantages of the integrated design team approach go hand in hand with some significant restrictions and limitations, including the following:

1. A significant initial organizational investment is required for team members to learn enough to work together effectively.
2. The approach suits people who enjoy informality and taking initiative. It probably would cause problems in a turf-conscious hierarchical organization or in a highly directive managerial culture. The goal is getting things done and done right—not following established procedures, or doing only as you are told.
3. Personal knowledge of other participants and functions is very important. Thus the approach may work less well in large firms.
4. The team must have a long-term, high-priority time commitment from all its members, in particular the expert.
5. The approach was evolved for large-scale generic expert system products. It may not be applicable for development of small shell-based single-application systems by or for individual users.

6. Substantial management attention is required. With so much going on so fast and so informally, management must monitor communication channels and spend a lot of time "walking the halls" to stay current, catch potential problems early, and make sure everything is under control.

7. Significant management time also is required to deal with resource bottlenecks and to obtain consensus on short-run changes in priorities. For example, having a product manager involved wherever in the organization his or her pragmatic knowledge and experience are needed will not work if everyone wants help at the same time. Someone must manage the conflicts to minimize overload and thrashing.

8. Although the design teams have proven remarkably resilient under conditions of extreme stress and pressure from deadlines, there obviously are limits here, too. Exceed those limits, and the development process quickly exhibits a high level of thrashing, which in turn can result in a precipitous drop in morale.

9. Because the approach depends so heavily on adequate relations among the team members, if personal friction or turf conflicts become serious, prompt and decisive management intervention is mandatory.

10. Finally, there is a natural tension between encouraging individual initiative, professional pride, and involvement, and maintaining the directiveness necessary to achieve a coherent quality software product. Striking a good balance between these objectives is a recurring problem.

COMMERCIALIZATION OF GENERIC EXPERT SYSTEMS: CURRENT STATUS AND PROSPECTS

Applied Expert Systems, Palladian, and Syntelligence, the three initial developers of high-end commercial expert system products, are all privately held companies, and they do not release detailed figures on their sales. Nonetheless, it seems clear that commercial generic expert system products have yet to achieve general market acceptance. Having completed our discussion of the managerial issues involved in building such products, we will conclude this chapter by considering what we can learn from the market's initial reactions to them. Once again, these observations are based primarily on Palladian's experience.

We mentioned earlier the premises underlying these enterprises, the belief in the broad applicability of generic expertise, and the sense that this expertise could be tailored to the requirements of many different users, thus making its benefits available at a fraction of the cost of custom-built systems. If we accept these premises, the commitment to building the Advisors follows naturally. After all, these experts were paid substantial sums to help management solve its problems. Their time was limited. They had to be scheduled far in advance. This meant that they could be used only for the most important problems, and only for those that did not involve numerous reiterations and a tight time schedule. Why not clone the experts, building their knowledge into systems that would be available for problems throughout a company and around the clock?

Some of the difficulties involved in carrying out this idea were anticipated from the start. The conventional computing environments available in 1984 would not support large-scale expert systems. This meant that, initially at least, the products would have to be delivered on unfamiliar hardware, using unfamiliar languages and running unfamiliar operating systems. The initial versions of the products would not mesh with users' other hardware and software, or with their existing data bases.

It also was understood from the start that marketing and selling these products would not be like marketing and selling soap. The market for soap exists. It is well defined. It does not need to be educated about the value of soap. If you come up with a new and better soap, the market is likely to be able to understand and evaluate the claimed advantages and to decide whether they justify their cost. By contrast, the market for generic expert systems for management did not exist in this well-defined sense. Business organizations had people evaluating business opportunities or manufacturing plans, but these people were not using comparable products or technologies, and they had no ready framework for evaluating and cost justifying generic expert systems. In other words, there might well be a large potential market, but the companies building these products could only guess as to who would use them, and the companies considering buying them were not sure who the users would be, either. In effect, the developers of these products were aware that market acceptance would require a significant change in how prospective customers conducted their management planning, but they counted on the obvious advantages of their new approach to carry them through.

As things turned out, however, the developers underestimated the forces of organizational inertia. Many prospective customers viewed demonstrations of the products, pronounced themselves interested, and then asked to be contacted further once the products had been reengineered for conventional computers. Others, typically top management people impressed with the concepts and their potential, or advanced technology people impressed with the technical merits, bought the products and then could not find people in their companies willing and able to use them on a regular basis.

Equally significant, the developers substantially underestimated the difficulties of bridging the gap between generic expertise and the working frameworks of individual users. There are several reasons for this. The most obvious one was the failure to notice that they were not just modeling their experts. The experts, as we have seen, worked with their clients at a fairly high level. It generally was up to the clients to implement this high-level guidance in the context of their own financial, accounting, or operating systems. The expert systems were required to do substantially *more* than their expert models in this regard. They not only had to provide general guidance and direction. They also had to carry out the analyses to completion. This meant, as we have already seen, that they had to incorporate substantially more pragmatic knowledge than the developers had envisioned initially.

Solving this pragmatic interfacing problem is now understood to be absolutely critical for market success. There is a core of users who are very happy with the Advisors as they stand. Over and over again, however, prospective customers have expressed enthusiasm, even awe, at the analytic capabilities of the products; and then, if they have reservations about their ability to describe their problems to the Advisors exactly the way they are used to thinking about them, they elect to stay with their existing methods, the superior analytic powers of the Advisors notwithstanding.

It remains to be seen how successful generic expert system developers will be in dealing with these difficulties. Palladian has introduced a new product, the Operations Planner, which runs on conventional hardware. The Operations Planner does not include all of the AI capabilities of the OA described earlier, but it does provide the OA's basic functional expertise on a widely accepted platform.

The issue of pragmatic knowledge probably will be harder to deal with. It is possible to continue to add pragmatic and analytic breadth, thereby accommodating increasing numbers of users. But the Advisors are basically closed systems. If a prospective customer is concerned about encountering a problem the Advisors do not accommodate, there is no way the customer can modify the Advisor to rectify the situation. It may be possible to redesign the Advisors to make them more open, and if future generic expert system products are to be fully successful, Palladian's experience would suggest that they will have to have this property. But this will entail substantial technical efforts. It also alters the product concept. No longer are we talking about off-the-shelf products that can be used unconditionally by nonprogrammer managers. Now we have to do with systems that may require significant in-house development efforts if they are to work effectively in a given corporate context. That is by no means a *bad* idea. But it is a different idea from the product concept that underlies the Advisors.

SUMMARY AND CONCLUSIONS

The Operations Advisor and the Management Advisor are large-scale management applications using expert system and AI technology. They break new ground for application software in incorporating large amounts of generic expert knowledge about operations planning and management, and the valuation of business opportunities.

To develop these systems, management had to confront issues and requirements falling under three distinct heads: knowledge engineering, technical implementation, and overall business requirements. To deal with these issues, and to expedite designing, implementing, and delivering the products, management evolved an integrated design team approach to development. This approach made effective use of the experts, product managers, and technical people comprising the team, and contributed to productivity levels far in excess of those normally observed in commercial software development. The integrated design team approach has its limits, but it is likely to yield comparable benefits for any organization whose goals, work style, and culture are compatible with its requirements.

The OA and the MA provide significantly enhanced analytic capabilities for users whose problems fit within the Advisors' descriptive frameworks. Market acceptance of these systems so far has been quite limited, however. Future generic expert system products will have to offer substantially more flexibility than these first products provide. But the Advisors have contributed significantly to our understanding of the requirements for developing and marketing such products successfully, and the next generation of generic expert systems products is likely to realize substantially more of the potential inherent in the concept as a result.

REFERENCES

BITRAN, G., and T. PAPAGEORGE. "Integration of Manufacturing Policy and Corporate Strategy with the Aid of Expert Systems," in M. Oliff, ed., *Proceedings of the International Conference on Expert Systems and the Leading Edge in Production Planning and Control,* Addison Wesley-Benjamin/Cummings, Menlo Park, CA, 1987.

DUDA, R. O., P. E. HART, R. REBOH, J. REITER, and T. RISCH. "Syntel: Using a Functional Language for Financial Risk Assessment," *IEEE Expert,* Vol. 2, No. 3, pp. 18–31, 1987.

MYERS, S. C. "Notes on an Expert System for Capital Budgeting," *Financial Management,* Vol. 17, No. 3, pp. 23–31, 1988.

STANSFIELD, J. L., and N. R. GREENFELD. "Planpower: A Comprehensive Financial Planner," *IEEE Expert,* Vol. 2, No. 3, pp. 51–60, 1987.

STEELE, G. L., Jr. "The Definition and Implementation of a Computer Programming Language Based on Constraints," Ph.D. Dissertation, MIT, Cambridge, MA, 1980.

WALSTON, C. E., and C. P. FELIX. "A Method of Programming Measurement and Estimation," *IBM Systems Journal,* Vol. 16, No. 1, pp. 54–73, 1977.

10

Development of Natural Language Processing Systems from a Manager's Perspective

ANTONIO ZAMORA, IBM Corporation
ELENA M. ZAMORA, IBM Corporation

INTRODUCTION

Since the introduction of computers, there have been tremendous changes in the ways in which mathematical problems are handled. Today, it would be inconceivable to approach a mathematical problem without considering the role that the computer will play. Similarly, in the last few years, the role of computers in natural language processing has increased so much that it will not be too long before linguistic processing by computers is an absolute necessity. This is already true in areas such as word processing and cryptography, but there are many other areas that are just emerging that will change completely the way we think about computers and language. Some of the factors that have contributed to the fast growth of this field are the lower cost of computers and their increased capabilities.

The manager or developer of natural language processing applications faces many problems for which traditional data processing techniques do not provide adequate methodology. The purpose of this chapter is to highlight some of the technical issues that affect the management of natural language applications and to suggest management strategies for coping with the intricacies of these applications.

In traditional data processing tasks, such as inventory control and accounting, one role of the manager is to make sure that the final computer programs preserve the integrity of the data. These applications may be viewed as models of the real world, where money or goods are being represented internally by the computer.

Natural language processing has some similarities to traditional data processing, but it also has aspects that are altogether different. Like traditional data processing programs, linguistic applications need to preserve the meaning of utterances; however, the meaning may be paraphrased, translated into other languages, changed into voice, or printed. Unlike traditional data processing, linguistic data may contain ambiguities and may be incomplete or inconsistent. The procedures used to manipulate language sometimes cannot be guaranteed to terminate and, generally, this forces the introduction of heuristics, which are partial, rule-of-thumb solutions for complicated problems. It is these uncertainties that make it hard to manage the design and installation of natural language processing systems.

APPLICATIONS OF LINGUISTICS

Computational linguistics provides many opportunities for basic research and for a broad spectrum of applications. This should not be surprising, given that the use of language is such a fundamental human activity. In spoken form, language can be mixed with gestures and body movements to extend the range of expressiveness. The dynamics of the human voice can also impart emotion or provide clues about the geographic origin of the speaker. Written language provides a long-term record of ideas and serves as an important means of communication.

These are some of the areas in which linguistics plays a role:

- word processing, document preparation
- spelling verification and aid
- synonym support
- syntactic analysis, parsing
- grammar checking, style aid
- text generation, paraphrasing
- lexicography, dictionary structures
- message handling, prioritizing communications
- telephony, cryptography
- voice synthesis and recognition

- automatic or computer-aided translation
- knowledge representation
- text understanding, intelligence gathering
- automatic abstracting
- data base generation, compression, query, and retrieval
- document classification, indexing, and ranking
- integration and manipulation of text, image, and voice

CHARACTERISTICS OF LINGUISTIC SYSTEMS

In general, systems dealing with linguistics are large; they require a long time to develop; they require coordination of programming and linguistic skills, and they are never complete. The complexities of natural language systems create conditions that require skilled management from the conception of the project through product development.

As an example, consider the spelling-checking software that is now available on most word processors. Although we now think of spelling checking as fairly trivial, it took a long time to get this technology into user products. Research into spelling verification and correction started around 1957, but some of the first application programs were developed only in 1971. Early spelling verification technology ran into problems; it was possible to verify words with a high degree of reliability, but it was not possible to generate candidates for correction because the dictionaries were compressed into irreversible hash codes. Designers had to invent ways of allowing the users to customize dictionaries. Methodologies had to be adopted for hyphenation support and for handling foreign languages with accented characters and word compounding. Interactive spelling aids did not appear in the market until the late 1970s. During the twenty years from conception to the availability of competitive products, there were many advances in hardware and software, but most crucial to the implementation of spelling verification were the organization and compaction of the dictionaries and the specification of adequate user interfaces (Peterson, 1980). Today, consumers can buy compact hand-held units that provide spelling verification and correction for vocabularies in the range of 100,000 words at prices comparable to those of portable radios.

After thirty years of experience in spelling-checking applications, one would expect that most problems would have been solved, but this is not the case. Providing word verification and spelling-aid candidates for compound words in Germanic languages is still a very challenging problem, and there are also many problems in the verification of Finnish words because of their highly productive morphological inflections.

Syntactic analysis and grammar-checking applications are now in a period of development similar to what spelling verification went through, but these processes are much more complicated (Cherry, 1978; Heidorn et al., 1982; Robinson, 1982). Syntactic analysis requires not only access to dictionaries but also formalization of the grammars. Although it was possible to adapt spelling-verification programs to several languages by swapping dictionaries and making minor software changes, the same is not true for syntactic analysis. Even related languages have substantial differences in syntactic structure. The development of syntactic analysis and grammar-checking software to handle multiple languages remains a formidable challenge for the future. Yet, these obstacles must be faced and conquered before more complex problems such as automatic translation between natural languages can become a reality. Automatic translation is so difficult that during the 1970s, a group of influential researchers concluded very convincingly that the translation problem could not be solved. Consequently, translation work virtually came to a standstill in the United States. It was only during the 1980s that significant new work resumed in this field.

Semantic analysis is at an embryonic stage. Although a lot of work has been done, general guiding principles for implementation of practical systems have not been developed. Scientists are now divided between formulating semantic representations from hand-coded data bases like dictionaries and designing self-learning, self-organizing systems with consistency checks. Models based on the human brain can go only as far as our understanding of how the brain works, which, in absolute terms, is not very much.

Since some problems in linguistics are very difficult to solve, progress depends on steadily improving dictionary data bases, algorithms, and grammars. All of these require many years of effort and the ability to use previous work. A lot of effort is wasted in linguistics. A great deal of good linguistic work has been done by many researchers throughout the world, but it is generally impossible to use someone else's work, either because the systems are proprietary or because they are incompatible. One researcher will code in Prolog, another one prefers Lisp, and so on. Even when the same programming language is used, the format of the dictionaries, the data structures, the program interfaces, or the hardware pose additional roadblocks.

Most linguistic software is specific to one language and cannot be extended to other languages. It is very difficult to integrate linguistic software from different vendors. Linguistic databases such as dictionaries are different for each application package and cannot be shared for different uses. Vendors impose restrictions on the use of their data bases. Many dictionary publishers permit their dictionaries to be used for research, but they do not allow their use in commercial products.

MANAGEMENT STRATEGIES

The manager of a linguistics or natural language application needs a clear understanding of the desired goals to establish project milestones and criteria to decide when each task has been satisfactorily completed. The manager also needs to be aware of the technical difficulties that are addressed by his or her staff so that their efforts can be directed to solve significant and relevant problems. A linguistic project is like any other program development project in that there is a project definition stage, an organization and management stage, and an implementation stage (Aron, 1983). During the project definition stage, the problem is characterized; this stage may even involve building a model of the solution. A model or prototype of a linguistic system is very useful because it makes it possible to evaluate the complexity of the problem, to visualize the interaction of the system components, and to determine the feasibility of developing a more complete implementation. Once the model has been constructed, it is possible to experiment with it to make refinements or generalizations.

A linguistic project can be managed either with a stepwise strategy or with a total-system strategy. The choice depends on the goals, the duration, and the scope of the project. If the linguistic project is relatively small, the manager may opt for a total-system design in which all the components are specified during the project definition stage. In general, this strategy is useful only for development of prototypes or highly specialized linguistic components.

The stepwise strategy is most useful for long-range linguistic projects where it is not possible to anticipate all the potential uses of the technology being developed. The stepwise approach emphasizes the design of components that can be used to produce immediately useful results and can serve as the foundation for subsequent work. For example, if a spelling-checking application requires a dictionary, the same dictionary and access subroutines should be used to service a syntactic parser. Of course, the spelling-checking dictionary might not contain all the information needed by the parser; it might be necessary to enhance it in a way that does not decrease the efficiency of the original spelling-checking application. Sometimes, it is not possible to satisfy conflicting demands, and in those cases duplication of system components is inevitable.

The manager must be prepared to assign a well-informed staff member to resolve problems arising from conflicting demands. The technical staff member must know both the short-term and the long-term goals to make the best decision. Some of the problems may seem trivial on the surface, but the wrong decision can have detrimental long-term consequences. Consider, for example, that it is necessary to manage the design of a natural language parser. The specifications call for passing an input sentence to the parser to obtain a data structure that represents one or more parse trees. The problem that is not reflected in the specifications is that identifying a sentence from natural language text is a complicated problem. Recognizing the role of periods is difficult. Periods may be embedded in numeric strings, they may occur in abbreviations, or they may indicate the end of a sentence. What happens when an abbreviation such as *etc.* is at the end of the sentence? Such problems must be resolved by a technical staff member, and the consequences of the approach must be documented. If the solution tends to categorize abbreviation periods as "end of sentence," the parser will receive less data than it is expecting and will not be able to complete a parse. On the other hand, if periods are generally considered "abbreviation periods," the parser will come to the end of a sentence, and there will still be text to be processed. Which approach is better depends on the application of the system. A solution that allows progressive refinements is sometimes the best solution. The paradoxical question, *What came first, the chicken or the egg?* has many manifestations in linguistics. This problem is just one of them: If you need a parser to determine the end of a sentence, how can you isolate a sentence to pass it to the parser?

The following sections describe three major aspects of natural language systems: lexicon, syntax, and semantics. A manager needs to have substantial knowledge of these areas to determine the best strategy to follow with the human resources and the time constraints that are available. If a manager is told by the technical staff that a year is needed to develop the grammar or that the application cannot be written in C language, how can the manager determine whether these statements are right? A manager who does not have enough technical knowledge of the field cannot judge what the right decision is and, consequently, will interfere with the performance of a good team or will lead an inexperienced team into technical difficulties.

Lexicon

A lexicon is a dictionary containing the words that are recognized by a natural language system. The scope of the lexicon may be expanded by morphological analysis procedures. In English, for example, words ending in -*ly* are typically adverbs; therefore, it is reasonable to guess that a word is an adverb if it is not in the lexicon but it has an -*ly* ending.

For a manager to be able to assign staff members, organize lexical work, and coordinate activities that depend on the lexicon, he or she should be familiar with some of the statistical properties of language. Zipf's law (Zipf, 1949) states that the frequency of a word and its rank are inversely related by a constant. This means that predictions can be made about the sizes of dictionaries needed for certain applications. Books containing word frequencies are also available (Carroll et al., 1971; Dahl, 1979; Francis and Kucera, 1982). These are useful in setting up small dictionaries that have large coverage. For example, a short list containing about fifteen English prepositions and articles is able to match around 25 percent of the words in an average paragraph, whereas a dictionary of 3,000 words is able to match approximately 80 percent of the words, and a dictionary of 100,000 words generally matches about 95 to 98 percent of the words. Taking into consideration these figures, a manager can concentrate available resources on aspects of the linguistic work that have the greatest benefit.

It is necessary to define what a word is before a lexicon can be constructed. The technique for isolating words affects the content of the dictionary and the applications that use the dictionary. Should the dictionary include contractions like *can't* or hyphenated words like *mother-in-law*? If capitalized words are allowed, will there be a distinction between *Victor* and *victor,* and *Bill* and *bill*? Will the dictionary contain multiple words such as *hot dog* or abbreviations like *etc.*? Will words with numeric characters, such as *42nd* or *B-52* be allowed?

The procedure to identify words may consist of isolating strings delimited by blanks and then removing leading and ending punctuation characters, but it may be preferable to isolate only alphanumeric strings that contain embedded hyphens or apostrophes. The choice depends on the area of application. The first procedure, for example, will reduce fragmentation of technical vocabulary that contains embedded punctuation.

If the lexicon is designed for languages other than English, the word isolation procedure should be modified to accommodate language-specific conventions. In French, contracted prefixes are found on many words, such as *l'enveloppe* ("the envelope"); the prefixes should not be included as part of the dictionary entries. Similarly, some hyphenated French words, such as *permettez-moi* ("permit me") may need to be recognized as two separate words. However, the equivalent word form in Spanish (*permítame*) is fused and does not use explicit hyphenation. For Spanish, recognition of the component words *permita* and *me* requires identification of the pronoun ending and removal of the accent from the verb root. Word compounding in German presents still harder problems because the mechanisms for word formation are very productive.

The manager of a natural language processing task should strive to have a single interface for accessing dictionaries. The interface may include parameters to customize the output for particular applications. Enforcing access through a single interface is the only way to guarantee that all functional requirements for the lexicon are consolidated. Sometimes, it will be necessary to upgrade the interface to support new functions or even to redesign the dictionary structure, but the advantage of establishing standardized access to the dictionaries will pay off as the applications that use the interface grow in number.

How do you build a lexicon? What do you put in it? The simplest way to start is to create a prototype of the application. Select a small sample of text and process it manually in the same way that the finished system would process it. Next, build a computer model. In this model, the contents of the lexicon can be represented as program data structures, or they can actually be external files. The idea is to externalize the lexicon eventually so that it can be augmented without changing the programs. (Most linguistic applications consist of a set of internal rules and external lexicons. The lexical information can be accessed from the external files as needed.) The process being prototyped can be repeated with a different sample of text. This iterative process makes it necessary to determine the essential contents needed in the lexicon. From this experience, one can generalize and create a lexicon structure that fulfills the needs of the application.

While it is relatively easy to create a test lexicon, it is extremely laborious to create a full-size one. The manager must evaluate whether the staff should be involved in the lexicographic work or whether contractors should do the work. It may even be possible to obtain data bases containing syntactic or semantic attributes from publishers or other suppliers, but the manager should be aware of copyrights, use restrictions, and royalties. It is always a good idea to work several hours on the creation of dictionary entries to determine the rate at which they can be generated. After such a trial run, realistic estimates can be made about the size of the lexical task and its approximate cost. If the dictionary is to contain word frequencies, it is a good idea to estimate the corpus of text that would be required to get the size of the vocabulary and the precision desired for the final system.

Morphology

Some aspects of the lexicon can be expanded by morphological analysis procedures. Although these procedures are useful, they are of limited value because there is always an element of doubt when a word is not found in the lexicon. The reliability of morphological procedures can be enhanced by introducing specialized dictionaries that contain exceptions to the morphological rules. Assume, for example, that it is necessary to determine whether an English word is the past tense of a verb. This can be accomplished by first looking for the word in a list of exceptions and then checking to see if the word ends in -*ed*. The list of exceptions needs to contain irregular verb forms such as *took* and *wrote,* as well as *embed, shred,* and other words with -*ed* endings that are not past-tense verb forms. English has approximately 270 irregular verbs and, in general, about 5 different forms for each verb. Romance languages, by contrast, have around 50 different forms for each verb and many more irregularities.

The type of morphological process depends on the application supported. If the application requires a lemma, elaborate processing is needed to convert a word form to its lemma. A lemma is the base word form to which all the inflections are related. For example, *type* is the lemma of the words *typed*, *typing*, and *types*. For English, it is possible to design morphological programs that will transform words into their lemmas (Kucera, 1987). The lists of words must be large (on the order of 13,000 words) to be able to identify most exceptions. Phenomena such as doubling (*gasses* → *gas*) and irregularities (*babies* → *baby,* but *rabies* does not change) need to be handled. Many reference books provide complete conjugations for irregular verbs and patterns for regular conjugations (Kendris, 1971; Quirk et al., 1985).

The lemma of a word provides a convenient index point for storing grammatical attributes, synonyms, and other data. The lemma is the basis for ordering most commercial dictionaries. Generally, dictionaries will list a highly irregular word such as *went* and relate it to its lemma *go*, but most dictionaries will not do the same for a word whose morphology provides intuitive clues. Thus, even though the word *building* may be listed in a dictionary, only its function as a noun will be described; the fact that it is also a present participle will be mentioned only under the lemma for the verb *build*, if at all.

Syntax

Syntax is the branch of linguistics that deals with the formation of phrases, clauses, and sentences. A natural language parser is a computer program that attempts to identify the grammatical role of the words of a sentence. To the manager of a natural language project, a parser should be like a utility program, such as a sort, which has standard interfaces to make its use as simple as possible by any number of applications. A manager would also wish to have the parser well integrated with dictionaries that have other uses. The standard interface of the parser should consist of well-defined data structures and easy-to-use subroutines that access these data structures to provide parse trees, part of speech, or other information required by any application program.

In planning work on a parser, the manager will face several roadblocks to the division of the tasks into manageable portions such as the following: (1) Syntax is not separable from semantics; therefore semantic processing has to be done concurrently with parsing; (2) the choice of the parsing strategy plays a major role in the skills required to code the parsing engine and to code the grammar; (3) a grammar is a highly interconnected logical structure; therefore it is impossible for more than one person to develop the grammar; (4) a separate grammar has to be developed for each different application because there are many interdependencies between the structure of the grammar and the semantic requirements of the application.

Although there is much truth in these generalizations, a manager has to be able to divide the work to be able to add or reassign personnel to speed up the completion of a project, if necessary. The question of whether syntax is separable from semantics can be answered *yes* or *no,* depending on the type of sentence; different types of ambiguities require different types of information. For example, it is possible to guess that both "xxx" and "yyy" are nouns in the sentence "The xxx was at yyy," even though "xxx" and "yyy" are unknown words. It can further be deduced that "yyy" is a location because that is what the preposition *at* requires. The sentence "I see the man with the telescope" can be parsed correctly, but the attachment of the prepositional phrase remains unknown. Do I have the telescope, or does the man have the telescope? Finally, in a sentence such as "I saw her duck," *saw*, *her*, and *duck* each have two different interpretations. *Saw* is a verb with two meanings, *her* can be either a possessive or an objective pronoun, and *duck* can be either a noun or a verb. If we knew which semantic meanings were associated with each word, it would be possible to select one of the alternative parses.

Many researchers in natural language would argue that it is impractical to code a syntactic parser without semantic information, and it is true that knowing the semantic context makes it possible to provide more accurate syntactic information. However, morphological, syntactic, and semantic features usually form a continuum along which it is difficult to define discrete boundaries. Therefore, the question of how much semantic processing is done in a syntactic parser is one of degree, rather than something that can be expressed in absolute terms. The separation has to be based on the scope of the linguistic project and the needs of the application. For small, specialized projects, the integration of syntax and semantics is more practical than for projects that expect to serve many applications and for which a modular structure is more advantageous.

A manager is faced with many choices during the design phase of a natural language parser. Should the parser be procedural or interpretative? Should it process the text from left to right or from right to left? Should the grammar be interpreted from the bottom up or from the top down? Should the grammar be procedural, phrase structure, Augmented Transition Network (ATN), Recursive Transition Network (RTN), or something else? Should it be coded in Lisp, Prolog, or in some language like C, which offers more portability between mainframes and workstations? What role should word frequencies play in the determination of the part of speech?

A manager should recognize that the parser structure and its optimization are computer programming problems, whereas writing grammar rules is a linguistic problem. A procedural parser encodes the grammar rules as program statements; thus, development of a procedural parser needs to be staffed by individuals who are proficient programmers and who are also good linguists. This is a rare combination for which the manager will be hard pressed to obtain qualified candidates. An interpretive parser, on the other hand, separates the "parsing engine" from the grammar and makes it possible to divide the work among individuals with different specialties.

The choice of programming language for the parser depends on the environment in which the application will run. If the parser is to be a subroutine that is going to be used in a question-answering system or a text-processing application, it may make sense to choose a language that will make the interfacing relatively simple. There are other options, such as allowing the parser to reside in a fast service machine connected through a network to the applications requesting parsing services. In this type of detached mode, the language in which the parser is coded is not a major interface issue.

The direction of the parsing (left to right versus right to left) is not a critical design problem. Good results can be obtained with both approaches (Sager, 1981). The bottom-up versus the top-down option has been resolved in some parsers by combining both approaches. Top-down analysis tries to parse text by matching the expected sentence structures against the input text. Bottom-up analysis, by contrast, looks at the input text, and, based on the words found, tries to find sentence patterns that are appropriate. In general, bottom-up analysis is more efficient for an initial analysis, but top-down is better during the later stages when the presence of a verb, for instance, gives some clues about the types of complements that can be expected.

The choice between context-free, transformational, phrase structure, ATN, RTN (Marcus, 1980; Winograd, 1983; Woods, 1970), or any other grammatical analysis approach is normally justified on the basis of "parsing power." Parsing natural language requires a powerful mechanism that is able to examine as much context as necessary to arrive at a successful parse. Thus, any mechanism that allows full context sensitivity and has a clear grammatical notation will be satisfactory. Many times, the choice is made on the basis of whether there already exists an application or a prototype with a specific grammar. If a completely new project is being started, the choice depends on the experience of the grammar developer and the support environment that is adopted. Several commercial firms provide linguistic development workstations with facilities for generating and testing grammars.

DEVELOPMENT OF A GRAMMAR

Grammar is the study of the relationships of words to create phrases, clauses, and sentences. Grammar may include disciplines such as syntax, morphology, phonetics, semantics, and pragmatics. A computational grammar is a highly interconnected logical structure that expresses dependencies and constraints imposed by these disciplines and which enables a computer either to analyze or to generate correct utterances.

Creating the grammar rules is probably the hardest task in the development of a natural language system. One major problem is that there are no good and comprehensive grammars of any natural language that are suitable for direct input into a computer. The traditional grammars do a fairly good job of describing linguistic phenomena for a human reader, but they are not detailed or systematic enough to be transcribed into computational grammar rules. Many times, a collection of grammar books is needed to resolve questions about the usage of a particular word. On some occasions, the information needed to resolve a problem is not in any book. Personal intuition must be used to create grammar rules that satisfy the computer's need for exact, nonconflicting specifications. It is tempting to say that the real problem in computational linguistics is that grammar does not exist. Language exists, but grammar is only our attempt at finding regularity within the variation of human expression. Languages grow and change with time and, therefore, the grammar must also change. Grammar reflects accepted usage, but it is never up to date.

Development of grammar rules generally starts with a fairly broad definition of what a sentence is. Almost every book on the subject has examples indicating that a sentence consists of a noun phrase plus a verb phrase (S → NP VP). The grammar development process continues with definitions of prepositional phrases, complements of the verb phrase, compound subjects, and relative clauses. When it comes time to handle relative clauses (e.g., "The man *who lives by the park* came yesterday,"), the use of recursion in the grammar rules can be very helpful in reducing the number of rules, but it also increases the complexity.

Grammar writers must not only have a native knowledge of the language; they must also have an instinct for parsing techniques that are computationally efficient. A manager may be able to assign several persons to develop the grammar, but the interactions between them must be well coordinated to prevent conflicts in the resulting rules. Sometimes it is better if persons have complementary assignments so that they will not get in each other's way. One person may work on grammar rules and another may prepare the lexical entries or samples of natural language text on which to test the rules. As the rules of the grammar evolve, it may be necessary to change the supporting dictionary. A good data base mechanism can be very useful if there is a lot of dictionary activity.

Testing a grammar is a tedious, time-consuming job; it involves the examination of the parse trees generated by the parser to decide whether the text was processed properly. Is the part of speech correct? Were the phrase boundaries properly identified? Were the dependent phrases properly attached? During the initial development of the grammar, these questions can be answered easily in an interactive mode, but as the grammar grows, it is necessary to use some type of batch process and an automatic scoring mechanism. The batch mechanism makes it possible to test previous examples to make sure that changes in the rules have not caused regression in the quality of the results. The automatic scoring mechanism helps the grammar writers to focus on the features that changed from the preceding run, or on the differences from manually coded "ideal" output.

The progress of a parsing project can be measured by monitoring the types of linguistic phenomena that can be handled successfully and by evaluating the performance of the parser on samples of random text. The first verifies the list of features included in the grammar, whereas the second is a results-oriented analysis. The text can be categorized according to the phenomena coded in the grammar, and the correct and incorrect handling of each feature can yield percentages that reflect both the coverage and the robustness of the system.

How do you know when you are done developing a grammar? You are never done, but you can get closer and closer to the results you need. The needs of the applications that use the grammar dictate when a sufficient level of performance has been achieved. An interactive natural language front end, for example, will require the grammar to address discourse structure problems such as the use of pronouns to refer to something mentioned previously, the use of fragmentary input and ellipsis in response to system queries. A grammar-checking application, on the other hand, may need to be able to recover from ungrammatical input by postulating a likely cause of the error, and then proceed in spite of the error. In the ideal case, both applications would be handled by the same grammar. However, the time and cost of grammar development is large enough that it is not possible to do everything at once. There are also system constraints such as file storage for dictionaries and grammars, speed of execution, and computer memory limits that make it necessary to aim for modest, but achievable, goals. In the current state of the art, it is not unusual to have separate grammars for each different application. The major reason for this is that there are many interdependencies between the structure of the grammar and the syntactic and semantic requirements of the application. Also, different grammars can be developed by different teams in about the same amount of time. Although redundant activity is wasteful, sometimes it can be of tactical importance to meet business needs.

A manager should realize that a linguist experienced in writing computational grammars using good support tools will require at least one year to develop a passable grammar. A grammar with good coverage may take two or more years of development and many more years of support for testing the grammar and updating dictionaries. The lack of standardization in grammar writing systems and parsing technologies makes it almost impossible to use published work or even to buy any technology from vendors. This will probably be remedied in the future, but now there are few practical alternatives to in-house grammar development.

Semantics

Semantics is the study of the relationship between symbols and their meaning. The technology to handle artificial languages, such as programming languages, has advanced to such a degree that a language can be transported to different types of machines and be interpreted in exactly the same way. By contrast, semantics for natural language systems is in a very early stage of development: There is no generally accepted theoretical foundation and there is no standardized technology. Natural language contains many idioms and metaphors that add color to the language but also create ambiguities. An idiom such as "on the other hand," for example, is used to indicate an alternative and does not have anything to do with "hand," except in special cases. Distinguishing these special cases is not easy. Metaphors such as "Time flies like an arrow" would make one think that "time" is a type of winged creature, if one did not know better. That is the nature of metaphors; they are merely analogies, and it is necessary to distinguish them from reality to understand the meaning of a passage of text. Scientists, mathematicians, and lawyers attempt to develop precise terminology to achieve universal clarity. Comedians, on the other hand, like to exploit the ambiguities of language to create puns. The old joke that asks "How do you get down from an elephant?" and comes back with the answer "You don't get down from an elephant—you get down from a duck!" is based on different ways of parsing sentences. The richness of natural language and the many purposes for which it is used will remain a formidable challenge to any attempts toward its mechanization for years to come. The programs that handle semantics successfully today are those that limit themselves to a narrow subject area to reduce ambiguities.

Some of the basic problems of semantics include the representation of concepts within a computer, ways to handle alternative meanings of expressions, the relationship of logic and world knowledge to natural language expressions, and the interpretation of discourse (Jackendoff, 1983; Kamp, 1981; Minsky, 1975; Schank and Ableson, 1977; Schank, 1980; Simmons, 1972, 1984; Sowa, 1984). Natural language semantics needs to incorporate world knowledge of the type found in expert systems, and at times it requires inference mechanisms from artificial intelligence (AI) systems. Semantics is a field that offers many opportunities for basic research. A manager interested in product development will need to set clear, limited objectives in order to succeed. Narrowing the domain of the problem or creating a specialized solution is one way to achieve this. Narrowing the domain simplifies the problem to be solved. This can be seen, for example, by examining the meanings of the word *execute*. In one sense, *execute* means "to carry out"; in another sense, it means "to put to death." An unrestricted system would have to sort out these meanings for a phrase such as *execute the program*. Such a system would have to figure out that only living things can die, that programs are not living, and that therefore the first meaning is intended. All the complications of making the logical deductions to make the meaning unambiguous can be avoided by preparing a restricted lexicon where *execute* simply has the meaning desired for the application.

Once the meaning of a natural language expression is known, it can be stored in the computer as a conceptual network, a list structure, or any number of knowledge representation formats. This is virtually a necessary step for any modular system. A knowledge representation format makes it possible to paraphrase a natural language query—that is, to verify that what was understood by the computer is what was intended by the user (Harris, 1978). These internal knowledge representations have also been used as a kind of focal point or "transfer structure" for automatic translation. When a natural language statement is parsed, its syntactic and semantic constituents are converted to the transfer structure. The structure is then mapped by an appropriate generative grammar to the desired target language.

What role do world models, world knowledge, and domain expertise play in a natural language system? The answer depends on how ambitious the goals of the project are. Clearly, if a reasonable attempt is made to understand text, it is necessary to access as much relevant information as possible. Some of this information may be in the form of semantic networks, mathematical models, or data bases. The information needs to be structured to avoid redundancy and to provide useful functions. The world knowledge information records facts that may be used to make deductions. For instance, if we know that animals are living things and that a whale is an animal, we can deduce that whales are also living things. The inheritance of attributes is an important aspect of knowledge representation that simplifies the contents of these data bases, but it also introduces the complexities of dealing with logical expressions and contradictions in the data base.

Some of the current approaches for building world knowledge into natural language programs use methods for predicting the structure of text based on scenarios and on discourse conventions (Brady and Berwick, 1983; Dyer, 1983; Grimes, 1972; Mellish, 1985; Sidner, 1979). Both of these approaches assume that discourse has a structure and a theme; that is, sentences within a unit of discourse are related in some intelligent way. The discourse analysis methods assume that a sequence of statements represents progressive time frames or that the order is a logical sequence for the presentation of the facts. The theme structure methods depend on the logical continuity provided by a model of the theme expressed as scripts, schemata, or thematic abstraction units. One good feature of the theme structure methods is that they make it possible to establish meaningful dialogues between computers and humans. Since the computer has at its disposal a scenario of world events and their sequences and relationships, the computer may prompt a user for missing information.

Consider the following three sentences:

John went to a restaurant.

He ordered soup.

He left a big tip.

A human reader has no problem concluding that John ate soup and that he liked the service. However, a program would need to associate the pronoun *he* with *John*, and it would have to know that the purpose of going to a restaurant is to eat and that a customer first orders food and then eats it. The program also needs to know the role of waiters and the events associated with them. If the sentences were in a different order, a theme-oriented method would be able to identify a discrepancy, whereas a discourse analysis method might not be able to work at all. This example, small as it is, illustrates the complexity that needs to be built into a natural language system with modest goals. The solution of natural language problems requires the ability for relating and manipulating conceptual entities. This is an area that is so close to artificial intelligence as to be virtually indistinguishable from it. Artificial intelligence, however, deals with many problems that do not need natural language.

A Case Study

When one examines a project after many years have passed since its completion, one is able to judge its achievements and its failures from a broad perspective. The events that transpire in the course of a decade make it possible to determine whether a problem was easy because somebody solved it or whether it was hard because nobody solved it yet. The development of new technology in the course of ten years also makes it possible to verify whether the predictions made in the project regarding the trends in technology have been fulfilled or whether they were falsely grounded. The following section reviews an automatic abstracting project that did not get beyond the research stage, and it examines some of the reasons that contributed to this.

In 1969, as part of a thesis project, one of the authors started working on a method for producing abstracts from natural language text automatically (Rush et al., 1971). The work was motivated to some degree by the fact that the author worked for Chemical Abstracts Service, a publisher of scientific abstracts related to chemistry. Several years after the thesis was completed, additional work was supported by the company to explore the possibility of using the technology as part of the publishing system (Pollock and Zamora, 1975).

All the conditions were right for a natural language project of this type. There was a business need and the work was relevant to the main thrust of the business; also, there was sufficient prior literature on the subject, the domain was restricted to scientific text, and there were clear editorial policies about what should be or should not be in the abstracts. The abstracting procedure relied on what would now be called rudimentary parsing techniques and semantic categorizations. Nevertheless, the results met the objectives of being inexpensive to produce (about 50 cents of computer time per abstract) and of being easily postedited to meet the company policies (the machine abstracts were about three times longer than manually produced abstracts but contained most of the relevant information).

Some of the problems of the project had been anticipated. First of all, there was a lack of machine-readable primary journal data that could be input to the automatic abstracting program. The tapes that were available had typesetting conventions that required elaborate decoding procedures. At that time, optical character recognition as a form of data acquisition was out of the question because it was not reliable for the different font types that needed to be processed. Manual keying of the source documents was not a good alternative either because of its labor-intensive nature. It was anticipated that, as the publishers of primary journals started computerizing their editorial processes, a significant number of relevant scientific articles would be in suitable machine-readable form. What was not foreseen clearly was that the author summaries that were required by the editors of the primary journals would tend to obviate the need for automatic abstracting. However, at that time, we felt that the authors of the primary journals did not always write abstracts that met the strict editorial requirements of the abstracting service, but we had to accept that, in general, the author abstracts were good.

One significant point that was recognized and was intentionally never addressed by the project was the multilingual nature of the source material. Although a large percentage of the primary journals were written in English, there was an enormous volume of foreign literature that needed to be translated into English. Clearly, it would save a lot of money if we were able to handle automatically the majority of the English journals, but the complications mentioned above about getting the input data posed a large roadblock. The translation problem was a much larger problem that we dared not even address.

At the time of this study, chemical literature had been growing at a compounded rate. It was anticipated that the introduction of a mechanical aid would be welcomed by the technical staff, but this was not the case. An analysis procedure was set up to evaluate the results of the program. Manually-produced abstracts were intermixed with computer-produced abstracts so that the reviewers did not know which had been prepared by the computer. The purpose of the test was to determine whether the editors would notice the difference in the manually produced or machine produced abstracts. We also wanted to record the editors' suggestions for improvements. Of course, in many cases, it was obvious which abstracts had been created by the computer because they contained redundancies or well-known facts that a human abstractor would have avoided. Although the results of the test were favorable, the editorial staff was very disturbed because they feared that their jobs might be eliminated. This caused consternation among the editors and a tendency to overcriticize the program results and question its benefits.

The text-handling technology that was developed for the automatic abstracting project was eventually used in other machine editing tasks that had more general applicability and that resulted in improved productivity for all types of abstracts. The fact that there were limiting factors in the application of the automatic abstracting technology, such as the unavailability of input, the foreign language text, and the reticence of the editorial staff to embrace the approach, made it hard to justify its implementation. The project results themselves indicated that unless there was a breakthrough in the handling of semantics, the accomplishments would never be completely satisfactory or equal to manually produced abstracts.

One can only ask whether anything would be different if the project were conducted today. The answer is probably *no*. Although today we have better parsing technology and we can handle semantics better, there have not been any breakthroughs that would have a significant impact on the results. One can conclude reluctantly from this and similar experiences that progress in linguistics will continue to proceed at a snail's pace. Our only hope is that all of these small, incremental improvements will eventually enable us to solve today's problems satisfactorily.

SUMMARY

It is not easy to give general advice on a topic as broad as managing linguistic projects, because what is right in one situation may be wrong in another one. However, there are some general trends in linguistics that are broadly supported by many practitioners, and there are also techniques that have been tried and have failed to produce the desired results. This experience may be summarized as a list of *do*s and *don't*s which, on the whole, can serve as a general guideline for someone who is starting in the field. The recommended strategy is to try to develop a unified linguistic technology that is independent of the applications that it supports. The linguistic components should be like utility programs that have multiple uses and standard interfaces to maximize their use and reduce the overhead of developing dictionaries, access code, and so on. It is important to realize that since a linguistic task is seldom completed to satisfy all requirements, the components need to be designed in a modular fashion so that they can be upgraded. If these components become too complex to be understood, no further enhancements are possible.

Linguistic technology must be developed under a centralized management to assure that the overall goals of consistency and multiplicity of uses are realized. Such a coordinated effort will prevent waste of resources. Because every application has unique requirements, the linguistic technology must be capable of being tailored with a minimum of effort. A development group should be able to take the kernel of linguistic functions and superimpose application-dependent features. When the management of the linguistic effort is not centralized, it is not uncommon to have competition within internal company groups or even between internal groups and vendors hired by another branch of the same company. The divisiveness created by such improper management is demoralizing to the staff and inhibits the orderly development of company resources.

It is important for management to support a sustained, long-term linguistic effort and the standardization of linguistic technology. As was discussed earlier, linguistic projects require a lot of time; if the management is not willing to make a long-term commitment, the result is usually a product of small coverage and limited utility that cannot be upgraded. Long-term planning and standardization of the interfaces for the technology help to guide software and linguistic development toward tangible goals in a systematic way. Where appropriate, intermediate milestones may be established to provide accountability for the developers and to guarantee that the results of the project are in a usable form. Adequate planning and a sound base of software and linguistic data make it possible to delegate some portions of a project to subcontractors or to temporary staff.

Progress in linguistics traditionally has been slow, and there have not been any great breakthroughs to revolutionize the field. Nevertheless, there is a need for the staff to be well informed by participating in linguistic meetings and keeping abreast of new publications. Sometimes the progress in a peripheral field, such as computer hardware or a new programming language, can have a substantial impact on linguistics by making feasible previously impractical tasks. Meetings provide a good forum for the exchange of ideas and are a good source of new approaches, applications, and trends. Often, new commercial systems or their prototypes are demonstrated at technical meetings, and this enables one to evaluate competitive technology and measure it against one's own development efforts.

The following checklist provides some ideas for a manager to keep in mind.

- Develop a list of linguistic tasks to solve practical problems.
- Evaluate existing technology.
- Identify lexical and syntactic requirements of each problem.
- Determine whether simpler, nonlinguistic solutions are possible.
- Plan the activities for each area.
- Acquire relevant external technology and data bases.
- Encourage collaboration of groups with similar interests, including vendors, universities, and government agencies.
- Centralize linguistic efforts to develop standards where possible.
- Promote convergence of competing technologies.
- Encourage data sharing by groups working on related projects.
- Provide state-of-the-art technology for researchers.
- Hold information-exchange meetings periodically.
- Review new technology systematically for marketable ideas.
- Keep in mind the type of prevailing hardware in the marketplace.
- Get a broad base of users to test linguistic products.
- Work with government agencies toward the establishment of linguistic data bases that can serve as national resources.

REFERENCES

ARON, J. D. *The Program Development Process—The Programming Team, Part II,* Addison-Wesley Systems Programming Series, Reading, MA, 1983.

BRADY, M., and R. C. BERWICK, eds. *Computational Models of Discourse,* The MIT Press, Cambridge, MA, 1983.

CARROLL, J. B., P. DAVIES, and B. RICHMAN. *The American Heritage Word Frequency Book,* American Heritage Publishing Co., New York, 1971.

CHERRY, L. L. "PARTS—A System for Assigning Word Classes to English Text," Bell Laboratories Computing Science Technical Report No. 81, Bell Laboratories, Murray Hill, NJ, 1978.

DAHL, H. *Word Frequencies of Spoken American English,* Verbatim, Essex, CT, 1979.

DYER, M. G. *In-Depth Understanding. A Computer Model of Integrated Processing for Narrative Comprehension.* The MIT Press, Cambridge, MA, 1983.

FRANCIS, W. N., and H. KUCERA. *Frequency Analysis of English Usage: Lexicon and Grammar,* Houghton Mifflin Co., Boston, 1982.

GRIMES, J. "The Thread of Discourse," NSF Tech. Rep 1, Cornell University, Ithaca, New York, 1972.

HARRIS, L. R. "The ROBOT System: Natural Language Processing Applied to Database Query," Proceedings ACM 78 Annual Conference, 1978.

HEIDORN, G. E., K. JENSEN, L. A. MILLER, R. J. BYRD, and M. S. CHODOROW. "The EPISTLE Text-Critiquing System," *IBM Systems Journal,* 21, No. 3, 305–326, 1982.

JACKENDOFF, R. *Semantics and Cognition,* The MIT Press, Cambridge, MA, 1983.

KAMP, H. "A Theory of Truth and Semantic Representation," in J. A. G. Groendijk, T. M. V. Janssen, and M. B. J. Stokhof, eds., *Formal Methods in the Study of Language,* MC Tract 135, Amsterdam, p. 277, 1981.

KENDRIS, C. "Dictionary of 501 Spanish Verbs Fully Conjugated in all the Tenses," *Barron's Educational Series,* Woodbury, NY, 1971.

KUCERA, H. "Textual Database System Using Skeletonization and Phonetic Replacement to Retrieve Words Matching or Similar to Query Words," U. S. Patent No. 4,674,066, June 16, 1987.

MARCUS, M. P. *A Theory of Syntactic Recognition for Natural Language,* The MIT Press, Cambridge, MA, 1980.

MELLISH, C. S. *Computer Interpretation of Natural Language Descriptions,* Halsted Press, NY, 1985.

MINSKY, M. "A Framework for Representing Knowledge," in the Psychology of Computer Vision, P. Winston, ed., McGraw-Hill, New York, 1975.

PETERSON, J. L. "Computer Programs for Detecting and Correcting Spelling Errors," *Communications of the ACM,* 23(12), 676–687, 1980.

POLLOCK, J. J., and A. ZAMORA, "Automatic Abstracting Research at Chemical Abstracts Service," *Journal of Chemical Information and Computer Sciences,* 15(4), 226–232, 1975.

QUIRK, R., S. GREENBAUM, G. LEECH, and J. SVARTVIK. *A Comprehensive Grammar of the English Language,* Longman Group Ltd., 1985.

ROBINSON, J. J. "DIAGRAM: A Grammar for Dialogues," Comm. of the ACM 25, No. 1, 27–47, 1982.

RUSH, J. E., R. SALVADOR, and A. ZAMORA. "Automatic Abstracting and Indexing. Production of Indicative Abstracts by Application of Contextual Inference and Syntactic Coherence Criteria," *Journal of the American Society for Information Science,* 22(4), 260–274, 1971.

SAGER, N. *Natural Language Information Processing. A Computer Grammar of English and Its Applications,* Addison-Wesley Publishing Co., Reading, MA, 1981.

SCHANK, R. C. "Language and Memory," *Cognitive Science,* 4, 243–284, 1980.

SCHANK, R. C., and R. P. ABLESON. "Scripts, Plans, Goals, and Understanding," Lawrence Erlbaum, Hillsdale, NJ, 1977.

SIDNER, C. "Disambiguating References and Interpreting Sentence Purpose in Discourse," in *Artificial Intelligence: An MIT Perspective,* Volume 1, P. H. Winston and R. H. Brown, eds., The MIT Press, Cambridge, MA, 231–252, 1979.

SIMMONS, R. F. *Computations from the English.* Prentice-Hall, Englewood Cliffs, NJ, 1984.

———, "Semantic Networks: Their Computation and Use for Understanding English Sentences," CAI Lab Report NL-6, Computer Science Dept., The University of Texas, Austin, TX, 1972.

SOWA, J. F. *Conceptual Structures: Information Processing in Mind and Machine,* Addison-Wesley Publishing Co., Reading, MA, 1984.

WINOGRAD, T. *Language as a Cognitive Process.* Volume I: Syntax. Addison-Wesley Publishing Co., Reading, MA, 1983.

WOODS, W. A. "Transition Network Grammars for Natural Language Analysis," *Comm. of the ACM* 13(10), 591–606, 1970.

ZIPF, G. K. *Human Behaviour and the Principle of Least Effort,* Addison-Wesley, Reading, MA, 1949.

11

Strategies for Managers to Reduce Employee Fear When Introducing a New Technology

DEBORAH A. GLAZER, Independent Consultant
in Social and Organizational Behavior

TECHNOLOGY DEFINED

What is technology? Harvey (quoted in Champion, 1975) refers to technology as "the mechanisms or processes by which an organization turns out its product or services" (Champion, 1975, p. 101). Regardless of a company's size, shape, or composition, technology is a segment of all organizations (Champion, 1975). Inventions are a principal cause of technology.

An organization with any hope of remaining competitive in a rapidly changing society such as ours must constantly be prepared for continuously changing technologies and innovations. This is the key to advancement in productivity and, ultimately, the key to success. Realizing their important function in society, teachers are now insisting that students obtain at least a minimal knowledge of computers, in order to be prepared for the future job market (Gardner, 1981).

To exemplify the extent to which civilization has advanced technologically, Laird (1985) claims that of all the information taught in high schools today, only 25 percent of it was known and accepted in 1945. Furthermore, in 1960, 10,800 computers specifically used in companies existed in the United States, whereas in 1980, 10 million could be accounted for (Laird, 1985). According to *Careers Tomorrow,* such new technologies will affect more than 45 million jobs over the next 20 years. Such a phenomenon, however, is not without complications. Research available on the social effects of technology suggests that there is a likely connection between organizational structure change and technological change. Sultan and Prassow claim that "there are significant conceptualization obstacles to overcome" (Champion, 1975, p. 102). Such structure modifications include changes in spans of control, hierarchies, and job change or elimination.

FEAR OF CHANGE

Companies which use computers are composed of employees who have numerous fears and anxieties about using and learning about these new technologies. They are resistant to change for fear of losing their jobs, and they lack the motivation for taking the time and effort necessary to be trained.

The proper training of these employees is a vital role of management in these organizations. Some managers may feel that they do not want to invest in what they believe may be unnecessary training—that their employees will just "get the hang of" new equipment (Nadler, 1980). They feel that some changes are just not significant enough to warrant the expense. An example of why this is a poor idea occurred in a plastics plant, where machinery was used to draw plastic into certain shapes and a change needed to be made in the type of plastic used. Managers at the plant did not regard the change as significant enough to justify additional training, as the same equipment would be used with the new plastic; only a change in the material was made. During the first few days of the change, no problems occurred. The new plastic caused only a minor difference. Previously, sometimes a machine would have to be stopped when the material did not separate from the dye, a change that usually involved simple correction. The operator would contact the nearby mechanic who would then stop the machine and clear the dye. The process took about ten minutes. However, the new plastic caused one major problem, requiring that several machines stop at once. The mechanic could not service all the machines quickly enough, as different repair methods were necessary. The machine *operators* did not require training; however, the *mechanics* did, and this was a major oversight on the part of the managers (Nadler, 1980). A training program was hastily implemented that corrected the problem, and it needed to last only half an hour. Correcting the problem cost much more than the entire cost of training.

Not long ago, managers used an "adapt by fire and hire" policy (Pepper, 1982, p. 7). When a new technology or innovation was introduced, managers would retain employees who already knew how to use it, and would fire those who did not. They would even hire new employees with pertinent experience, instead of training existing ones.

ENHANCEMENTS TO LEARNING

Various methods exist for enhancing this often tedious process of training; many involve generating the proper level of motivation necessary to interest employees in learning these new technologies in order to attain higher levels of performance. One of the few reasons why such advancement in new technology has not spread more rapidly is that such changes cause widespread obsolescence among equipment. This reason, however, is rapidly decreasing in importance when weighed against the value of maintaining a competitive balance with other organizations (Galati, 1986).

The computer is a major new technology that allows for new avenues to communicate more efficiently. Its capacities for word processing, computer conferencing, and electronic mail will eventually replace many soon-to-be "reptiles," such as meetings, business calls, and standard correspondence (Galati, 1986). New laptop computers, while maintaining the efficiency of desktops, can fit into a briefcase and now weigh under thirteen pounds (Fletcher and Perry, 1986).

PROGRESS

Not long ago, progress in the business sector lagged far behind agriculture and manufacturing, which had invested $254,000 –$500,000 per worker in equipment, and a comparable increase in productivity. By comparison, only about $2,000 per employee was invested in the domain of management. This latter figure has recently jumped to $50 billion spent on new technology annually. In addition, International Data Corporation claims that business computer usage has increased 50 percent in merely two years (Fletcher and Perry, 1986). In an attempt to solve the problem of actually measuring the amounts of technological changes, Amber and Amber (quoted in Champion, 1975) have attempted to measure the "degree of automation" as "the degree to which first energy and then information are provided by machines rather than by man" (Champion, 1975, p. 102).

Modern businesses are rapidly learning that a computer is a major necessity for their successful and smooth operation (Lambert, 1986). This new technology supplies data for key decisions and enhances control. Although even a small computer represents a great monetary expense, the results outweigh the initial costs, producing significant savings in the long run. In fact, computers have much more potential than what they are currently used for; their use is often limited because of the small amount of computer knowledge of their users. This is why training is essential.

ADAPTABILITY AND ANXIETY

Before a new technology is introduced into an organization, managers must agree as to what should and should not be updated. They must also keep in mind that new methods and technologies will not make great progress if they are introduced insensitively (Pepper, 1984). It is vital that the proper training needs be established.

Another important arena where change occurs rapidly is in sales. When a company's products are updated, the salespeople must be fully briefed as to the capabilities of the new products in order to adequately inform customers. Thus, their training should be continuous. However, since salespeople are frequently on the road and have little time to spare for training, training can be a problem. One company came up with the ingenious idea of providing its salespeople with training cassette tapes to play as they travel (Nadler, 1980).

A main issue to deal with is that of adaptability in the working environment—the ability to successfully cope with changes. Adaptation must occur whenever a new technology is introduced; employees must be trained and retrained. Some individuals may react only to specific types of equipment or tasks. Frequently there are also the changes resulting from promotions or transfers, as well (Pepper, 1984). This involves changes in knowledge and skills, number of employee hours, time, and money. Individual limits must be realized in order to develop appropriate expectations for ability to adapt. These limits are determined by many variables, such as emotions, intelligence, and personal background.

Women are being especially affected by computers (Rogers, 1986). Cambre and Cook (1987) claim that both gender and age are related in some way to computer anxiety, particularly among college students. More research is necessary before generalizations can be applied to the general adult population; however, similar findings are likely. According to Rogers (1986), far fewer women are learning about computers than their male counterparts, thus decreasing the chances for women to achieve status and salary equal to that of male employees. Rogers discovered, in a recent survey, that females composed merely one-quarter of computer camp enrollees out of twenty-three such camps; one-seventh of the enrollees of advanced classes; and one-twentieth of the other advanced classes (Rogers, 1986). A racial difference is also noted in results of computer tests; white test-takers score higher than other races, with the exception of Asian-American students. Also noteworthy is the finding that Asian-American females score higher than white males. Rogers suggests that efforts should begin at the high school level to promote equality in this area, particularly through using computers to teach some of the classes, thus making computer interaction difficult to avoid.

Another possible individual difference related to use of computers is aptitude. Adams and co-workers (1987) found that students with higher aptitude make more effective use of computers, specifically when using them for computer-assisted instruction (CAI), than those students characterized by a low aptitude. The researchers claim that the type of subject matter being taught via the computer is an additional factor. Also, many students' interest in learning computers is dependent upon how important their teachers perceive computers to be (Reed, 1986). For example, if teachers do not value and use computers that are available in the schools, then more computers will not be purchased for the schools' use later on.

One reason some individuals are hesitant to learn about computers is that they believe that if they are not programmers, they will not be able to use the system. They also tend to believe that much more time is involved in the computer-training process than is actually the case. Others fear losing valuable information through the touch of a wrong button or a glitch in the system (Galati, 1986).

Other employees resist learning computers for different reasons. For example, those in upper management often feel that it is below them to operate a computer—that "menial" work should be saved for their secretaries. Such executives may resist because they lack typing skills. Others find it difficult to adjust to computer composition instead of using dictation (Galati, 1986).

Employees who are older than the average age of workers in the work force are particularly prone to anxiety about learning new technologies. Donald Rogers (Smith, 1982) believes that such fear of learning is taught in the schools early in life. A description of such anxiety by Carlos' Castaneda's Don Juan appears to be quite accurate:

> A man goes to knowledge...as he goes to war, wide awake, with fear...He slowly begins to learn—bit by bit at first, then in big chunks. His thoughts soon clash. What he learns is never what he pictured, or imagined, and so he begins to be afraid...Every step of learning is a new task, and the fear begins to mount...Fear! A terrible enemy—treacherous and difficult to overcome (Smith, 1982, p. 46).

A very good reason to try to reduce such anxiety levels, according to McKinley (Smith, 1982), is that anxiety acts as a distraction to learning; much more information can be retained in a more relaxed state. Such uneasiness could stem from fears of being compared to other co-workers, and being found deficient in intelligence. Even the late Abraham Maslow spoke of "the need to know and the fear of knowing" (Smith, 1982, p. 89), caused by fears of inadequacy. There are numerous causes for such a problem, and attempts need to be made to minimize them.

Frequently, support staff fear losing their jobs upon the introduction of more advanced equipment (Galati, 1986). They wonder what they will do if they are not typing on a typewriter. Management must redefine their expectations of support staff to help their workers retain confidence in job security. It must be made clear that they will be expected to have greater responsibilities, including editing, performing graphics tasks, and manipulating data bases (Strohmer, 1987). Such redefinitions of roles and assignment of increased responsibilities should motivate support staff to become more interested in their work. Additionally, this usually means increased compensation. Any fears of ability to perform should be diminished through appropriate training programs.

Some employees have been known to display severe characteristics of so-called computer anxiety, as illustrated by responses on self-report instruments or measured by physiological changes (Cambre and Cook, 1987). Emotional reactions such as apprehension, a distrust of technology, a feeling of personal threat, and fear have all been displayed. These reactions can be initiated through attempts to use a computer or merely the thought of it. According to Spielberger (Cambre and Cook, 1987), however, anxiety is more a temporary state than a permanent one; this is beneficial because a temporary state is more apt to be altered. Powers, Raub, Jordan, and Stroup (Cambre and Cook, 1987) claim that computer anxiety can be decreased by mere exposure to a computer; once the employee is shown some basics of computer functioning, he or she witnesses its simplicity and becomes familiar with it.

Attitude is basically the root of whether or not an employee accepts or resists new technologies. Gardiner (1980) claims that attitude influences behavior, so the latter can be altered by changing the former. Thus it is vital that positive attitudes toward innovation be reinforced in order to create wider acceptance of new technologies.

Gardiner (1980) describes ten common reasons why individuals have negative attitudes toward new technologies. The first reason is *obsolescence* ("The technology may replace me"). As equipment becomes more and more advanced, increasing numbers of jobs may be threatened by replacement by such machines. Of course, on the positive side of this, innovations also create new jobs. For example, there is currently a high demand for computer programmers, and positions in new types of disciplines are evolving, such as in human engineering, cybernetics, robotics, and bionics (Gardiner, 1980). Of course, training is important here, as many employees may otherwise not qualify for such positions. In addition, numerous conventional positions can be transformed or upgraded into jobs that involve a person-machine interface. For instance, a librarian can become an intermediary between data terminals and library users; secretaries can become go-betweens for managers and word processors (Gardiner, 1980).

Gardiner's second reason for negative feelings toward new technologies is *exploitation* ("The technology may be used to exploit me"). There is always the potential for any technology that processes information to be used by someone to exploit another person or organization. This can possibly cause a monopoly on information; however, information is usually only available on-line, meaning that the information is classified, available only to those who can afford the expense of an electronic data terminal.

A third reason for negative attitudes toward new technologies is *privacy* ("The technology may be used to invade my privacy"). This is a legitimate reason in that an increased amount of information is now available to a larger number of people through the use of computers. Individuals fear the loss of their right to decide upon their preferred level of privacy.

Technophobia ("The technology is vaguely threatening") is the fourth reason. This means that many individuals have a conscious or an unconscious fear of machines; many people do not even know why they possess such a feeling. Attempts to analyze this phenomenon have occurred through research on a similar fear, math phobia (Gardiner, 1981). Learning math is a function of attitude more than level of intelligence. Such a fear, similar to that of computers, causes the exclusion of many individuals, particularly females, from higher level professions.

Similar to technophobia and math phobia is *neophobia*, an unjustifiable fear of new things or of change, which could actually be an umbrella to the two aforementioned types of fears. This underlies the idea that the unknown is often a cause for apprehension and curiosity. Thus, many individuals fear computers because they fall into the same category as the unknown, which is a cause for uneasiness.

Champion (Cambre and Cook, 1987) offers additional causes for barriers to change, such as the notion that changes may affect employee relationships. Some individuals may be transferred away from their current co-workers, who have become their friends. Others dislike the idea of having to undergo further training. Those of a higher status may fear a lowering of their perceived level of authority. Others, however, may appear to gain prestige or advancement from such changes. To overcome this fear, or at least to diminish it, managers should attempt to involve their employees in as much of the decision making as possible when the time comes to consider a potential addition or innovation to the working environment. Management should also allow for plenty of advanced notice when such changes occur so that employees will have time to get used to the idea and learn about it and its future effects upon the environment. Champion (Cambre and Cook, 1987) even encourages the idea of the innovation occurring in small steps or phases, so as to avoid feelings of being overwhelmed.

Gardiner refers to his fifth reason as *technophilia* ("The technology may involve me too deeply"). This reason has a slightly different perspective. Technophilia, or the love of machines, is characterized by those who fear that once they are exposed to the new technology, they will never leave it since they will enjoy using it so much. Gardiner compares this occurrence to drug addiction. This is likely to be where the expression "computer nerd" was derived, "one who talks, lives, and breathes computers."

A sixth reason why individuals display resistance to innovation is *dependence* ("The technology may become a 'crutch' "). This is not dissimilar to the previously mentioned technophilia, except that in this case, the idea is more that one can become dependent on the technology as a need, rather than continued use from mere enjoyment. An appropriate analogy would be any other modern technology that has evolved over the years, such as a dishwasher or an automobile. These inventions greatly reduce time and effort. However, at times, dependence on them can be negative, such as when one drives a car to go half a block, or when an unmarried person uses a dishwasher to avoid washing a dish by hand. A computer could be abused in this sense to perform a simple math problem, allowing the brain to become lazy. Others (Gardiner, 1980) argue that the brain should not have to be "cluttered" with such unnecessary content when it can easily be stored in computers and diskettes.

Overload ("The technology may generate too much information") is a seventh reason people reject new technologies. The basic idea here is that society is receiving more information than it knows what to do with. In other words, input must equal output, and this is not so. However, instead of reducing amounts of information, the skill of being selective in choosing certain valuable portions of the available information is becoming important. Individuals need to learn how and what to choose to get the most use out of this thrust of information.

Gardiner's eighth reason for resistance, *informediation* ("The technology may depersonalize me"), describes the fear of becoming depersonalized when a machine intervenes between what used to be communication between people. For example, two people talking on the telephone, or more so the intervention of a telephone answering machine, becomes more impersonal than a face-to-face conversation. Some fear that this effect will worsen further with increasing new technologies.

Media-as-Message ("The technology may change me") is the ninth reason, which is characterized by the fear of dehumanization. Anthropological evidence shows how those living in a media-saturated environment may prove to vary extensively from those living in more innate or lifelike surroundings. Thompson (Gardiner, 1980) claims that the former is no longer nature—just information. Gardiner (1980) thus suggests adapting to the advent of technology by developing attitudes to adjust appropriately to rapid increase in new technologies, so that we do not become "poor imitations of the mechanisms we have created," but rather "fine examples of realized human potential."

Gardiner's tenth reason for the resistance of new technologies is *opportunity cost* ("The technology may take too much time"). Some resist new technologies solely on the basis that they are surrounded by so many time-saving devices that they do not have time to use them, let alone learn them. To help guard against this attitude, training must be made very concise, easy, and enjoyable.

People must be persuaded that they will save money in the long run by investing in the new technology. They must also be convinced that something similar was not previously on the market, in order to diminish the belief that an equivalent technology may have already been in existence, creating the possibility that the new technology might not be worthwhile.

Gardiner's ten reasons for barriers to change cover a lot of ground. However, even more reasons exist. For example, certain employees who do only borderline performance on their current job display deep concern about attempting any new type of task for fear of failure to display satisfactory performance, possibly leading to their unemployment.

FACTORS AFFECTING ADAPTABILITY

Cytrynbaum, Lee, and Wadner (Wedman and Strathe, 1985) describe another variable affecting the ability to adapt to new technologies, as the particular life stage that the person is currently in. They recognize three separate stages. The first is the *early entry and career stabilization stage,* in which an individual attempts to find a particular niche within the environment and strives to achieve his or her desired position. The second stage, involving less of an interest in change, is the *midlife development stage.* Here one's needs are geared more toward the personal spectrum over that of the organizational. Professional security is important here, causing resistance to change. The third and final stage, the *senior life change,* is characterized by a preparation for retirement. Here, one's needs are focused upon support of institutional change, as well as an active involvement in participation towards the institution's goals. These stages are helpful in recognizing reasons for resistance to change by various individuals. Hall and co-workers (Wedman and Strathe, 1985, p. 17) have proceeded a step further by developing the Faculty Development in Technology (FDT) Model, which addresses individual faculty members' development needs in relation to computer technology. The three dimensions along which this model is organized are as follows:

1. the *concerns dimension,* characterized by the concerns that the individual has about the change or innovation, which is computer technology in this instance;

2. the *faculty context dimension,* where the major contexts in which a faculty member may use a computer technology are described;

3. the *organizational dimension,* involving the different levels of organizational structure where faculty development interventions can be identified.

Within the concerns dimension are four levels through which an employee advances while experiencing an innovation. The first level, *information concerns,* is characterized by the individual who is new to, in this case, computers, being "curious, but cautious about computer technology, preferring to view computers in a noncommittal fashion." Level 2, *exploration concerns,* involves those who are exploring computer applications that are of personal interest. Level 3, *utilization concerns,* describes those who are interested in directing a computer project and concern themselves with the project's effect upon others. Finally, level 4, *collaboration and innovation concerns,* characterizes individuals who have an interest in developing and sharing new applications of computer technology.

The context dimension is also characterized by four contexts in which a faculty member may experience computer technology, as follows:

1. *instructional context,* which involves the use of computer technology in the instructional process as a tool;

2. *creative context,* where computer technology is used creatively, such as in publishing and research, and as an object of study;

3. *management context,* is characterized by the involvement of computer technology in activities using information processing, such as scheduling and advising;

4. *personal context,* in which computer technology is used where it is not directly related to professional activities. Recreation and personal finance are examples of this.

The third dimension of the FDT model, the organizational dimension, contains four components. *Individual level* is the first one, which stresses the significance of each faculty member's individual needs in connection to computer related tasks. Level 2 is *group level,* indicating the idea that faculty members usually fluctuate between individual and group settings, the groups serving as a way of communicating with several individuals within a given context. Level 3 is *department/school level,* in which, as the first formal level of this dimension, departments and schools dispense resources and rewards necessary for faculty activities. The results of the development effort are dependent upon how support for computer-related faculty participation is perceived. The last level of the organizational dimension, level 4, the *college/university level,* is actually the main means for support of developmental activities. The college or university sets the tone for the development effort, thus illustrating that college or university faculty are involved with profitable actions.

These three main dimensions can effectively be used as a support structure for faculty who are attempting to include computer technology into their professional and personal lives.

In effect, many organizations are creating their own training and development departments to accommodate such multiplying training needs. With the advent of so many new technologies in companies today, employees who were formerly top-notch performers quickly become unable to perform their jobs properly. The proper training is necessary to help employees perform their jobs correctly for their own satisfaction, as well as for that of the company. Such training and development departments consist of training and development officers who assist managers of given departments within organizations to solve such employee performance problems (Laird, 1985). These specialists begin their training plan by collecting information on who needs the training, what type of training is needed, and why it is needed (Rogoff, 1987).

It is wise for any trainer to determine the composition of the target audience in advance. It is helpful to know, for instance, whether some of the employees hold engineering degrees or have had extensive job experience (Rogoff, 1987). These are necessary to know so that the subject matter may be altered accordingly. The size of the group should also be determined ahead of time, as this can also cause variance in the manner and type of training used. Separate training groups may be warranted. Another important component in the training process involves the ability to integrate the new knowledge into existing job functions (Rogoff, 1987). It is one thing to be able to use a new tool; it is another to be able to effectively incorporate the new ability into the current job duties. This could mean the difference between teaching robots to perform a skill without understanding the reasons for doing it, and training intelligent employees to learn certain skills in addition to understanding the accompanying concepts to comprehend what they are doing (Rogoff, 1987). This is where on-the-job training can be very beneficial; employees are able to immediately and directly apply their newly acquired knowledge to their specific tasks.

SOLUTIONS

Champion (Hoole et al., 1981) has studied the effects of informal groups as a means for reducing anxiety from changes or additions in the work environment. One bank that implemented a new electronic data processing (EDP) system exemplifies this effect (Champion, 1975). There had apparently been a discrepancy between what managers remembered informing the employees and what information had actually been disseminated. The employees had initially been informed of the change through informal "grapevine" groups before they were formally informed through supervisors. Not until later did management make such a formal announcement about the acquisition of the new EDP system as well as the date it would be installed. This announcement, of course, created various questions from employees as to whose jobs would be affected. Orientation meetings were set up in phases; during one of them it was announced that no one would lose his or her job. Films were also shown that displayed the process of an EDP installation at other companies around the nation. Still, in spite of this seemingly satisfactory dissemination of information, there were mixed feelings about the addition. Employees still did not feel assured about what their jobs would entail, and negative reactions were becoming widespread. They disliked the new system and also claimed that they were not being kept adequately informed about what was occurring. Some claimed to be informed about some job changes only five minutes in advance and that adequate time to allow for training was not available.

This case exemplifies how receiving differing amounts and types of information about a change can affect reactions and behaviors. The informal group apparently was more involved with reducing anxieties about the EDP system than was management. Of course, merely receiving such information does not necessarily automatically reduce apprehension; it can also worsen it, as informal groups may also spread incorrect information. Thus, two important factors here are the degree to which the information is threatening, such as causing job changes, as well as the level of accuracy involved. Some companies publish monthly newsletters for employees in all their branches. This is a beneficial way of maintaining open communication and keeping everyone informed in advance of any upcoming changes (Champion, 1975).

A good way for managers to begin training is to identify the new technology itself and provide descriptions for the materials and equipment involved (Gardner, 1981). Each step required in the proper operation of the equipment should be elaborated upon as necessary; however, this should not be drawn out to the point of causing boredom or frustration. If these initial phases provide the proper meaning and concept to the trainees, then learning how to operate the machine will be less tedious and easier to comprehend. Lambert (1986) refers to this as "focused learning."

Following this should be a description of how the employee will use and apply it to his or her particular job. This will display a logical connection and purpose between the new technology and the actual job tasks (Gardner, 1981). The main goals of the trainer are to reduce the employees' anxiety with regard to the innovation and to train them so that they will attain optimal job performance.

A successful trainer will comprehend and bear in mind principles of applied learning. Lambert (1986) defines learning as "knowledge gained through observation and study, resulting in a modification of attitude or behavior" (36). Learning should also be a continuous process, as new job tasks in relation to new innovations will always be occurring. Trainers must also realize that individuals learn at different rates, depending upon age, level of education, level of experience, and personality variables.

Following any training process, it is vital for the individual to practice on the job in order to retain the newly acquired knowledge and skills and to avoid forgetting what has been learned. Additionally important, a common oversight may be for the trainee's work to pile up during the training process. Provisions should be made for maintaining the continued work flow during this time. It has not been uncommon for the trainee to return to work to find that he or she must work extensive hours to catch up; this extra time requirement can be perceived as a penalty for attending the training class. At times, this cannot be avoided; however, steps toward its prevention will reduce existing stress to the employee who is being trained against his or her will. Management should offer as much support as possible to enhance these transitions.

The ideal size of a training staff should be determined by the budget, training expectations, management priorities, the perceived value of training by management, the size of the organization, and the size of its groups to be trained (Lambert, 1986). Good planning is an essential step in this decision. Current programs must be reviewed, and new programs must be implemented as necessary. A thorough planning department will consist of a program designer to determine course content and objectives; a task analyst to determine which skills are needed to perform certain tasks; an instructional writer, who prepares and coordinates all the training materials to be used; and a media specialist to suggest or acquire certain audio-visual software to enhance program content.

After carrying out appropriate courses in the correct manner, program evaluation should be implemented to measure the quality and effectiveness of the training. This should be done through feedback from the trainees, and they should offer recommendations for future program improvement. In this manner, the program can be enhanced each time it is offered. Laird (1985) emphasizes participative learning in order to achieve effective absorption of information. He feels that if individuals actually experience rather than merely listen, they will absorb and retain more information, and it will be more meaningful. B. F. Skinner (Laird, 1985) agrees: "To acquire behavior, the student must engage in behavior" (p. 29). Also in agreement is Carl Rogers (Laird, 1985): "Learning is facilitated when the learner participates responsibly in the learning process...Significant learning is acquired through doing" (p. 29).

Motivation is also important to include in the training process. In one major high-tech manufacturing corporation, a new data processing system was to be added to three different departments, which incidentally contained three different types of groups (Rogoff, 1987). Employees in one department had no computer skills and high computer anxiety, and this department was to be the one to use the new system the most. Those in the other two departments already possessed appropriate skills to use systems similar to the new one, and they were looking forward to using the new system. Motivation to learn the new system in the first department was quite low. These employees were not even forewarned about the acquisition of the new system, and they were supposed to learn entirely new tasks in addition. Meanwhile, employees from the other two departments who were used to controlling all the data entry were hesitant about having inexperienced employees assume this responsibility. To increase the motivation of these employees, the system's benefits had to be explained very carefully and put forth as a benefit to all who were involved. Everyone had to be made aware of what each person's responsibilities were, and everyone had to be made to feel that they were a single team attempting to achieve the same goal.

Mayer (1981) theorizes that "meaningful learning" must occur in order for knowledge to be absorbed. According to Bran (Rogers, 1986), this type of learning is a process in which an individual understands a relationship between new knowledge and that which is already present in the memory, called a schema. Such a relationship is referred to as assimilation (Mayer, 1981). What Mayer emphasizes is the ability of the individual to apply what he or she learns to new situations; this proves that he or she truly has learned the information. This phenomenon is compared to rote learning, in which material is merely memorized, not actually absorbed. The use of concrete models is recommended to achieve better absorption of information. Word problems commonly used in teaching elementary math exemplify this, such as adding and subtracting oranges and apples instead of abstract numbers. du Boulay (Mayer, 1981) offers additional suggestions for teaching computer operation. One is the idea of simplicity; the computer operation should be explained in a manner that describes the simple interaction of just a small number of parts in an easily comprehensible manner. Second is the idea of visibility—that the trainees should be able to see certain parts and functions of the system during operation. Mayer (1981) suggests an additional method of effective learning, which he refers to as elaboration. In this sense, the individual is encouraged to explain in his or her own words what has just been learned. This is similar to applying this new knowledge to other new situations. Here, if one relates the new knowledge to other familiar ideas, it shows that he or she does have the ability to comprehend and work with the new concept.

On the lighter side of easing the training process for new technologies, humor can make or break a training course. Strohmer (1987) emphasizes that individuals are able to learn at a higher rate when the stress level is minimal, and Jalongo (Strohmer, 1987) suggests that humor aids in decreasing stress. Humor helps to motivate the individual to maintain a positive attitude toward training, and Colwell (Strohmer, 1987) adds that it also causes the trainer who makes the jokes to present himself with a more positive appearance. In addition, humor can serve as a context with which to store information, in that it provides a "memory hook," according to Colwell (Strohmer, 1987). For example, if a fact is taught about a specific computer operation and the fact is delivered simultaneously with a joke, the two ideas are stored in a trainee's memory together. Upon future retrieval of the information, the joke will be remembered easily, and the accompanying fact will automatically be remembered.

A trainer should, however, add humor in a carefully planned manner. Since the trainee is most attentive at the beginning of a class, this time should be wisely used to teach valuable information, with the possible exception of some minimal humor. More amusing jokes should be reserved for later, when fatigue begins to set in, or else following the delivery of a difficult concept (Strohmer, 1987). Wakshlay and co-workers (Strohmer, 1987) recommend distributing short, evenly spaced humor throughout the lesson, as opposed to longer, less frequent humor. This is suggested in an effort to maintain rapport, participation, and attention, remembering to end the program by summing up what has been taught, and not with a joke, since the end is what trainees will remember. It is also advisable, if possible, to use humor that relates in some manner to the content being presented, so as not to cause distractions.

In a similar fashion, the use of games as a training tool has become both popular and effective. Laird (1985) suggests the use of computer games to add fun and excitement to what can often be dull learning. The fact that the trainee receives points or rewards from the computer for each correct answer serves as immediate gratification and thus retains his or her interest in the subject matter as a result of a high level of motivation to learn. A good resource for such games is *The Guide To Simulations/Games for Education* (Laird, 1985), in which can be found more than 400 pages of descriptions of commercial games commonly used as tools for training and development specialists. Games are also beneficial in the development of spontaneity skills in addition to others.

Company G, a medium-sized accounting firm, was able to make effective use of computer games in its training process. Initially, the three main users of the new computer attended a training session at the computer company. They were the only three trainees in the session, so the training was very personalized. Sharing one computer terminal, the three were able to work together in a cohesive group, assisting one another to achieve the goals set by the instructor. This course was continued on-site at the accounting office by the same instructor. The first thing she did there was to give the trainees computer games to play, which achieved several purposes. First, it provided the trainees with a feeling of comfort with the keyboard, helping them realize that touching an incorrect key would not destroy any data. Second, they acquired ease in handling and loading diskettes as well as how to turn the machine on and off. One of the games involved printing out graphic pictures, which enabled the employees to learn to use the printer. This situation exemplifies how certain types of training can ease computer anxiety and be fun while motivating employees to learn a new technology.

Another effective motivator is positive reinforcement. When appropriately applied, this can increase the amount and quality of learning that occurs. This can be achieved in numerous ways. One trainer attempted to maintain a very nonthreatening environment, then even gave out certificates on the last day of the course (Cambre and Cook, 1987). This should also be carried from the training process all the way to when the employee is actually working on the job. This can be done in many ways—verbally, monetarily, through assignment of increased responsibilities, and so on.

Another aid in the enhancement of the computer training process is through computer-assisted instruction (CAI). This system has proven to be quite effective and non-anxiety provoking, as it is a self-paced program and does not have preconceived ideas about a trainee, as might a human instructor. A series of learning segments is displayed on the computer, and the trainee makes responses accordingly (Nadler, 1982). The computer, through the CAI software, then provides appropriate feedback, and no one but the trainee knows how many errors have been made. According to some researchers (Reed, 1986), those learners who are not as gifted particularly benefit from CAI, probably for this reason.

Along the same lines is programmed instruction (PI), involving teaching machines and textbooks. This type of system operates in much the same manner as CAI in that it is self-paced and discrete with regard to visualizing errors to responses. Because cognizant trainees can move along quickly and inexperienced ones can move slowly and not hold up the others, trainer time is saved considerably. All PI programs have been tested so that every trainee should get about 95 percent of the responses correct (Bass and Barrett, 1981). Another advantage to this method of learning is that trainees are active, as opposed to passive, learners. Motivation to learn is high in this situation, mainly because of immediate feedback and because of the system's discretion and nonthreatening manner. No reprimands are given for errors. Information is disseminated in such a manner that simpler material is at the beginning phases and more difficult material is introduced step by step. Trainees redo each incorrect response until it is correct.

Company I performed a study in which forty-two employees took the regular training course, while seventy others used programmed texts. Results showed that those in the latter group acquired 90 percent mastery in nineteen hours. The group that took the regular class acquired only 45 percent mastery in a fifteen-hour period (Bass and Barrett, 1981). Thus, even though some individuals missed a human trainer and the classroom atmosphere, PI was still preferable by 87 percent of the trainees, and was more effective. It should also be noted, however, that the initial programming for PI involves much time and effort but should later prove to be well worth the effort.

Company D discovered a simplified manner in which to train its employees to learn AI. Peacock-Gillooly refers to this process as "eliminating the magic" (Dunkerly, 1987). She accomplishes straightforward training through direct experience through the use of models to which individuals can relate. Also used in attempts to ease what can be a complicated and tedious training process are videos, demonstrations, and lectures. All of these training methods are used to accomplish the goal of providing means for interest and for effective learning. During part of this process, each trainee learns at his or her own computer terminal, repeating what is shown by a trainer, step by step. Minimal time is invested in the entire training process—usually only about four days. After successful training of the basics, a follow-up class is then held to teach knowledge engineering, and a help line and consultations are available when needed. Such training techniques described here have proven quite effective at this company, and transference to other settings is recommended for trial.

All the techniques mentioned thus far can be carried out either on the job or at the site of the company that is installing the equipment. The former is usually the most popular method used, especially in smaller organizations (Bass and Barrett, 1981). An advantage of such training is that employees can still earn their salary while they are being trained, and can also be productive. In addition, they learn on the same equipment that they will be using after the end of training. There are also disadvantages to this method. The training process may tend to be disorganized, too casual, and not thorough enough. In addition, production on the job is usually given more attention than the training, and the pace is often more hectic than a setting used only for training. The instructor is also usually not a professional trainer.

I was an employee in "Company T," where I initially received on-the-job training, followed by formal training at the corporate training center, which was not added until a few months later. Initially, someone worked with me on a one-to-one basis in a conference room for a few days. This was quite effective. However, the following week, my training was switched to a small branch office that was extremely hectic. Production was prioritized over training, causing high anxiety and slower learning. Actually, some of the learning did come faster through this method, but it was through trial and error, which was not always beneficial to the company, since dealing directly with customers was a large facet of the position. Other segments of this position were learned through observation of other co-workers, which was effective.

The formal training at the corporate office a few months later was good; however, it was partially a review and correction of errors found in job performance, as well as formal presentations, with class participation encouraged, and a higher level of training, geared toward the next level of employment within the company. The classes were small but very formal and high pressured. Participation was mandatory, and evaluations of each employee were sent back to supervisors and placed in permanent records. The trainers included high-level executives from the corporate office. Professional dress was required during these sessions, which lasted for very long durations each of the three to five days. A break from the pressure did not occur during meals, as we all ate together, sometimes all three of the daily meals. My anxiety level was so elevated that I was usually unable to eat much at these so-called breaks.

Another source of training comes from the vendor supplying the new equipment. For example, when I worked at "Company F," the manager purchased a new word processor. The manager in turn sent me right to the vendor's training center to properly learn the correct skills for using the equipment. I found this to be a very worthwhile method; what better teacher could there be than the original manufacturers of the equipment?

Bass (Bass and Barrett, 1981) encourages the use of teaching aids such as videotapes, films, and slides, even though these tend to be costly. They tend to save money in the long run, however. Error rates in employee performance have been found to decrease significantly with the use of films because they can actually observe the job being carried out by other employees. Such aids are even more effective when accompanied by classroom discussion and act as worthwhile substitutes when professional trainers are unavailable.

Gardiner (1980) suggests the possibility of distributing questionnaires to employees to do some consciousness-raising, such as asking them to estimate the number of machines that are in their homes. This is effective, as most people underestimate the number; this sparks an awareness that we use a lot more machines than we realize in everyday life.

Robert Smith (1982) presents six optimum conditions for an employee's learning, which are as follows:

1. they feel the need to learn and have input into what, why, and how they will learn;
2. learning's content and processes bear a perceived and meaningful relationship to past experience and experience is effectively utilized as a resource for learning;
3. what is to be learned relates optimally to the individual's developmental changes and life tasks;
4. the amount of autonomy exercised by the learner is congruent with that required by the mode or method utilized;
5. they learn in a climate that minimizes anxiety and encourages freedom to experiment;
6. their learning styles are taken into account (p. 47).

CONCLUSIONS

All of these means for more effective training techniques in efforts to decrease employee anxiety in the learning of new technologies are beneficial. Some are more helpful in particular environments than others—hence, the benefit of having access to a variety of methods and solutions. Before we know it, these new innovations and ideas will be the antiques of the future. Such technological progress is inevitable, as all organizations and employees must advance and adapt with time if they are to succeed.

Managers need to switch their ways of thinking to prioritize and strongly consider human needs and fears (Miner, 1982) through one or more of these methods. For the most part, such solutions will well be worth any initial investment of time and money, in an effort to enhance the advancement and success of modern organizations.

REFERENCES

ADAMS, T. M., P. B. WALDROP, J. E. JUSTEN, II, and C. H. MCCROSKY, "Aptitude-Treatment Interaction in Computer-Assisted Instruction," *Educational Technology,* Vol. 27, No. 12, 1987.

BASS, B. M., and G. V. BARRETT. *People, Work, and Organizations.* Allyn & Bacon, Inc., Boston, 1981.

CAMBRE, M. A., and D. L. COOK. "Measurement and Remediation of Computer Anxiety," *Educational Technology,* Vol. 27, No. 12, 1987.

CHAMPION, D. J. *The Sociology of Organizations,* McGraw-Hill Book Co., New York, 1975.

DUNKERLEY, J. "Secret to AI Training: Start Simple," *Applied Artificial Intelligence Reporter,* Vol. 6, 1987.

FLETCHER, C., and T. PERRY. "Why Future-Friendly Thinking is a Must," *Working Woman,* Vol. 11, 1986.

GALATI, T. "Electronic Communication; Implications for Training," *Training and Development Journal,* Vol. 40, No. 10, 1986.

GARDINER, W. L. *Public Acceptance of the New Information Technologies: The Role of Attitudes,* Information Society Project, Gamma, Université de Montreal, McGill University, Montreal, Canada, Paper No., I-9, 1980.

GARDNER, J. E. *Training Interventions in Job-Skill Development,* Addison-Wesley Publishing Company, Reading, MA, 1981.

HOOLE, F. W., R. L. FRIEDHEIM, and T. M. HENNESSEY, eds. *Making Ocean Policy: The Politics of Government Organization and Management,* Westview Press, Inc., Boulder, CO, 1981 (Chap. 4, "Organizing for Marine Policy: Some Views from Organization Theory," Stuart A. Ross).

LAIRD, D. *Approaches to Training and Development,* Addison-Wesley Publishing Co., Inc., Reading, MA, 1985.

LAMBERT, C. *Secrets of a Successful Trainer: A Simplified Guide for Survival,* John Wiley & Sons, Inc., New York, 1986.

MAYER, R. E. "The Psychology of How Novices Learn Computer Programming," *Computing Surveys,* Vol. 13, No. 1, 1981.

MINER, J. B. *Theories of Organizational Structure and Process,* The Dryden Press, New York, 1982.

NADLER, L. *Corporate Human Resources Development: A Management Tool,* Van Nostrand Reinhold, New York, 1980.

———. *Designing Training Programs,* Addison-Wesley Publishing Co., Reading, MA, 1982.

PEPPER, A. D. *Managing the Training and Development Function,* Gower Publishing Company, Ltd., Aldershot, Hants, England, 1984.

REED, W. M. "Teachers' Attitudes Toward Educational Computing: Instructional Uses, Misuses, and Needed Improvements," *Computers in the Schools,* Vol. 3, No. 2, 1986.

ROGERS, E. M. "High-Tech Threats to Sexual Equality," *USA Today,* Vol. 115, 1986.

ROGOFF, R. L. *The Training Wheel,* John Wiley & Sons, New York, 1987.

SMITH, R. M. *Learning How to Learn: Applied Theory for Adults,* Follett Publishing Co., Chicago, 1982.

STROHMER, J. C. "ITV Design: Leave Them Laughing?" *Educational Technology,* Vol. 27, No. 12, 1987.

WEDMAN, J., and M. STRATHE. "Faculty Development in Technology: A Model for Higher Education," *Educational Technology,* Vol. 25, No. 2, 1985.

INDEX

A

ADL, 10
ADS. (*see* Application Development System)
Aetna Life & Casualty, 8
AI and:
   Lisp machine makers, 2
   MIS, 14. (*see also* AIC and AION)
   Wall Street, 11. (*see also* Business)
AIC. (*see* Artificial Intelligence Corp.)
AION, 15. (*see also* IBM)
American Cimflex and Teknowledge, 89
American Express, authorizer's assistant, 97

American Management Systems, Inc., 53
Amoco, 8, 9
   and Intellicorp, 82
AMS. (*see* American Management Systems)
Analysis. (*see* Methodology)
APEX. (*see* Applied Expert Systems, Inc.)
Apple Computer, 16
   MAC II and Lisp, 86
Application Development System, 140
Applied Expert Systems, Inc., 2, 146
ART, 5, 15. (*see also* Inference Corp.)
Arthur Anderson, 10
Arthur D. Little, Inc. (*see* ADL)

Artificial Intelligence. (*see* AI)
Artificial Intelligence Corp., 15
  (vs. ADS and ESE, 140)
  KBMS development consortium, 142
  Knowledge Base Management System, 139
  Intellect, 139
  Southern California Edison, 144
  Transamerica Insurance Group, 143
Automated Reasoning Tool. (*see* ART)

B

Bachman Systems, 16
BBN. (*see* Bolt, Beranek & Newman, Inc.,)
Boeing, 6, 7
Bolt, Beranek & Newman, Inc.,7
Business. (*see also* Experts; Knowledge
    engineering)
  adaptability of employees, 196
  AI and core business, 12, 96, 100
  AI Corp. product strategy, 139–41
  contracting, 131–33
  cost/benefit, 101, 115
  expertise as a resource, 29, 94
  funding consortium for KBMS, 142
  funding of Intellicorp, 82
  investment per employee, 191
  liability theory, 125–27
  market growth, 4, 82
  NPV, IRR, and ROI, 91–100
  organization of AI companies, 17
  ownership, 135
  Palladian Software:
    business requirements, 159–60
    reasons for using AI, 154
  productivity, 109
  taxability, 124
  technological changes, 190
  universal commercial code, 132

C

CAI. (*see* Computer Aided Instruction)
Carnegie Group, Inc. and "big four," 89
Carnegie Mellon University. (*see* CMU)
Chemical Abstracts Service, Inc., 183

CMU, 2, 5
Computer Aided Instruction (CAI), 202
Consulting. (*see also* Business organization)
  by AMS at the National Archives, 53
  at Intellicorp, 23
  at Lockheed, 8
  as a replacement for AI staff, 3
  types of services, 10, 90

D

DARPA, 7, 11
DEC, 2
  DEC 10 computer, 2
  XCON, 12, 97
Department of Energy, 95
Digital Equipment Company. (*see* DEC)
Direct models of costs and revenues, 101
Documentation:
  specialtists, 18
DOE. (*see* Department of Energy)
Domain of a problem. (*see also*
    Methodology)
  defining in layers, 27
  lexicons, 175
  natural language grammars, 179
  in project initiation, 40–41
DuPont:
  expert system shells, 13
  University of Maryland, 13
Dynamic simulation of expert system,
    business effects, 100

E

Earth Radiation Budget Satellite, 47
EC2 et cie., 95
Environmental Protection Agency:
  CORRECTIVE ACTION expert system, 97
  prototyping, 117
EPA. (*see* Environmental Protection Agency)
ERBS. (*see* Earth Radiation Budget Satellite)
ESE. (*see* Expert Systems Environment)
Europe, distribution of KEE, 83
Experts:
  building expert systems, 12

Experts (*cont'd.*)
  building language semantics, 182
  expert's view of KE, 65
  liability, 130
  "semi-experts," 28
  within a team, 13, 54
  working with, 28–29, 57–60, 71
Expert Systems. (*see also* AI)
  mainframe shells, 15
  packaged applications, 16
  as part of the work force, 134
  PC shells, 15
  structure of, 30
  transcending decision support, 158
Expert system applications. (*see also*
        Operations advisor; Management
        Advisor)
  abstracts from text case, 183–85
  ACE, 127
  application assistant, 97
  archivist's assistant, 53
  authorizer's assistant, 97
  capital budgeting assistant, 97
  consultant, 97
  CORRECTIVE ACTION, 97
  EVIDENT, 49–51
  factory scheduler case study, 35–36
  Intelligent secretary, 134
  mentor, 97
  MUDMAN, 96
  MYCIN
  network configuration system, 33–34
  power plant diagnostic system, 31
  probe-design assistant, 34
  Process Diagnostic System (PDS), 97
  propellent process expert, 31–33
  prospector, 127
  requirements engineering automated
        development, 46–47
  remote diagnosis and service scheduler,
        36–37
  remote repair advisor, 35
  R1/XCON, 12, 97
  Strains Management System, 82
  TOPSCO, 47–49
Expert Systems Environment (ESE), 140
Exploitation fears, 194
Exxon, 9

F

Faculty Development in Technology (FDT)
        Model), 196–98
FDT Model. (*see* Faculty Development in
        Technology Model)
Financial services, appeal of AI, 10
FMC, 7
Fortune 500, spread of AI into, 14. (*see also* MIS)
Framatone, 9

G

Games as a training tool, 201
General Electric, 8
Grammar and natural language, 179
  developing, 180
  testing, 180
GTE, 6
Guide to the National Archives of the United
        States, 63

H

Honeywell:
  Mentor expert system, 97

I

IBM:
  AION corporation, 15
  Amoco, 8
  consultant expert system, 97
  expert systems environment, 140
Immigration and Naturalization Services, 95
  application assistant, 97
Indirect models of costs, 101
Inference Corporation, 4. (*see also* ART)
  and Lockheed, 8
  and TI, 12
Information Science Institute, 2
Informediation, 195
INS (*see* Immigration and Naturalization
        Service)
Intellect. (*see* Artificial Intelligence Corp.)

Intellicorp, 3. (*see also* KEE; Methodology;
 Technology transfer)
 technology transfer methods, 22–24
 and TI, 12
IntelliGenetics, 81. (*see also* Intellicorp)

J

Jacobson, Alex, 4. (*see also* Inference
 Corporation)
Japan, distribution of KEE, 83

K

KBMS, and SQL, 141. (*see also* AIC)
KEE, 15, 21 (*see also* Intellicorp)
 features, 83–84
 as part of a layered product, 84
Knowledge acquisition:
 through interviews, 32, 58
 for natural language, 182–83
Knowledge engineer:
 attribute of, 14, 26, 43–45
 hiring, 4–7
knowledge engineering:
 bottlenecks, 45, 57
 by experts, 12
 by a team, 13, 25–26
Knowledge system vs expert system, 81
 (*see also* AI; Expert systems)
 Knowledge Systems Engineer (KSE), 21

L

Lexicon, 175
 defining 175
 testing, 176
Lisp. (*see also* AI; LMI)
 vs C, 89
 hardware platforms, 86–87
 and Lisp machine makers, 2
LMI, 2
Lockheed, 6, 7
 with Inference and NASA, 8

LES, 8
Lotus, 16

M

M.1 system shell. (*see Teknowledge)*
Management advisor, 147
 mapping to business, 151–53
Managers. (*see also* Business, Methodology,
 Project)
 guidelines for, 39
 participation in knowledge acquisition, 30
 overcoming employee fear, 190
 as users of expert systems, 147
Marketing:
 AI marketing staff, 18
 considerations in cost justification, 104
Martin-Marrietta Corporation, 9
Media-as-message, 195–196
Methodology. (*see also* Domain)
 analysis, 24–25
 technology transfer, 22
Minsky, Marvin, 2
MIT, 1
 and Marvin MInsky, 2
Mitre, 6
Morphological analysis, 176–77

N

NARA. (*see* National Archives and Records
 Administration)
NASA, 8
 and EVIDENT application, 49–51
 and READ application, 46–47
 and TOPSCO application, 47–49
National Aeronautics and Space
 Administration. (*see NASA*)
National Archives and Records
 Administration, 53

O

Operations advisor, 147, 148–50
Overload of technology, 195

P

Palladian, 16, 146. (*see also* Operations Advisor; Management Advisor)
PARC, 2, 6. (*see also* Xerox)
Personal consultant, 15. (*see also* TI)
Programmed Instruction (PI), 202
Project. (*see also* Domain and Methodology)
  benefits, 104
  cost estimation guidelines, 110
  description, 105
  FDT Model, 196–98
  initiation issues, 24
  justification guidelines, 118–19
  productivity (at Palladian), 164
  prototyping, 39, 117, 173
  stages, 40–42, 173–74
  testing the Archives' prototype, 76
Prototype. (*see* Project)

R

Robots and liability, 128, 133

S

S.1 system shell. (*see* Teknowledge)
Schlumberger-Doll, 2
SDI. (*see* Strategic defense initiative)
Selling AI and expert systems:
  gaining internal commitment, 39–41, 114, 193–94
  leveraging Intellect for KBMS product strategy, 141
  Palladian's market definition, 167–68
  selling KEE, 82–83
Semantics:
  and expertise, 182
  representation, 181
Southern California, Edison Company and AI Corp., 144
Spelling verification, 172
Sperry and Intellicorp, 82–83
SRI International, 4, 7

Staffing and organizing the AI team. (*see also* Business; Knowledge engineer; Managers; Project)
  advisory committee (at the National Archives), 4
  composition, 42, 161–62
  culture, 104
  evolution (at Palladian) 162–63
  mission, 102–3, 160
  professionals' "wish list," 5
  responsibilities, 116
  restrictions, 165–66
  training and planning, 199
Standard Oil of Ohio, 9
Stanford University, 2
  and Edward Feigenbaum, 14
  and Intellicorp, 81
Strategic Defense Initiative, 129. (*see also* DARPA)
Syntax and natural language systems:
  and managing natural language software projects, 178
  and parsers, 177
  syntactic analysis, 172–73
Syntelligence, 16, 146
Systems analysis. (*see* Methodology)

T

Technology transfer:
  within DEC, 3
  and Intellicorp apprenticeship, 22
Technophilia, 195
Technophobia, 194. (*see also* Managers; Selling; Staffing and organizing the AI team)
Teknowledge, 3
  and American Cimflex, 89
  selling M.1 and S.1, 15
Texas Instruments. (*see* TI)
TI, 12. (*see also* Personal Consultant)
  capital budgeting expert system, 97
Training (*see also* Computer aided instruction; Programmed Instruction; Staffing and organizing the AI group)
  adapting to new technology, 192–93

Training (*cont'd.*)
  at Apex, 4
  at Arthur Andersen, 10
  Boeing Model, 8
  at Intellicorp, 21
Transamerica Insurance Group, 143
TRW, 7

U

UNISYS. (*see* Sperry)

University of Maryland, and DuPont, 13

W

Westinghouse, PDS expert system, 97
Work value analysis in cost justification of
  AI, 101–2

X

Xerox, 2. (*see also* PARC)